Black
Votes
Count

D1500004

The research for this
book was supported
by the generosity of
the Joint Center for
Political Studies.

Frank R. Parker

Foreword by
Eddie N. Williams

Black
Votes
Count

Political Empowerment
in Mississippi after 1965

The University of North Carolina Press

Chapel Hill and London

The paper in this book meets the guidelines for permanence
and durability of the Committee on Production Guidelines for
Book Longevity of the Council on Library Resources.

94 93 92 91 90   5 4 3 2 1

Library of Congress Cataloging-in-Publication Data
Parker, Frank R.
   Black votes count : political empowerment in Mississippi
after 1965 / Frank R. Parker ; foreword by Eddie N. Williams.
      p.   cm.
   Includes bibliographical references.
   ISBN 0-8078-1901-8 (alk. paper).—ISBN 0-8078-4274-5
(pbk. : alk. paper)
   1. Afro-Americans—Mississippi—Politics and government. 2. Afro-Americans—Suffrage—Mississippi. 3. Mississippi—Politics and government—1951– . 4. Voting—Mississippi—History—20th century. 5. Political participation—
Mississippi—History—20th century. I. Title.
E185.93.M6P37   1990   89-39074
323.1'1960730762—dc20   CIP

Excerpt from Calvin Tomkins, "Profiles (Marian Wright
Edelman): A Sense of Urgency," The New Yorker, March 27,
1989, reprinted by permission. © 1989 Calvin Tomkins.
Originally in The New Yorker Magazine.

Map 2.1, Land Areas of Mississippi, adapted from James W.
Loewen and Charles Sallis, eds., Mississippi: Conflict and
Change, rev. ed. (New York: Pantheon Books, 1980) and used
with permission of the editors.

Design by April Leidig-Higgins

To Anne
and for Ian,
Barbara,
Stephanie,
and Kevin

Contents

Tables

Maps and Figures

Maps

Figures

Acknowledgments

This book was begun while I was at the Joint Center for Political Studies as a MacArthur Foundation Distinguished Scholar. I am indebted to President Eddie N. Williams, Research Director Milton D. Morris, and the staff at the Joint Center for their hospitality and support and to the John D. and Catherine T. MacArthur Foundation for supporting my work during my year at the Joint Center.

I am also indebted to many individuals for their criticisms, encouragement, and helpful comments. The comments and suggestions of Morgan Kousser, Allan Lichtman, and David Colby have been particularly beneficial. Neil McMillan, Alex Willingham, Linda Williams, Katherine McFate, Anthony Scott, James Loewen, Peyton McCrary, and Robert Smith also offered ideas, comments, and encouragement along the way. I was very fortunate that the Joint Center provided me with the assistance of an excellent editor, Susan Kalish, who with Katherine McFate, also of the Joint Center, contributed substantially to making sense out of what I had to say. I am also appreciative of the excellent editorial support and assistance provided by Lewis Bateman, Ron Maner, and Stephanie Wenzel of the University of North Carolina Press. Debts of gratitude also are due to Carolyn Parker, for her enormous support and encouragement of my work in Mississippi; Henry Kirksey for showing me the importance of these issues and for drawing many of the original maps on which the maps herein are based; Jan Hillegas for her diligent research assistance over long periods of time, for coming up with newspaper articles I otherwise would have missed, and for collecting, keeping, and making available the files of the Mississippi Freedom Information Service; Sarah Smith for sending me boxes of files from Jackson; and Emily Epstein and Lucia Gill for additional research and graphics assistance.

My colleagues at the Lawyers' Committee for Civil Rights Under Law also provided helpful support, including former executive director William Robinson, who gave me the time off to start writing; Samuel Issacharoff, who made suggestions on how the story should be told; and Robert McDuff and Brenda Wright. Special thanks go to "Cuppy" Wilson for her always reliable and efficient secretarial support. Finally, this work would not have been completed but for the steadfast encouragement and support of my friend Anne Burlock Lawver.

Foreword

Few events in American political life have had as profound or as far-reaching consequences as has passage of the Voting Rights Act of 1965. That law ended a century of denial to blacks of the most basic right of American citizenship—the right to vote. Within a short time of its enactment, blacks in large numbers throughout the South were registering to vote, and voting levels quickly shot up to match and, in some cases, surpass black voting outside the South. Currently, voting levels of black Southerners are less than five percentage points below those of whites; more than half of the over 7,000 black elected officials in the nation are elected in the South; and black voters are a formidable force in the electoral processes throughout the region.

But as stunning an achievement as enactment of the Voting Rights Act was, it did not end the effort by white Southerners to curtail the political rights of their black fellow citizens. Throughout the South, white public officials took the view that although they could no longer deny blacks the right to vote, they could certainly reduce the impact of their vote, especially in electing black candidates to office. Thus, these public officials quickly shifted their efforts, from denying the right to vote to diluting the vote of blacks. They did this by creating at-large and multimember districts, redrawing district boundaries, and even changing some offices from elective to appointive.

In the two decades since the Voting Rights Act, civil rights advocates have vigorously and successfully fought against these and other devices aimed at diluting the impact of the black vote. In the process, they have not only eliminated most official impediments to the full exercise of the franchise; they have also clarified and deepened our conception of the one-person, one-vote principle by emphasizing the right to cast an effective vote.

The voting rights struggle involved all of the southern states and now reaches outside the South, but Mississippi was easily the most challenging arena of struggle. There the black population was largest, the resistance to all forms of civil rights the most vigorous, and not surprisingly, the efforts to dilute black political influence the most massive. There, too, the gains have been among the most dramatic. For these reasons, it is especially appropriate that this study focuses on that state in studying the epic struggle for full voting rights that followed enactment of the Voting Rights Act.

No one I know is better equipped to study Mississippi's massive resistance to black political empowerment than Frank Parker. In fact, it is rare when subject and author are so well matched. Attorney Parker has spent virtually all of his illustrious legal career in the cause of voting rights for minorities, including twelve years in Mississippi, leading the fight for political rights for blacks in the courts there. He, therefore, comes to this study with considerable familiarity with the issues, the strategies, and the actors.

The Joint Center for Political Studies is pleased to have had the opportunity to host Mr. Parker as a MacArthur Foundation Distinguished Scholar for fourteen months while he wrote this book. We are grateful for the foundation's generous support of our Distinguished Scholars program, to the members of the program's advisory and selection committees headed by Professors John Hope Franklin and Michael Winston, respectively, and to the staff of the Joint Center who assisted in facilitating Mr. Parker's work. It is my hope that the result of our joint efforts will be a better understanding of the remarkable achievements of our society, the state of Mississippi, and the many individuals, black and white, whose deep commitment to justice and equality made the voting rights revolution possible.

Eddie N. Williams
President
Joint Center for Political Studies
Washington, D.C.

Black
Votes
Count

Introduction
The Quest for Black Political Equality in Mississippi

Since 1965 America has witnessed a renaissance of black political participation. Nationwide, more than 12 million black Americans are registered to vote. The number of black elected officials has increased about fourteenfold, from about 500 in 1965 to more than 7,200 in 1989.[1] The 24 black members of Congress, more than 400 black state legislators, and more than 300 black mayors—more than at any other time in American history—symbolize this dramatic upsurge in black political participation. This tremendous increase in black political participation has had important implications for national politics and has been an essential element of the realignment of southern politics for the past twenty-five years.

This dramatic progress is due in large measure to the passage by Congress of the Voting Rights Act of 1965; 67 percent of these black elected officials are in the South.[2] The Voting Rights Act swept away the primary legal barriers to black registration and voting in the South, eliminating the literacy tests and the poll taxes and allowing the Justice Department to dispatch federal registrars and poll watchers to insure the integrity of the voting process. Yet, in the years following the passage of the Voting Rights Act, despite the dramatic increases in black voter registration, black voters in southern states found that, generally, they were unable to elect more than a few black candidates to public office. The reason was that immediately after the act was passed, southern states—led by Mississippi—adopted "massive resistance" strategies designed to nullify the impact of the black vote. The devices that had been used before 1965 to deny black citizens the right to vote—the literacy tests and the poll tax—were replaced with a second generation of disfranchising devices designed to nullify and dilute the black vote. These included such devices as at-large elections, racial gerrymandering of district lines, abolishing elective offices and making them appointive, and increasing the qualifying requirements for candidates running for public office. This campaign required the civil rights movement to adopt new strategies to deal with these new threats to the black franchise. The Voting Rights Act, which previously had focused on the denial of the vote to blacks, became the primary safeguard against these new efforts to dilute the black vote.

A number of valuable and insightful books have been written about southern politics and black voting after 1965, including Bartley and Graham's *Southern Politics and the Second Reconstruction*, Bass and DeVries' *The Transformation of Southern Politics*, Lamis's *The Two-Party South*, Lawson's *In Pursuit of Power*, and, most recently, Black and Black's *Politics and Society in the South*, and most of these books touch on the new barriers to black participation following the passage of the Voting Rights Act. But none of these books fully describes or analyzes these new barriers in detail, focuses on them as a massive resistance strategy of the entrenched white political leadership seeking to perpetuate its power, or thoroughly explores their impact as a primary impediment to black political participation during this period.

The purpose of this book is to fill a gap in the existing literature and to provide a new perspective on the political struggles of black citizens in the South by focusing on the central role of the voting rights movement after 1965 in the struggle for black political empowerment. The book describes the dramatic increase in black registration in Mississippi following passage of the Voting Rights Act, Mississippi's official, state-sponsored program of massive resistance to nullify the newly gained black vote, the impact these vote-dilution devices had on the opportunities of black voters to elect candidates of their choice, the successful strategies employed by black Mississippians to overcome the state's massive resistance campaign, and the impact these struggles have had on both state politics and national policy.

Mississippi is an appropriate focus for this analysis for several reasons. First, of all the states, the changes that have occurred in Mississippi have been the most dramatic and far-reaching. Mississippi has had a higher proportion of black people than any other state—42 percent in 1960, 37 percent in 1970, and 35 percent in 1980—and politically has been the most repressive state for black people. Before 1965, discriminatory voter registration laws prevented all but 6.7 percent of Mississippi's black adult population from registering to vote—the lowest black registration rate of any state in the nation—and there were no more than six black elected officials in the state. As of January 1989, Mississippi had 646 black elected officials—more than any other state—including a black member of Congress, a black state supreme court justice, 22 black state legislators, almost 70 black county supervisors, more than 25 black mayors, and 282 black city council members. Having started so far behind, Mississippi had further to go than any other southern state to begin to attain some semblance of democracy and political justice for black citizens.

Second, after 1965 Mississippi, the scene of so many civil rights struggles in the past, once again became the testing ground for whether the promises of the Fourteenth and Fifteenth Amendments and the Voting Rights Act could ever be fulfilled. Mississippi led the South in the adoption of discriminatory new electoral mechanisms designed to render ineffective the new black vote. The tenfold increase in black voter registration after 1965, from 6.7 percent to over 60 percent of the eligible black population, triggered a massive resistance reaction from the white political establishment that was more intense than in any other southern state. The Mississippi Legislature enacted a series of state statutes aimed, not at denying blacks the right to register and vote—for this was now prohibited by the Voting Rights Act—but at diluting the effectiveness of the black vote. In 1966 the state legislature gerrymandered the congressional district lines to prevent the election of a black member of Congress; denied black voters representation in the state legislature by creating large, multi-member state legislative districts in which black voting strength was diluted; authorized counties to switch to at-large elections for members of the county boards of supervisors and county school boards to prevent the election of black candidates; abolished elections for county school superintendents in numerous counties; and increased the qualifying requirements for independent candidates to prevent black independents from qualifying to run for office.

Events in Mississippi thus demonstrate that after 1965 the focus of voting discrimination shifted from preventing blacks from registering to vote to preventing them from winning elections. Success in overcoming this new black disfranchisement effort was critical to the future of black political participation, for without it all prior victories— over the white primary, the literacy tests, and the poll taxes—would be negated. In the face of these new discriminatory electoral barriers black voters would be able to vote but would be unable to elect candidates of their choice to office.

This shift in white supremacists' strategies from denial to dilution of the black vote then raised a whole new series of questions: Would these new structural barriers be as successful as outright denial of the franchise in preventing blacks from gaining access to the political process? What strategies were available to the newly enfranchised black voters to overcome these new barriers? Could the legal standards that were developed in the struggle for black voter registration be adapted to defeat these new barriers, or did new legal standards have to be developed to meet these new challenges to the right to vote?

The struggle in Mississippi was critical, not only because of the intensity of the white resistance, but also because the first court cases challenging the new dilution of black voting strength were brought there. The results of those test cases would determine whether similar tactics could be employed elsewhere, and the successes in the Mississippi voting rights litigation have to a large extent established the legal standards applicable to the current voting rights litigation. To be sure, the struggle to overcome new forms of dilution of black voting strength was not limited to Mississippi. After 1965 such techniques as racial gerrymandering and at-large elections were used and continue to be used throughout the South and elsewhere to dilute black and other minority voting strength. But what happened in Mississippi is particularly important because the first legal battles to overcome these new structural barriers were fought there, and therefore the future prospects for elimination of these new barriers throughout the South were critically dependent upon the results in the Mississippi cases.

Third, what has happened in Mississippi, historically the national symbol of white resistance to blacks' civil rights, is a barometer of whether the civil rights movement and its successes has had any real impact on American politics. As Mary King, a former civil rights worker and author of *Freedom Song: A Personal Story of the 1960s Civil Rights Movement*, noted in a 1987 *New York Times* interview: "People often ask me if I believe any progress has really been made in civil rights. . . . I tell them that it may have taken 23 years, but a black lawyer, Mike Espy, was elected last fall to Congress from a majority black district in the Mississippi delta. Back in 1964 those black counties didn't have a single black registered voter."[3]

Thus, this book also examines the consequences of the increase in black political participation in the state. An analysis of the consequences of this struggle is important to provide answers to the more general questions concerning the emergence of blacks as a political force in the post-1965 period: Are black voters merely tangential to the political process, or do they have real power? What difference do black elected officials make? Have white attitudes toward blacks changed?

The research for this book grew out of the writer's experience, first, as a staff attorney for the United States Commission on Civil Rights assigned to survey barriers to black participation for the commission in 1967–68, and, second, as a participant-observer of the emergence of black electoral politics in Mississippi as a civil rights lawyer with the Lawyers' Committee for Civil Rights Under Law in Jackson from 1968 to 1981. This early research and participant observations were supplemented by surveys of secondary materials relating to southern politics, black politics, and the civil rights movement. Contemporary accounts of the events portrayed were also found in journal articles and magazine articles for the period.

Original research was conducted through an analysis of newspaper accounts of the Mississippi Legislature's 1966 massive resistance session, litigation records, the archives of post-1965 black political participation assembled by Jan Hillegas and Ken Lawrence for the Mississippi Freedom Information Service, and through interviews with a number of the participants in the events described and observers of politics in Mississippi.

Because Mississippi politics has been so racially polarized, this book uses numbers of registered voters by race and numbers of black elected officials as indicators of black political progress or lack thereof. This methodology is consistent with academic writings that use the number of black (or other minority) elected officials as the principal measure of the impact of structural barriers on black political participation.[4] This is not to say that this is the only measure of black political progress. Black voters can also elect white officials who are responsive to their needs, but since there are no quantitative data available on the number of white officials in this category, political analysts generally have used the number of black elected officials in measuring black electoral success.

As used in this work, the term "structural barriers" refers to election laws, practices, and methods that diminish the effectiveness of black voters' voting strength, in contrast to barriers that prevent blacks from registering or casting a ballot. "Vote dilution"—the effect these structural barriers have on minority voting strength—is the denial or abridgment of the opportunity of minority voters to influence the electoral process and to elect candidates of their choice. "Racially polarized voting" refers to white and black voters voting for different candidates for office, usually white voters voting for white candidates and black voters voting for black candidates, regardless of the causes or motivations for such voting behavior. Thus, racially polarized voting is demonstrated statistically by a consistent relationship between the racial composition of the voting precincts and the votes for candidates.[5]

The analysis of the political emergence of Mississippi's black population after 1965 and the white resistance to black political participation described in the following chapters sheds important light on a number of conceptual issues relating to the nature of political change in America and the black struggle for political equality. The underlying conceptual and analytical themes described below provide a framework for the detailed discussions in the succeeding chapters.

The power struggle thesis. A number of scholars have described the political and social advancement of blacks in American society as a power struggle between competing racial groups.[6] This power struggle is a contest between, on the one hand, a powerful white elite, struggling to maintain its dominant position in society, and, on the other hand, disadvantaged blacks, in a subordinate position, striving to achieve their desired goals of political, social, and economic advancement. As summarized by political scientist Mack H. Jones:

> What we have is essentially a power struggle between blacks and whites, with the latter trying to maintain their superordinate position vis-a-vis the former. Since the political system is the arena in which societal conflicts are definitively resolved, black politics should be thought of as the manifestation of the power struggle between these two groups. However, we need to add one other specifying condition to further distinguish black politics from other extensions of the universal power struggle. That condition is the stipulation that the ideological justification for the superordination of whites is the institutionalized belief in the inherent superiority of that group.[7]

This view was confirmed by William J. Simmons, head of the Citizens' Council, the all-white group committed to maintaining racial segregation in the South, in a speech he gave in the early 1960s:

> I was born in Mississippi and the United States and I'm the product of my heredity and education and the society in which I was raised, and I have a vested interest in that society, and I along with a million other white Mississippians will do everything in our power to protect that vested interest. It's just as simple as that. . . . It's primarily a struggle for power and I think we would be stupid indeed if we failed to see where the consequences of a supine surrender on our part would lead.[8]

This conceptualization does not exclude the social and economic class dimensions of the conflict. Race and class in Mississippi are strongly linked. The vast majority of blacks who had jobs in Mississippi in the 1960s worked in positions of unskilled labor as house servants and field hands, and their political oppression was part of the larger scheme to maintain their economic oppression as well. To this extent, black people's struggle for political rights also had elements of a power struggle between economic classes in the society.

But as Mack Jones and William Simmons point out in the passages quoted above, the struggle of blacks for political equality and the white resistance to that effort were largely defined by race. Although Mississippi's franchise restrictions had an impact upon poor whites as well as blacks, the voter registration cases of the 1960s showed that illiterate and marginally literate whites were permitted to vote, while educated blacks were denied the right to vote.[9] White politicians were dependent on the votes of poor whites to win elective office, and racial campaigning was a proven technique for dividing the poor whites from the poor blacks and gaining the white vote. Although there may have been poor whites who were sympathetic to the efforts of blacks to gain political equality after 1965, few poor whites participated in the black political organizations or voted for their black candidates for office.

Consistent with this theoretical framework, the analysis of the black political emergence in Mississippi necessarily involves an investigation of the positions within the society occupied by the racial groups in terms of their political power, the resources available to each group to maintain or change its power relationships, and the strategies that might be employed by the dominant group to maintain its position and by the subordinate group to improve its position. The analysis that follows lends support to this concept. The increase in black voter registration produced by the Voting Rights Act provided a direct threat to the entrenched political power of Mississippi's white ruling elite. Whites in power then took steps to negate this increased black voting strength; these steps took the form of a series of political massive resistance statutes enacted by the Mississippi Legislature designed to dilute the black vote. Having virtually no influence in state government, black citizens were forced to resort to litigation in federal courts as the only means at their disposal to counter these efforts.

The critical importance of structural barriers as a determinant of black political success or failure. When the Voting Rights Act was enacted, many assumed—as some still believe today—that all the formal, legal barriers to black voting and equal black political participation in the South had been eliminated. For example, the historian Steven F. Lawson in his book *Black Ballots*, which describes the black struggle for voting rights from 1944 to 1969, concluded that the Voting Rights Act had removed the last remaining legal barriers to black political progress. The burden was now on black voters to take advantage of the new opportunities presented: "With the overt legal barriers destroyed, lack of political consciousness remained a major obstacle on the road toward enfranchisement."[10] Lawson concluded that the primary barriers to black political gains now were the need to negotiate and compromise with statewide white majorities, the lack of financial resources among blacks, and black economic dependence.[11]

Lawson failed to anticipate or acknowledge in *Black Ballots* that states covered by the Voting Rights Act were not about to roll over and play dead, and that the enfranchisement of blacks in the South would be met with new forms of state-sponsored discriminatory electoral barriers to black political participation. Thus Lawson was forced to write a sequel to his first book. In *In Pursuit of Power* he acknowledged that his earlier conclusion that all of the overt legal barriers had been destroyed was premature, and that "while most southern jurisdictions complied with the letter of the 1965 law, many attempted to violate its spirit by grafting sophisticated forms of bias onto existing electoral institutions. Unless the underlying structural impediments blocking the franchise are removed, the considerable, but as yet limited, amount of success southern blacks have enjoyed in pursuit of political power will not go much further."[12]

The post-1965 white reaction to black enfranchisement in the South has prompted social scientists to assess the impact of electoral arrangements such as at-large voting and legislative redistricting on the opportunities for minority voters to gain legislative representation of their choice.[13] As political scientists Richard L. Engstrom and Michael D. McDonald have concluded: "When voting patterns are polarized along racial lines (as is often the case in the South), electoral competition can be structured in a manner that impedes a minority—even a sizable minority—from converting its voting strength into the election of minority candidates."[14] This book analyzes the methods employed by the Mississippi Legislature in 1966 to structure "electoral competition" to impede black voters—even in counties in which they constituted a majority of the population—from converting their voting strength into the election of black candidates and the impact of those methods in the subsequent elections. As such, the study provides additional empirical evidence of the strength of these structural barriers as a determinant of black political success and failure. Such an analysis has important implications for the study of black political behavior and for election law reform efforts.

The role of litigation in removing structural electoral barriers to black participation and producing political change. In the post-1965 period, black political leaders and voters in the South used voting rights litigation in the federal courts as the principal vehicle for overcoming these structural barriers. An analysis of this litigation has important implications for the study of litigation as a means of producing political and social change and for the role of the federal courts as protectors of the democratic process.[15]

Since the end of Reconstruction, civil rights litigation has been a necessary component of the civil rights struggle in America. Some of the most important victories of the civil rights movement have been litigation victories, striking down the white primaries and the grandfather clauses,[16] desegregating public transportation and the public schools, and the like. But the voting rights litigation of the post-1965 period was qualitatively different from the litigation that preceded it in terms of the position of the black litigants and their attorneys, the actual gains that were made, and the development of new legal doctrines protecting black citizens' right to vote.

Prior to 1960, voting rights litigation focused on discriminatory restrictions on the right of black citizens to register and cast ballots. Although a number of these restrictions were struck down by the courts, including the white primary and the grandfather clauses, these court decisions had little real impact on black electoral participation. As legal scholar Mark Tushnet has observed, particularly in the Deep South "blacks gained little effective political power as a result of the invalidation of the white primary."[17] Blacks continued to be excluded from the political process by intimidation and violence, and the principal restrictions of the literacy tests and the poll tax remained in place until they were struck down by the Voting Rights Act in 1965.

Beginning about 1960, the civil rights movement switched its emphasis from a litigation strategy to a mass-based protest strategy to overcome the remaining franchise restrictions. In this political organizing and protest phase, the primary role of the civil rights attorneys was defensive: to protect the political organizing and protest efforts of the civil rights workers by contesting police harassment, by challenging the anti-protest laws that curtailed these activities, and by getting the civil rights workers out of jail when they were arrested. This protest effort succeeded in accomplishing what case-by-case litigation against registration restrictions failed to do. It produced the 1965 Voting Rights Act that struck down the primary restrictions on the right to vote. Thus, the dramatic increases in black voter registration that occurred after 1965 were produced by legislative action, not judicial action.

The passage of the Voting Rights Act triggered a new era of voting rights litigation designed to overcome the barriers that diluted the voting strength of the newly enfranchised black voters. Although this litigation was in reaction to initiatives taken by state and local officials to restrict black electoral success, it was also proactive in the sense that it involved minority plaintiffs aggressively filing lawsuits that mounted direct challenges to barriers to minority political participation. Backed by Supreme Court decisions of the 1960s establishing rights to equal representation and by the Voting Rights Act, the civil rights lawyers went on the offensive to challenge the state statutes that curtailed the opportunities of black voters to elect candidates of their choice. After 1965, the transition was one from litigation protecting the protest movement designed to achieve political and social change to litigation actually achieving political change by eliminating the structural barriers to full political participation. The black political leaders went from being defendants in criminal prosecutions designed to suppress their political organizing efforts to being plaintiffs in voting rights lawsuits seeking remedies that would allow black candidates to be elected to office.

For the first time, as a result of this post-1965 voting rights litigation, black voters gained effective political power as measured by substantial increases in the number of black officeholders. The first Supreme Court victory over elements of Mississippi's massive resistance program (*Allen v. State Board of Elections*) struck down the state's effort to switch to at-large elections of county supervisors, appoint county school superintendents, and increase the qualifying requirements for independent candidates, resulting in a doubling of the number of black county supervisors, the subsequent election of nine black county school superintendents, and an increase in the number of black candidates for office. The Mississippi state legislative reapportionment case (begun as *Connor v. Johnson*) forced the state to eliminate at-large voting in multimember legislative districts statewide and resulted in an increase in the number of black legislators from four to seventeen in the 1979 elections and additional increases since then. The lawsuit challenging a switch from ward elections to citywide elections in over forty cities (*Stewart v. Waller*) immediately resulted in a doubling of the number of black city council members, and subsequent lawsuits challenging at-large city council elections have contributed to increasing the number of black city council members to 282 as of January 1989.

This does not mean that voting rights litigation actually got black candidates elected, only that it was a necessary precondition to black political success. The normal rules governing political mobilization and political success still applied: the black community still had to recruit candidates to run who would appeal to a broad spectrum of the voting public, and these candidates still had to adopt platforms that would appeal to voters, campaign for votes, and win a majority of the votes to be elected to office. The litigation battles were primarily over the last element. As the white ruling elite sought to deny black voters the opportunity to elect candidates of their choice by depriving them of black majority districts in which they could win voting majorities, litigation was necessary to overcome these efforts. In this sense, voting rights litigation became the principal vehicle for black political entry and for political change.

Further, the voting rights litigation that came out of Mississippi

and that was commenced by black Mississippi plaintiffs and prose-
cuted by civil rights lawyers who lived in Mississippi played a major
catalytic role in the development of today's federal voting rights law.
In order to resolve the conflicts presented, the Supreme Court articulated new legal prohibitions against minority vote dilution and
against methods of election that deny minority voters an opportunity
to elect candidates of their choice, principles that have become an important part of American civil rights jurisprudence. Mississippi thus
became the crucible in which modern federal voting rights law was
largely forged, and these litigation successes have opened up the
once-closed political system to a new era of black political participation, with enormous consequences for state and national politics.

   *The validity of recent challenges to the new federal legal protections for mi-
nority voting rights.* In recent years, the legal principles protecting minority voters from dilution of their voting strength developed in this
post-1965 period have come under attack. During the congressional
hearings on extending and amending the Voting Rights Act in 1982,
several scholars criticized proposed amendments to the Voting Rights
Act that incorporated legal standards prohibiting methods of election
that deny minority voters an opportunity to elect candidates of choice
and measuring voting discrimination by effect, rather than intent,
for providing affirmative, race-based entitlements and a legal right of
minorities to proportional representation.[18] In a recently published
book, *Whose Votes Count? Affirmative Action and Minority Voting Rights*,
political scientist Abigail Thernstrom also attacks these developments.
She criticizes the landmark Supreme Court decision that first implemented the principle of minority vote dilution and enabled Mississippi black voters to overcome the state's political massive resistance
program, *Allen v. State Board of Elections*, as a distortion of the original
intent of the act.[19] She also contends that these legal developments
have "reshaped [the Voting Rights Act] into an instrument for affirmative action in the electoral sphere" and grant minority voters an
unjustified "entitlement" to "special protection from white competition" and "proportionate ethnic and racial representation."[20] Her solution to these supposed evils is that federal judicial protection for
minority voting rights should be cut back and limited to rare and extreme cases.[21]

   These arguments represent a threat to the progress described in
this book because they are part of an effort to roll back the advances
that have been made. Full judicial protection against minority vote
dilution has been critical to ensuring representative government and
the proper functioning of the democratic process. Thernstrom and
her fellow critics grossly mischaracterize the legal principles involved

in modern voting rights litigation; the prohibition against minority vote dilution grants minority voters a remedy from discrimination, not an entitlement to proportional representation.

These arguments cannot be fully evaluated without placing them in a particular context, and developments in Mississippi provide such a context. Should black voters have a right to cast ballots but not an opportunity to elect candidates of their choice? Should the elimination of at-large elections and gerrymandered districts that unfairly structure electoral competition to the disadvantage of black voters be condemned as granting black voters an "entitlement" to "special protection from white competition"? Do legal rules that have resulted in an increase in black officeholders from 0 percent of the total number of elected officials to 13 percent in a state that is 35 percent black unfairly provide black voters with "proportionate ethnic and racial representation"?

Contemporary legal principles protecting minority voting rights were not developed in the abstract but arose to meet a critical need in a particular historical context. This book is intended to shed light on this current debate by examining the historical context in which these principles were developed and by analyzing whether their protections are still needed.

The following chapters describe the struggle for black political equality in Mississippi and assess its results. Chapter 1 sets the scene by assessing the position of black people in Mississippi in 1965. It describes the pre-1965 strategies to deny black citizens the right to vote and the impact of the 1965 Voting Rights Act in enfranchising Mississippi's black citizens. Chapter 2 describes in detail the Mississippi Legislature's 1966 massive resistance legislation designed to negate the increase in black voting strength in the state, and its impact on the 1967 statewide elections.

Chapter 3 describes the litigation struggles of black candidates and voters to overcome Mississippi's massive resistance program and the response of the federal courts, including the United States Supreme Court, to these efforts. This discussion includes the unsuccessful challenge to the racial gerrymandering of the state's five congressional districts that was rejected by the Supreme Court. It also includes the successful challenge under section 5 of the Voting Rights Act to new laws providing for at-large county supervisor elections, appointment of county school superintendents, and increased qualifying requirements for independent candidates, resulting in the 1969 Supreme Court decision in *Allen v. State Board of Elections*, the *Brown v. Board of Education* of minority voting rights.

Chapter 4 describes the complex and lengthy litigation effort to eliminate racially discriminatory districts for the election of members of the Mississippi Legislature, litigation that went on for fourteen years, including nine trips to the Supreme Court, until black voters finally obtained relief in 1979. This litigation not only resulted in important gains for black political participation in Mississippi but also established important precedents in the southwide effort to eliminate discriminatory multimember state legislative districts.

Chapter 5 describes the impact of these successes on the politics of the state, including the impact of increased levels of black representation on the state legislature. This chapter also surveys the ensuing struggle of black voters to overcome resistance to black political participation and to gain representation in county and city government.

Chapter 6 describes how the black struggle in Mississippi has significantly influenced national voting rights policy. The Mississippi struggle to overcome the state's massive resistance program produced a new legal standard of minority vote dilution that has become embedded in our national jurisprudence. It also helped to secure the extension of the Voting Rights Act in 1970, 1975, and 1982; made the federal preclearance requirement of section 5 of the Voting Rights Act the primary safeguard against southern efforts to dilute the black vote; and resulted in a greatly expanded enforcement role for the Justice Department in reviewing voting-law changes. Chapter 6 also assesses the criticisms that have been made against the expansion of section 5 coverage and against the minority vote dilution principle.

Chapter 7 concludes the book with an overall assessment of the impact black political gains in Mississippi have had on the state, whether these black gains have significantly diminished racism as a factor in Mississippi politics, whether there are barriers to black political participation that remain, and the critical elements of the legal struggle for full black political participation.

1 Mississippi in 1965
The Struggle for the
Right to Vote

From the summer of 1962 to the spring of 1963, Leflore County, a predominantly black county in the Mississippi Delta in northwest Mississippi, was the testing ground for democracy for the civil rights movement. The Leflore County voter registration campaign was part of a massive effort of the Council of Federated Organizations (COFO), the Mississippi civil rights umbrella organization, and the Student Nonviolent Coordinating Committee (SNCC), the Atlanta-based activist civil rights group, in the predominantly black Delta region. As described by Lawrence Guyot, a SNCC worker and later chair of the Mississippi Freedom Democratic party, "Our objectives were very clear. It was not to desegregate the two or three good local white restaurants. It was simply to register people to vote."[1]

In 1962, on the eve of COFO's arrival, only 268 of the county's 13,567 black adults were registered to vote (1.98 percent), although 70 percent of the white adults were registered.[2] As a result of SNCC's organizing efforts, hundreds of black people attempted to register. Not only did the county registrar refuse to register black applicants, but this voter registration campaign was met with a reign of terror from the white community. The SNCC office was attacked by a group of armed whites, forcing the SNCC workers to flee through a second-story window; the county board of supervisors cut off the federal surplus food program upon which most black families were dependent; SNCC workers were arrested on trumped-up charges; and black homes were shot into and black businesses and the SNCC office were burned.

In February 1963, on the highway outside Greenwood, the county seat, three whites in a car pulled alongside of and fired a burst of gunfire into a car containing Robert Moses, SNCC leader and COFO voter registration director; Randolph Blackwell of the Voter Education Project (VEP) in Atlanta, the primary funding source for the campaign; and SNCC worker Jimmie Travis. Travis, the driver, was seriously wounded in the neck and shoulder.

These incidents of violence and intimidation spurred numerous protests and marches on city hall and the county courthouse by the outraged black community. In March, shots were fired into the home of Dewey Greene, a voter registration worker and father of two SNCC workers, and more than one hundred black people marched on city hall in protest. Even before the more highly publicized incidents in Birmingham, Alabama, the demonstrators in Greenwood were met by a line of armed police officers, and a police dog attacked the marchers. When the marchers retreated to a local black church, the police waded into the crowd and arrested Moses and seven other SNCC organizers of the voter registration effort who were then convicted of disorderly conduct, sentenced to four months in jail, and fined $200 each. The sense of terror evoked by the police suppression of the Leflore County voter registration campaign was recalled in a 1989 *New Yorker* interview with Marian Wright Edelman, who, as a third-year Yale Law School student, went to Mississippi during her spring break to provide legal assistance to the movement. As Edelman told author Calvin Tomkins,

> My last day in Greenwood, Bob [Moses] took a group of people down to the courthouse to register. He walked at the head of that scraggly bunch of courageous people; I was at the end of the line, behind an old man on crutches. This was the first time I'd seen police dogs in action, and I've been scared of them ever since. If I see a German shepherd on the street, to this day I'll cross over to avoid him. The cops came with the dogs, and led them to attack us. I remember seeing a dog jump on Bob Moses and tear his pants, and then it was just a terrifying scene—people running away, Bob and the other S.N.C.C. kids getting arrested, and throwing me their car keys as they were being led off.[3]

The Justice Department filed a lawsuit seeking to void the convictions and to enjoin police interference with the voter registration effort. But the lawsuit was dismissed when the Justice Department agreed to a deal under which all charges against the SNCC organizers were dropped, without any court order protecting the voter registration effort.

Justice Department statistics show that from March to June, 1963, at least 681 black citizens applied for voter registration but only 8 were registered.[4] From June 1962 to January 1964 there was a net gain of only 13 black citizens added to the county's voter registration rolls.[5] The VEP, the principal source of funds for voter registration efforts in Mississippi, concluded that without massive federal intervention further efforts were futile and refused to fund any additional voter registration activity in the state. After spending over $50,000 in

Mississippi during 1962 and 1963, the VEP-funded effort had registered no more than 4,000 black voters.[6]

Black voters in Mississippi were barred from participating as a significant force in the electoral politics of the state until 1965, when the Voting Rights Act was passed, and that year marks the starting point for measuring the new black political emergence. Although most southern states began to rid themselves of their "Jim Crow" political and social systems beginning in 1954, as late as 1965 little had changed in Mississippi. As *New York Times* reporter Anthony Lewis observed, "The revolution that so profoundly changed American race relations between 1954 and 1964 stopped at the borders of Mississippi."[7] Despite the *Brown v. Board of Education* decision of 1954 banning school segregation and the passage by Congress of the Civil Rights Acts of 1957, 1960, and 1964, Mississippi in 1965 was still a rigidly segregated and oppressive society for blacks.

Five years of statewide voter registration activity and black community organizing more intense than anywhere in the South had produced no more than 28,500 black registered voters out of an eligible black voting-age population of over 400,000, had not produced a single black elected official outside of the all-black Delta town of Mound Bayou, and had not desegregated a single school district. Black people remained economically and socially oppressed. The chief occupations of black males were field hand, yardman, and chauffeur, and the chief occupations of black women were maid, nursemaid, and cook. Civil rights protest efforts aimed at eliminating the rigid segregation of the society were ruthlessly suppressed by police harassment, economic reprisals, and Ku Klux Klan terrorism.

Socioeconomic conditions. For most of the South, the period from 1950 to 1960 was a time of substantial social and economic transformation. The populations of all other southern states had undergone a transformation from predominantly rural-based to predominantly urban-based, and manufacturing had replaced farming as the primary source of income. But economically, little had changed in Mississippi. The 1960 census revealed that almost two-thirds of Mississippi's population still resided in rural areas, making it the most rural state in the South, and farming remained the major source of income. Jackson, the state's largest city, had a population of less than 150,000.

In 1960 Mississippi was the poorest state in the nation, with a per capita income of only $1,119, compared with a national figure of $2,263. But black Mississippians, trapped in an economically and socially oppressive system, were the poorest of the poor. The extremes of white wealth and black poverty in Mississippi were vividly described by a *New York Times* reporter, Claude Sitton, in a 1963 *New York Times Magazine* article:

Mississippi offers a study in contrasts, especially in the Delta. Greek-revival mansions and rambling ranch houses in groves of shade trees look out on weather-beaten rows of clapboard cabins and tar-paper shacks, most of which have open privies and some of which lack even running water. A planter dressed in expensive western boots and hat gets up from a leisurely meal in a restaurant and displays a rare dime valued at $90 from his coin collection. Less than a mile away, a Negro mother arises and prepares a breakfast of sugar syrup and hoecake for her children, some of whom cannot attend school because they have no shoes.[8]

As table 1.1 shows, in 1960 the black median family income ($1,444) was only 34 percent that of whites ($4,209), while nearly 83 percent of all black families had incomes below the poverty level ($3,000 per year). Half of the black population had completed only six years or less of schooling, and over 32,000 black adults had no formal education at all. In contrast, half of all white adults in the state had completed eleven or more years of school. Less than 8 percent of adult blacks were high school graduates, compared with more than 42 percent of whites. Most blacks in Mississippi worked in menial and low-paying positions. More than 40 percent of all employed black men were farm workers and laborers, and almost 65 percent of all employed black women were maids, cooks, servants, and other service workers. Most black families (61.9 percent) lived in rented housing, while 69 percent of all white families owned their own homes. Blacks occupied three-fourths of all dilapidated housing in Mississippi, and one in four black-occupied homes was substandard. Almost half of all black-occupied housing units were overcrowded (more than one person per room) and had no running water. More than two-thirds of all black-occupied homes had no bathing facilities, while only slightly more than one-fourth of all white-occupied homes lacked bathing facilities.

Segregation in education. The Supreme Court's *Brown v. Board of Education* decision outlawed racial segregation in the public schools as contrary to the Fourteenth Amendment and required public school desegregation "with all deliberate speed."[9] Although resistance to the *Brown* mandate was southwide, Mississippi successfully avoided any school desegregation for ten years, longer than any other southern state. In the first two years after the school desegregation ruling, Arkansas, Tennessee, and Texas began to desegregate their public schools. North Carolina began the desegregation process in the 1957–58 school year, Virginia achieved some desegregation in 1958–59, and Florida, Louisiana, and Georgia followed in the next three school

Table 1.1. Selected Socioeconomic Characteristics of White and Black Mississippians, 1960

	All Mississippians	Whites	Percent of All Mississippians	Percent of All Whites	Blacks	Percent of All Mississippians	Percent of All Blacks
Family Income							
Median	$2,884	$4,209			$1,444		
Below $3,000	258,549	111,589	43.2	34.5	146,960	56.8	82.9
Over $10,000	25,924	25,149	97.0	7.8	775	3.0	0.4
Public Assistance							
All categories	115,462	44,272	38.3		71,190	61.7	
Aid to dependent children	20,898	3,937	18.8		16,961	81.2	
Education (adults)							
Median years of school completed	8.9	11.0			6.0		
No school years completed	40,640	8,444	20.8	1.2	32,196	79.2	8.4
Four years of high school or more	317,100	288,085	90.8	42.2	29,015	9.2	7.6
Four years of college or more	59,273	52,523	88.6	7.7	6,750	11.4	1.8

Table 1.1. (*continued*)

	All Mississippians	Whites	Percent of All Mississippians	Percent of All Whites	Blacks	Percent of All Mississippians	Percent of All Blacks
Occupations							
White-collar	199,324	182,160	91.4	42.3	17,164	8.6	6.8
Blue-collar	233,006	159,518	68.5	37.1	73,488	31.5	29.2
Service workers	95,765	25,633	26.8	6.0	70,132	73.2	27.8
Farm workers	137,157	57,995	37.9	12.1	85,162	62.1	33.8
Housing							
Owner-occupied	327,894	248,835	75.9	69.0	79,059	24.1	38.1
Renter-occupied	240,176	111,624	46.5	31.0	128,552	53.5	61.9
Sound condition	346,821	276,997	79.9	76.8	69,824	20.1	33.6
Dilapidated	76,237	18,624	24.4	5.2	57,613	75.6	27.8
More than one person per room	133,428	48,454	36.3	13.4	84,974	63.7	40.9
Hot and cold piped water	343,802	302,932	88.1	71.9	40,870	11.9	19.7
No piped water	175,056	74,918	42.8	17.8	100,138	57.2	48.2
Flush toilet	380,974	311,604	81.8	73.9	69,730	18.3	33.6
No flush toilet	247,971	110,090	44.4	26.1	137,881	55.6	66.4

Table 1.1. (*continued*)

	All Mississippians	Whites	Percent of All Mississippians	Percent of All Whites	Blacks	Percent of All Mississippians	Percent of All Blacks
Bathtub or shower	355,282	308,084	86.7	73.1	47,198	13.3	22.7
No bathtub or shower	273,663	113,250	41.4	26.9	160,413	58.5	77.3

Sources: U.S. Bureau of the Census, *1960 Census of Population.* Vol. 1, *Characteristics of the Population, Part 26, Mississippi* (Washington, D.C.: Government Printing Office, 1963): United States Commission on Civil Rights, *Hearings Held in Jackson, Mississippi,* 2:355–73.

years. Alabama and South Carolina desegregated some districts in the 1963–64 school year. As late as 1963, Mississippi stood alone among southern states in having achieved no public school desegregation.[10] Mississippi's white citizens and white public officials were determined to resist public school desegregation by all available means. Public school segregation was fundamental to maintaining racial segregation and the subjugation of blacks throughout the society. Resistance to the Supreme Court's mandate was considered essential to the survival of the "southern way of life."

Mississippi congressman (later governor) John Bell Williams set the tone of resistance in a vitriolic speech in Congress. Williams castigated the first *Brown* decision, calling the day it was handed down "Black Monday."[11] Two months after the *Brown* decision, a group of white businessmen and planters formed the first Citizens' Council, also called the White Citizens' Council, in the Mississippi Delta town of Indianola, to provide open, organized resistance to school desegregation. From 1955 to 1964, the influence of the Citizens' Councils spread throughout Mississippi and the South. Within a few short years these organizations had become the most powerful of the white Southern segregationist groups, and during the 1960s the Citizens' Council was the most powerful force in Mississippi politics.[12]

In February 1956, the Mississippi state legislature passed an "interposition resolution" protesting the Supreme Court's "usurpation and encroachment on the reserved powers of the States." This resolution declared the Supreme Court's decisions to be "unconstitutional, invalid and of no lawful effect within the confines of the State of Mississippi."[13] The state legislature also passed statutes repealing Mississippi's compulsory school attendance law,[14] required all state and local officials and law enforcement officers "to prohibit, by any lawful, peaceful and constitutional means" implementation of the *Brown* decisions,[15] and established a State Sovereignty Commission with investigation and subpoena powers "to protect the sovereignty of the State of Mississippi" from federal encroachment—code words for maintaining segregation.[16] Mississippi's entire congressional delegation joined seventeen other southern United States senators and seventy-seven other southern representatives in signing the "Southern Manifesto," which decried "the Supreme Court's encroachments on rights reserved to the States" and commended "the motives of those States which have declared the intention to resist forced integration by any lawful means."[17]

The Supreme Court's school desegregation decisions posed a fundamental challenge to the status quo in race relations in Mississippi and triggered a resurgence in racial rhetoric in state gubernatorial campaigns and other public discourse. From 1954 to 1967, racial seg-

regation was the predominant campaign issue, and strict segregationist candidates won each election.[18] In resisting James Meredith's
admission to the all-white University of Mississippi, in 1962 Governor Ross Barnett, one of Mississippi's most racist firebrand governors, proclaimed: "We must either submit to the unlawful dictates of
the federal government, or stand up like men and tell them 'Never.'
. . . Every public official, including myself, should be prepared to
make the choice tonight whether he is willing to go to jail, if necessary, to keep faith with the people who have placed their welfare in
his hands."[19]

The first Mississippi school desegregation lawsuits were not filed
until 1963, when the Justice Department commenced two lawsuits
against the Biloxi and Gulfport districts and the NAACP Legal Defense Fund filed three lawsuits against the Jackson, Biloxi, and Leake
County school districts. By the 1964–65 school year, only 57 of Mississippi's almost 280,000 black schoolchildren attended formerly all-
white schools. By 1965, the overall desegregation rate for Mississippi's schools stood at .02 percent—the lowest in the South.[20]

Voter registration and political organizing efforts. Although there were
pockets of hard-core resistance, most parts of the South outside of
Mississippi had made considerable progress in black voter registration by 1964. In Tennessee and Florida, a majority of voting-age black
citizens were registered (69.5 percent and 51.2 percent, respectively).
Black registration remained lower in the Deep South, but 31.6 percent
of the black voting-age population was registered to vote in Louisiana, 27.4 percent in Georgia, and even 19.3 percent in Alabama.[21]

In Mississippi, however, a combination of a history of exclusion
from the electoral process, discriminatory registration practices, and
vicious white resistance to black political organizing efforts produced
a black voter registration rate of only 6.7 percent—the lowest of any
state in the nation.[22] Civil rights organizing and voter registration
drives throughout the state from 1961 to 1965 and the filing of thirty
voter discrimination and harassment lawsuits by the Justice Department had failed to make more than a slight dent in the political exclusion of black citizens.[23]

Although there had been prior efforts in Mississippi to register
black people to vote, the first concerted efforts of the 1960s began in
the southwest Mississippi counties of Amite, Pike, and Walthall by
SNCC organizers at the invitation of local NAACP leaders and under
the leadership of Robert Moses. When that effort failed as a result
of white violence and harassment, the jailing of the SNCC organizers and their local supporters, and the resistance of local registrars,
SNCC in 1962 began a second registration campaign in the predominantly black plantation counties of the Mississippi Delta area, pri-

marily Bolivar, Coahoma, Holmes, Leflore, Marshall, Sunflower, and Washington counties. Moses indicated at the time that SNCC decided to reconcentrate its voter registration efforts in the Delta area because a majority of the population was black and there had been "a tradition of Negro organizations." Although Moses recognized that the Delta was the stronghold of the White Citizens' Council and that there would be strong resistance, nevertheless he expressed the hope that some day it would be possible to elect a black person to Congress from the Delta, an act which he anticipated "would have tremendous symbolic and political value."[24] To provide an organizational framework for the receipt of VEP funding for voter registration and to submerge interorganizational rivalries, the civil rights groups active in Mississippi—SNCC, the Congress of Racial Equality (CORE), the Southern Christian Leadership Conference (SCLC), and the National Association for the Advancement of Colored People (NAACP)—formed COFO. The coalition selected state NAACP president Aaron Henry as president and SNCC leader Robert Moses as director of voter registration; most of the COFO staff were SNCC personnel.

When the voter registration campaign in the Delta collapsed, COFO switched its emphasis to demonstrating the extent of black disfranchisement in Mississippi to the nation at large in order to persuade the federal government to take a more active role in securing the voting rights of black citizens. In 1963 two mock statewide "freedom elections" were organized. The first, held in the early summer of 1963, was a mock primary election between the two leading white candidates for governor, Paul B. Johnson, Jr., and James P. Coleman. The mock primary was open to everyone, regardless of whether they were officially registered to vote, and about 27,000 potential black voters participated. The second, larger and more publicized mock vote was held in the fall to coincide with the regularly scheduled state elections. In addition to the official candidates, COFO also offered a "freedom slate" of Henry running for governor and the Reverend Edwin King, a white minister at Tougaloo College who was active in the civil rights movement, for lieutenant governor. COFO staff recruited about 100 white college students from Yale and Stanford universities to help organize the effort, and about 80,000 black people participated. These "freedom elections" put COFO organizing activities on a statewide basis and demonstrated to the nation that black people in Mississippi were interested in voting but could not cast official ballots. They also helped overcome fear in the black community about participating in civil rights activities and educated blacks about voting procedures.[25]

In June 1963, state NAACP field director Medgar Evers, a critical state civil rights leader who appealed to a wide range of groups and individuals in the state civil rights movement, was murdered outside his home in Jackson. His brother, Charles Evers, returned to Mississippi to take his place and began to concentrate his voter registration and civil rights organizing efforts in the predominantly black Mississippi River counties in southwest Mississippi.

After the success of the 1963 mock elections, Moses and Allard Lowenstein, a white civil rights organizer who assisted with the freedom elections, supported by local black organizers, including Lawrence Guyot and Fannie Lou Hamer, who worked with SNCC in Sunflower County, began planning a massive organizing project for the summer of 1964. They planned to bring to Mississippi large numbers of white college students from outside the South, although some black SNCC activists opposed outside white participation. The objectives of the campaign included expansion of voter registration efforts and establishment of a parallel, unofficial "freedom registration" process as an organizing tool. The summer effort was also designed to build a statewide political organization that would be an alternative to the all-white state Democratic party and could challenge the official state party delegation to the 1964 Democratic national convention at Atlantic City in August. The alternative party organization, called the Mississippi Freedom Democratic Party (MFDP), was organized in April 1964 at a rally in Jackson.

Historian Neil McMillan describes the Mississippi Freedom Summer of 1964 as "easily the most spectacular and sustained single event of recent civil rights history."[26] Approximately 1,000 student volunteers traveled to Mississippi for the summer to assist with voter registration efforts and MFDP organizing, to open up "freedom schools" to educate black children, and to operate community centers. As a result of these efforts, 17,000 black citizens attempted to register to vote, but only about 1,600 were registered, half of them in Panola County where a federal court order prohibited discrimination in voter registration. In contrast, approximately 80,000 black citizens were enrolled in the freedom registration campaign. The Mississippi Summer Project of 1964 triggered a severe white backlash of violence and intimidation: more than 1,000 persons were arrested, at least 80 persons were beaten, 35 churches were burned, 30 homes and other buildings were bombed, there were 35 shooting incidents involving black people or civil rights workers, and 3 civil rights workers—Andrew Goodman, Michael Schwerner, and James Chaney—were murdered.[27]

When black citizens were denied full participation in the regular Democratic party delegation selection process in June, the MFDP held precinct meetings and county conventions for delegate selection in twenty-six of the state's eighty-two counties and a state convention in August which chose a racially mixed slate of delegates to challenge the regular all-white state delegation to the Democratic convention in Atlantic City.[28] The MFDP's challenge won national support from labor unions and liberal Democratic party leaders, and Fannie Lou Hamer gave eloquent and impassioned testimony at the nationally televised credentials hearings dramatizing civil rights denials in Mississippi. Nonetheless, the credentials committee, at the urging of President Lyndon Johnson and his supporters who were afraid sustaining the challenge would weaken Johnson's southern white support, rejected the MFDP challenge. The liberal Democratic leadership proposed a compromise in which two MFDP delegates, Aaron Henry and Edwin King, would be seated as at-large delegates and the other MFDP delegates would be received as honored guests. In addition, the regular Mississippi delegation was required to take a loyalty oath to support the Democratic party nominee, and the national party committed itself to adopting guidelines against discrimination in time for the 1968 party convention. Although the convention accepted the compromise, the MFDP delegation, by majority vote, rejected it as a capitulation to racism and segregation. As Hamer put it during the final debate among the MFDP delegates: "We didn't come all this way for no two seats."[29]

In January 1965 the MFDP, relying on congressional precedents from the Reconstruction period, challenged the seating of Mississippi's congressional delegation in the U.S. House of Representatives. The congressional seating challenge also focused national attention on voting denials in Mississippi and enabled over 150 volunteer lawyers to compile 10,000 typed pages of testimony from some 400 witnesses on voting discrimination in the state. Although the House rejected the challenge by a vote of 228-143, the extensive record of discrimination compiled in support of the challenge helped document the need for the Voting Rights Act of 1965 and helped dramatize for members of Congress the enormous scale of voting rights denials in the South.[30]

Mississippi's discriminatory voter registration laws. The discriminatory voter registration requirements that blocked black registration efforts prior to 1965 derived from the Mississippi Constitutional Convention of 1890, the first southern constitutional convention called to deny blacks the vote after Reconstruction. Black citizens in Mississippi had been denied electoral participation since 1875 by violence, intimidation, and vote fraud, but white political leaders thought the convention was necessary to "legalize" this exclusion of blacks from the political process. As one delegate to the convention stated, "The avowed purpose of calling [this] convention was to restrict the negro vote."[31]

The 1890 constitutional convention enacted the "Mississippi Plan" of southern disfranchisement that subsequently was copied by other southern states. Because the Fifteenth Amendment to the United States Constitution prohibited express denial of the right to vote to black citizens, the 1890 convention adopted a series of indirect measures that included requirements that an applicant for registration (1) must be able to read any section of the state constitution, or be able to understand a section when read to him, or give a reasonable interpretation of one (changed in 1954 to read *and* understand any section of the state constitution); (2) must live in the state for two years and in the election district for one year before being eligible to register; (3) must register to vote four months before an election; (4) must not have been convicted of a list of disfranchising crimes that the framers of the constitution thought blacks were most prone to commit; and (5) must pay a poll tax every year to be able to vote.[32] These requirements were later supplemented by subsequent constitutional amendments and state laws designed to stiffen the prohibitions against blacks registering to vote, including requirements that an applicant must demonstrate an understanding of the duties and obligations of citizenship and possess "good moral character."[33]

During the 1960s the literacy test was the chief instrument of black disfranchisement, and black applicants frequently were disqualified if the written responses on their voter registration forms were not "letter perfect." To register to vote in Mississippi before 1965, applicants had to demonstrate their literacy by filling out in their own handwriting and without any assistance a long, complicated voter registration form asking detailed questions regarding occupation and business, residence, and criminal record. Prospective voters had to copy any section of the Mississippi Constitution chosen by the registrar, write a correct interpretation of that section, and then explain in writing "your understanding of the duties and obligations of citizenship under a constitutional form of government." This was no easy task because, as Mississippi politician Theodore Bilbo once remarked, the Mississippi Constitution is a document "that damn few white men and no niggers at all can explain."[34] Any mistake or error in filling out the form, or any answer which the registrar considered to be incorrect, was cause for disqualification.[35]

One of the key features of Mississippi's registration procedure was the amount of discretion granted to county registrars to discriminate against black applicants. In some counties, blacks were given ex-

tremely difficult sections of the state constitution to write and interpret, while whites got easy sections and illegal assistance in filling
out the form. Registrars often failed black applicants for making simple mistakes, such as signing the form on the wrong line, while rou-
tinely passing whites who made similar or worse mistakes. Registrars
rejected black applicants who could not interpret long sections of the
state constitution that even some registrars could not interpret. In
one county, white applicants asked to interpret section 35 of the state
constitution ("The senate shall consist of members chosen every four
years by the qualified electors of the several districts") passed the test
even though they wrote only "equible wrights" or "The government
is for the people and by the people."[36]

If this obstacle course was not enough, under state laws passed in
1962 the names of those taking the voter registration test were published in a local newspaper once a week for two weeks. While the
stated purpose of this publication requirement was to permit voters
to challenge the qualifications of applicants, many black applicants
found that after their name had been published they were arrested
on spurious charges; subjected to physical violence, economic reprisals, or loss of employment; or found themselves unable to get jobs.[37]
Applicants were not informed whether or not they passed the voter
registration test; instead, they had to return to the registrar's office
thirty days after applying. Those who passed signed the voting rolls
and became registered voters. State law did not permit the registrar
to give failed applicants the reason for rejection (except for bad moral
character). Providing such information was considered to be illegal
"help" with the voter registration test.[38] To be fully qualified to vote,
voters also had to pay a $2 poll tax each year well in advance of the
election. In many counties, the sheriff simply refused to accept poll
tax payments from blacks.[39]

The exclusion of blacks from the political process had enormous
consequences for the politics of the state. During the first four decades of this century, Mississippi was the home of James K. Vardaman and Theodore G. Bilbo—two of the most vicious racial demagogues in the nation's history. From 1954 to 1967, gubernatorial
campaigns generally became exercises in race baiting. Candidates
won by appealing more effectively than their opponents to the racist
sentiments of white voters: Ross Barnett in 1959; Paul B. Johnson, Jr.,
in 1963; and John Bell Williams in 1967.[40] Blacks, who constituted 42
percent of the state's population in 1960—the highest percentage of
any state in the country—were all but totally unrepresented in elective offices. Occupants of the state capitol, the county courthouses,
and the city halls were all white; the only recorded black elected offi-

cials in the state in 1965 were the mayor and city council of the all-black Delta town of Mound Bayou.[41]

The passage of the Voting Rights Act. If the police attack on the civil rights marchers at the Selma bridge in March 1965 provided the catalyst for Congress to pass the Voting Rights Act, the record of official intransigence in Mississippi demonstrated the need. From 1960 to 1964 almost half of the Justice Department's lawsuits alleging racial discrimination in voter registration—twenty-two lawsuits involving twenty-seven counties—were filed in Mississippi, yet these cases failed to make more than a slight dent in the political exclusion of black citizens. Although the Civil Rights Act of 1960 gave the Justice Department a right to inspect and copy the records of county registrars, most registrars refused to make those records available without a court order, and months of litigation and lengthy delays were required just to gain access to the registration records. Further, a number of southern federal judges who were hostile to the Justice Department's efforts—notably District Judges Harold Cox of the Southern District of Mississippi and Claude Clayton of the Northern District of Mississippi—generally refused to grant any relief, necessitating appeals to the U.S. Court of Appeals for the Fifth Circuit, whose judges—also Southerners—were heroically dedicated to upholding the law.[42] Attorney General Nicholas Katzenbach, in his 1965 congressional testimony in support of the administration's bill, cited the slow rate of progress in registering black citizens and the excessive delays in litigating voting discrimination cases in Mississippi, along with Alabama and Louisiana, in support of his conclusion that "the judicial process, upon which all existing remedies depend, is institutionally inadequate to deal with practices so deeply rooted in the social and political structure. . . . Litigation on a case-by-case basis simply cannot do the job."[43] The House Judiciary Committee, in its report favoring passage of the act, relied on the same Mississippi statistics and litigation record described by Katzenbach in his testimony and also noted the "upsurge of public indignation against the systematic exclusion of Negroes from the polls."[44]

The Voting Rights Act of 1965 was the most far-reaching voting rights legislation ever enacted. In a section that was one of the most controversial during the congressional debate but that had the greatest immediate effect (section 4), the act automatically suspended all literacy tests and other discriminatory voter registration tests in seven southern states (Mississippi, Alabama, Georgia, Louisiana, South Carolina, Virginia, and forty counties in North Carolina). The act also declared the poll taxes unconstitutional and directed the Justice Department to file lawsuits to strike them down (section 10); authorized the Justice Department to dispatch federal examiners (voter registrars) and observers (poll watchers) to register voters and observe elections (sections 6, 7, and 8); and required the approval of the U.S. attorney general or the U.S. District Court for the District of Columbia for any new voting-law changes in covered states (section 5).

The Voting Rights Act was a great victory for the civil rights protest movement. It produced the massive federal intervention COFO and SNCC strategists hoped to achieve by their switch in tactics from county-by-county registration drives to statewide demonstrations of black political exclusion and to seating challenges at the Democratic National Convention and in Congress. In one piece of legislation, Congress struck down the discriminatory voter registration tests and the poll taxes that had barred black voting for so long.[45]

The "realization gap." In Mississippi, as a result of the elimination of voter registration tests, the dispatch of federal registrars to twenty-three Mississippi counties, and intensive voter registration campaigns by civil rights groups throughout the state, an estimated 235,000 black citizens were added to the voter registration rolls from August 1965, when the Voting Rights Act was signed into law, to September 1967. As shown on table 1.2, Mississippi's black voter registration rate rose from 6.7 percent of those eligible to an estimated 59.8 percent in 1967—the highest registration rate of any state covered by the suspension-of-registration-tests provision of the Voting Rights Act.[46] In this brief two-year period, black voters increased from 5 percent to 28 percent of the total Mississippi statewide electorate. By 1970, 66.3 percent of Mississippi's blacks of voting age were on the registration rolls. Although by 1980 the percentage of the black voting age population that was registered to vote had slipped slightly to 64.1 percent, that percentage was still the highest rate of any state covered by the Voting Rights Act.[47]

The goal of the Mississippi voter registration efforts was not simply to get black people registered, but to win elective office to change the oppressive conditions that prevailed in the state. As Fannie Lou Hamer put it: "We have to build our own power. We have to win every single political office we can, where we have a majority of black people."[48] But the dramatic increase in black voter registration after the passage of the Voting Rights Act did not immediately result in a commensurate increase in the number of black elected officials. The expectation that Mississippi's newly enfranchised black voters would now be able to elect their fair share of black officeholders was not realized, a phenomenon that may be termed a "realization gap." This is the gap experienced after 1965 by black voters in Mississippi (and other southern states) between their expectation that they could exer-

Table 1.2. Registered Voters in Mississippi, 1964–1980

Year	Number of White Voters	Percent of White Voting-Age Population Registered	Number of Black Voters	Percent of Black Voting-Age Population Registered
1964	525,000	69.9	28,500	6.7
1967	665,176	91.5	263,754	59.8
1971	670,710	71.6	268,440	62.2
1975	866,000	80.7	286,000	60.7
1980	1,152,000	102.2[a]	330,000	64.1

Sources: United States Commission on Civil Rights, *Political Participation*, app. VII, table 1; Voter Education Project statistics.

[a] Failure to purge the names of whites who have died or moved away results in a voter registration rate for whites of over 100 percent.

cise their newly gained voting power to elect black candidates to office and the actual realization of that expectation in terms of gaining black representation.

As the data on table 1.3 show, after 1965 the increases in black registration and voting power were not matched by significant corresponding increases in the number of black elected officials as a percentage of the total number of elective offices in the state. In the first statewide elections after the Voting Rights Act became law, held in 1967, despite the fact that blacks had population majorities in 28 counties and that black voters constituted twenty-eight percent of the statewide electorate, they were successful in electing only 22 black candidates to office. By 1968, taking into account the 1967 elections, school board elections, and other off-year elections, there were only 29 black elected officials in the entire state, or only 0.6 percent of the total number of elected officials. By 1972—seven years after the passage of the Voting Rights Act and after the statewide elections held in 1971—there were only 129 black officeholders who held only 2.7 percent of all elective offices. This included only 1 black representative in the 174-member state legislature and only 8 black members of the powerful county boards of supervisors out of a total of 410 county supervisors in the state.

This low success rate was not due to the lack of black candidates. As more fully described in chapter 2, in the 1967 statewide elections 127 black candidates ran, or attempted to qualify, for public office. Of these, 19 were disqualified by stringent new qualifying requirements, and 86 were defeated, including 7 of 8 candidates for the state legisla-

Table 1.3. Registered Black Voters and Black Elected Officials
in Mississippi, 1964–1980

Year	Percent of Black Voting-Age Population Registered	Blacks as Percent of Total Registered Voters	Number of Black Elected Officials	Blacks as Percent of Total Elected Officials	Black Legislators (Total = 174)	Black Supervisors (Total = 410)
1964	6.7	5	6	0.1	0	0
1967	59.8	28				
1968			29	0.6	1	4
1971	62.2	29				
1972			129	2.7	1	8
1975	60.7	25				
1976			210	4.4	4	16
1979	64.1	22				
1980			387	7.3	17	27

Source: Voter registration figures from Voter Education Project, United States Commission on Civil Rights; black elected officials statistics from Joint Center for Political Studies, *Black Elected Officials*, 1970, 1971, 1976, 1980.

ture, 14 of 16 candidates for countywide offices, 32 of 36 candidates for county supervisor, 14 of 23 candidates for justice of the peace, and 19 of 25 candidates for constable. Similarly, although in the 1971 statewide elections the number of black candidates more than doubled, again more than 80 percent of the black candidates went down to defeat. Of the 309 black candidates who ran, 259 lost, including 28 of 29 candidates for the state legislature, 10 of 10 candidates for chancery clerk, 14 of 14 candidates for sheriff, 10 of 10 candidates for county school superintendent, and 67 of 74 candidates for county supervisor.[49] Most of the black candidates who were elected were concentrated in relatively minor, non-policymaking positions, such as justice of the peace and constable, while the vast majority of the black candidates who ran for the most significant positions, such as state legislator and county supervisor, went down to defeat.

What is the explanation for this high rate of black electoral defeat after 1965? Donald R. Matthews and James W. Prothro, in their 1966 report based on 1961 southwide survey data, attributed low levels of black electoral participation to the low socioeconomic status of blacks, individual socioeconomic characteristics, and individual political attitudes, including lack of political partisanship, lack of interest, and lack of information.[50] But the dramatic increases in black participation in COFO's organizing efforts after 1963 and in black voter registration rates shortly after passage of the Voting Rights Act indicate that there was no lack of interest by black people in Mississippi in electoral participation. Political scientists Lester Salamon and Stephen Van Evera, in a later Mississippi study, found that after 1965 black voter turnout in the majority-black counties was not uniform and rarely exceeded 50 percent of the black voting-age population.[51] They concluded that the lack of black electoral success in Mississippi's majority-black counties was primarily associated with blacks' economic dependence on whites and with vulnerability to economic intimidation, which made blacks fearful of participating in the electoral process.[52]

Undoubtedly, a number of factors were involved, including the refusal of whites to vote for black candidates; the extensive history of exclusion of black citizens from the political process; low income and education levels; continuing white harassment and vulnerability of blacks to economic intimidation, which contributed to low turnout rates in some areas; and election irregularities. But studies of black political participation after 1965 have tended to disregard the fact that racial discrimination in the electoral process continued to play a critical role. The Voting Rights Act, while it struck down the most prominent legal barriers to blacks' registering to vote, did not immediately eliminate all the formal, legal barriers to black voters' electing candidates of their choice, and the post–Voting Rights Act white political counterinsurgency played a major role in the electoral defeat of black candidates. Nowhere is this more evident than in Mississippi, and the next chapter describes the new barriers enacted by the Mississippi Legislature immediately after passage of the Voting Rights Act to prevent black voters from gaining representation of their choice.

2 Mississippi's Massive Resistance to Black Political Empowerment

As early as 1958 Mississippi's leading newspaper, the Jackson *Clarion-Ledger*, urged the "custodians of Mississippi's 'white supremacy' machinery" to "take a serious, studied look" at the racial composition of the state's congressional districts "in view of the NAACP's vigorous drive for Negro voting rights." The newspaper's city editor noted that with a black majority in Congressman Frank Smith's Third District ("every one of the 11 counties . . . has a negro majority") and substantial black concentrations in the Fourth District ("seven of the thirteen counties have negro majorities") "it can be readily seen that the full employment of the ballot by the negro would represent a serious threat to 'white supremacy.' "[1]

Four years later, although black candidates for Congress in the 1962 election got few votes and the *Clarion-Ledger/Jackson Daily News* concluded that the results showed "rather clearly that there is no sizeable Negro bloc vote in Mississippi," the paper nevertheless predicted "the Legislature can be expected to re-district the state so as to split the Second District if a Negro's election ever appears imminent there."[2] Thus were the "custodians of Mississippi's 'white supremacy' machinery" forewarned of the "serious threat to 'white supremacy' " posed by the potential black vote.

The tremendous increase in black voter registration following passage of the Voting Rights Act triggered a "massive resistance" reaction by white political leaders aimed at nullifying the newly gained black vote. Deprived by federal legislation of the legal authority to prevent blacks from registering to vote, the state's white leadership resorted to a massive resistance strategy of employing numerous devices to perpetuate white control at all levels of government:

1. From 1966 to 1982 the Mississippi Legislature gerrymandered Mississippi's five congressional districts to prevent the election of a black member of Congress by dividing the predominantly black Delta region among three of the five districts, denying black voters a voting majority in any district.

2. From 1966 to 1979 the Mississippi Legislature denied black vot-

ers the opportunity to elect candidates of their choice to state legislative seats through the use of multimember legislative districts. These multimember districts employed at-large voting for two or more state senators or representatives in majority-white countywide or multi-county districts to submerge black population concentrations that were large enough for separate legislative representation.

3. Pursuant to state legislation enacted in 1966, fourteen counties switched from district to at-large elections for county boards of supervisors (the county governing boards), and twenty-two counties switched from district to at-large county school board elections. After at-large county elections were blocked by lawsuits and Justice Department objections under section 5 of the Voting Rights Act, almost half of Mississippi's eighty-two counties gerrymandered county supervisors' district boundaries to dilute black voting strength and to prevent the election of black county officials.

4. Beginning in 1966, the state legislature enacted a number of statutes designed to prevent the election of black candidates, including bills that increased the filing requirements for independent candidates and eliminated elections for certain offices. In 1966, 1970, 1975, 1976, and 1979 the legislature also enacted discriminatory "open primary" bills that eliminated the opportunity to win a general election with less than a majority of the vote and instituted a general election runoff requirement.

5. Anticipating black registration increases, forty-six cities and towns switched to at-large city council elections to prevent the election of black city council members beginning in 1962. In addition, many of Mississippi's cities and towns—including Jackson, the state's largest city—retained preexisting at-large election systems after the Voting Rights Act became law, resulting in the exclusion of black representation in city government.

6. Other devices, such as discriminatory municipal annexations and last-minute polling place changes, also have been used to dilute black voting strength.

Most of these vote-dilution stratagems were products of the 1966 regular and special sessions of the Mississippi Legislature, referred to as the political massive resistance session. This chapter focuses on that session of the Mississippi Legislature and analyzes the political context in which these vote-dilution devices were conceived, the legislative history of their enactment, and their impact on the first statewide elections following passage of the Voting Rights Act in 1967.

Political commentators have previously applied the term "massive resistance" primarily to the efforts of southern states to resist the Supreme Court's *Brown v. Board of Education* school desegregation decision by preaching defiance and refusing voluntary compliance, enacting pupil placement laws to avoid desegregation, providing financial assistance to segregated private schools, and closing or threatening to close desegregated public schools.[3] But the term equally may be applied to Mississippi's efforts to undermine the black franchise. Like the massive resistance campaign against school desegregation, the political massive resistance campaign was borne of an effort to frustrate a federal desegregation mandate (the Voting Rights Act of 1965), received its primary impetus from white state legislators who represented majority-black districts, was effectuated by a comprehensive series of state laws designed to avoid desegregation, and was couched in legalistic language and a facade of respectability. As it developed in Mississippi, the political massive resistance strategy was as encompassing and extreme in its impact on the state's election laws as the earlier effort was on the state's education statutes.

There were some differences, however, between massive resistance in education and massive resistance to voting rights. The open defiance, emotional public appeals, and blatant white supremacist rhetoric that characterized the legislative nullification strategy against desegregating the public schools were largely absent in the campaign against the black vote. White political leaders had found that their racial statements could be used against them in court to strike down such openly racial legislation, and therefore overt racial rhetoric was replaced by coded language, a reluctance to provide opportunities for public debate on proposed changes, and often transparent denials as to what was being attempted. Further, many of the political massive resistance statutes did not require immediate statewide changes but were targeted to particular counties where the threat, in the view of the county's legislative delegation, was thought to be the greatest.

Mississippi, which was one of the leaders of the black disfranchisement movement in the South with the "Mississippi Plan" of 1890, once again led the way with the black vote dilution strategy developed and implemented in Mississippi's massive resistance legislative session in 1966. Before the session ended, the all-white state legislature enacted thirteen major pieces of legislation which radically altered Mississippi's election laws and made it more difficult for black candidates to get elected and for the newly enfranchised black voters to gain representation of their choice. These bills incorporated a wide range of stratagems: racial gerrymandering of district lines, switching from district to countywide elections, multiplying the qualifying requirements for independent candidates to run for office, changing elected positions to appointed posts, and consolidating majority-black counties with majority-white counties. Then, in a later special session, the legislature enacted a new state legislative reapportionment plan for the election of state senators and representatives that increased the number of multimember districts, that is, districts electing two or more legislators countywide or districtwide from districts that combined two or more counties.

Outright denial to black Mississippians of the right to vote, now prohibited by federal law, was replaced with these more subtle strategies to dilute and cancel out the black vote. Mississippi's massive resistance to black political participation proved extremely effective. Not until these legal barriers were removed through court battles many years in duration would Mississippi's newly enfranchised black voters be able to exercise a meaningful vote. Initially, the federal courts were uncertain how to respond to these new strategies for nullifying the black vote. But, ultimately, the passage of this legislation resulted in an expansion of the protections of the Voting Rights Act by the Supreme Court, which established the present legal framework used by civil rights forces to counter new efforts to dilute the minority vote.

The first section of this chapter describes the political situation in Mississippi as the 1966 legislative session began and then details the massive resistance legislation of 1966, showing how it was designed to get around the black franchise. The second section analyzes the political mobilization of the black community for the 1967 elections and suggests that, although the minimal gains Mississippi blacks won were widely hailed as historic firsts, and rightly so, the limits on their successes actually amounted to a victory for massive resistance.

Mississippi's Massive Resistance Legislation

When the Mississippi Legislature convened for its regular biennial session in Jackson in January of 1966, the Voting Rights Act and its implications for Mississippi politics were very much on the minds of the state legislators. The stage was set for a new kind of battle between change and status quo. On one side were Mississippi's black citizens, already registering to vote in massive numbers. Federal registrars, dispatched by the federal government, were registering black citizens in twenty-three counties, and the state's civil rights organizations—the NAACP, the MFDP, CORE, and others—were organizing voter registration drives and encouraging black candidates to run for public office.

On the other side was the state's white power structure. Having lost the effort to prevent passage of the Voting Rights Act the previous year, as well as a futile attempt to prevent Mississippi from being covered by its suspension of voter registration tests,[4] the state's political leaders now stood in a much weaker position. Despite the setbacks of 1965, however, the leadership of the 174-member, all-white state legislature was determined to find new ways to minimize black electoral participation. Many of the key legislators were holdovers from the Ross Barnett "Never!" era, and many of them listed Citizens' Council membership in their official state biographies.[5] Indeed, the situation was a challenge to the inventiveness of the state's white supremacist leadership in circumventing the new law.

An additional factor contributed to the crisis atmosphere. In October 1965, the MFDP had filed a "one-person, one-vote" lawsuit, *Connor v. Johnson*, challenging the constitutionality of the state's five congressional districts and the state's legislative districting for gross population disparities among the districts and for exclusion of black representation. Objectively, the state's white political leadership knew that these grossly malapportioned districts were likely to be struck down by the federal court, and legislative action had to be taken or the federal court would draw new districts itself. All five members of Mississippi's U.S. House of Representatives delegation were up for election in 1966—the Democratic primary, the decisive election, was scheduled for June 7—and all 174 state legislators faced upcoming elections in 1967.

The effort to nullify the newly gained black vote was the dominant theme of the Mississippi Legislature's 1966 regular session and the special session later that year. Altogether, approximately thirty bills concerning elections and the political process were introduced.[6] Most of the bills were introduced in early January, indicating that they had been drafted prior to the start of the legislative session. The bills had a number of different sponsors, although there was some overlap. But most of the sponsors were from the majority-black counties, primarily in the Delta area and along the Mississippi River, where the white political leadership apparently thought it had the most to lose from black electoral participation. Before the year ended, the all-white legislature had enacted thirteen major pieces of legislation that radically altered Mississippi's election laws, making it more difficult for black voters to elect candidates of their choice to office.

The legislative deliberations on these bills provide a rare but interesting glimpse into the dynamics of post–Voting Rights Act white supremacy politics. The stereotype of a unified white leadership marching in lockstep does not always apply here. Although there was unity of purpose in the legislature that the black vote had to be nullified, sometimes there was disagreement on the exact tactics to be employed, and not all of the bills were passed without some dissent.

In striking contrast to the racially inflammatory rhetoric that characterized the debate over school segregation, both houses of the legislature attempted to maintain a conspiracy of silence regarding the racial motivation behind this legislation. Contemporary press accounts sometimes noted the coded language of the debates. There were a number of civil rights lawsuits pending in the state at the time, including the MFDP's reapportionment case, and it is apparent that the managers of these bills wanted to avoid creating any public record of their discriminatory intent that might be used later in legal proceedings. Although there were occasional references to the racial purpose of the bills, as during the state Senate debate on the bill providing for at-large county supervisor elections, and instances in which opponents broke the code of silence to dispute the wisdom of the tactics employed to nullify the black vote, the thirteen measures generally were enacted with little floor debate or mention of race as an issue. Public hearings that would have provided a forum for black leaders to give public testimony about the discriminatory impact of these measures were also scrupulously avoided.

Finally, there is little evidence of strong gubernatorial leadership similar to that provided earlier by Governor Ross Barnett or Virginia governor Lindsay Almond in massive resistance to school desegregation. Governor Paul B. Johnson, Jr., had been elected in 1963 because, as Barnett's lieutenant, he personally (but unsuccessfully) attempted to block James Meredith's enrollment at the all-white University of Mississippi. But, despite his record of resistance to desegregation, Johnson appears to have provided little direction to this 1966 political massive resistance effort, even going so far as to veto one element, the "open primary" bills.

The major bills comprising Mississippi's political massive resistance program to black political participation are listed in table 2.1. It is important to note that—unlike the discriminatory voter registration laws struck down by the Voting Rights Act—none of these bills directly denied anyone the right to vote. The 1966 bills, which focused on electoral rules, procedures, and structures rather than voting per se, presented more veiled obstacles to black political participation. In the following pages I will describe the rationale behind each bill, the circumstances under which the bills were enacted, and the effect on black political successes.

Table 2.1. Massive Resistance Legislation (1966 Regular and Special Sessions of the Mississippi State Legislature)

Racial Gerrymandering of Congressional Districts

House Bill 911. Gerrymandered the boundaries of Mississippi's five congressional districts to divide the black population concentration in the Delta area.

Changes in Methods of Election and Electoral Rules

County Officials to Be Chosen in Countywide Elections
House Bill 223. Authorized county boards of supervisors to change system for electing supervisors. Traditionally, Mississippi counties had been divided into five supervisors' districts, each electing one supervisor. Now, supervisors would be chosen in at-large, countywide elections.

Senate Bill 1966. Reenacted 1964 statute authorizing countywide referendums to switch from district to at-large county school board elections, required at-large school board elections in six counties, and permitted school boards to adopt at-large elections without referendums in two additional counties.

House Bill 275. Authorized switch from district to at-large county school board elections in Coahoma and Washington counties, and increased the qualifying requirements.

House Bill 1074. Authorized switch from district to at-large county school board elections in Leflore County, and increased the qualifying requirements.

School Superintendent Changed from Elected to Appointed Position
House Bill 183. Authorized countywide referendums on changing the position of county school superintendent from an elected position to an appointed position, and made the office appointive in eleven counties.

House Bill 200. Authorized appointment rather than election of a municipal school board trustee in Grenada County.

Counties Combined
House Concurrent Resolution 35. Constitutional amendment allowing the Mississippi Legislature by a two-thirds vote to combine counties.

Qualifying Requirements for Independent Candidates Increased
House Bill 68. Increased the qualifying requirements for independent candidates for office, including increasing the number of signatures required on nominating petitions tenfold or more and prohibiting anyone who has voted in a party primary from running as an independent candidate.

Nominating Procedure for School Trustees Changed
House Bill 446, Senate Bill 1880. Changed the nominating procedures and increased the qualifying requirements for school district trustees.

Open Primary Procedures Adopted
House Bills 436 and 793. Mississippi's open primary bills abolished party primaries and required a majority vote to win office. (Vetoed by Governor Johnson.)

Table 2.1. *(continued)*

Multimember Districts and At-Large Elections for State Legislature

Senate Bill 1504. Redistricted the state House of Representatives and state Senate districts by increasing the number of discriminatory multimember districts based on whole county units and combinations of counties. All members were to be elected at-large, countywide and districtwide, thus submerging the votes of black population concentrations in majority-white legislative districts. (Passed in special session of Mississippi state legislature in the fall of 1966.)

Racial Gerrymandering

As blacks began to achieve "the full employment of the ballot" about which the Jackson newspapers had warned, Mississippi's legislators were extremely concerned that black Mississippians might use their newly won voting power to elect one of their own to the U.S. Congress. Of all the regions of Mississippi, the one in which the newly enfranchised black Mississippi voters had the greatest potential electoral strength was in the northwest, heavily black quarter of the state known as the Mississippi Delta.

The Delta area, shown on map 2.1 along with the state's other geographic regions, is one of Mississippi's unique geopolitical regions.[7] Formed from the rich, black flood deposits of the Mississippi River and the ancient Ohio River, the Mississippi Delta stretches from the Tennessee line just south of Memphis to Vicksburg in the northwest portion of the state. Here is where Mississippi's largest and richest plantations developed, and where a few white plantation owners accumulated great wealth from the labor of large numbers of black workers, who were kept—and continue to be kept—in great poverty. In consequence, overall the region is one of the poorest in the country because of the great poverty of the Delta's black population, and it is no accident that this region gave birth to that uniquely American music known as "the Delta blues." Despite the great black outmigration resulting from the mechanization of cotton production, in the 1960s the Mississippi Delta still had the largest concentration of black people in the state; seventeen of the state's twenty-eight majority-black counties were located in whole or in part in this region.

The Delta region had been the heart of a congressional district in Mississippi for more than eighty years, since 1882. In each redrawing of congressional district lines necessitated by a reduction in the number of House seats allocated to Mississippi—in 1932, 1952, and 1962—the state legislature had kept the Delta district intact. In the last redis-

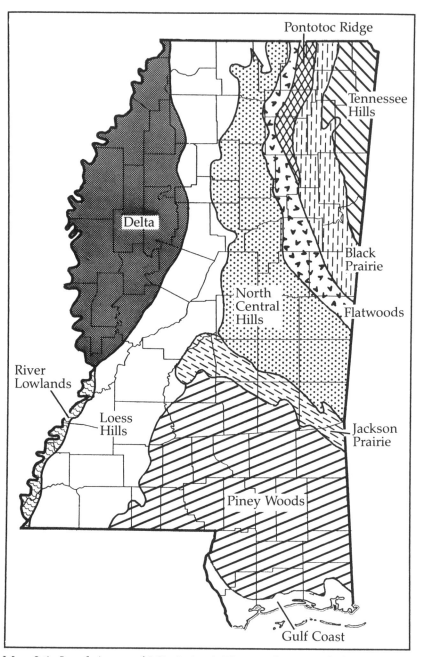

Map 2.1. Land Areas of Mississippi. The predominantly black Delta region is in the northwest corner of the state.

tricting in 1962, Mississippi's segregationist forces, led by Governor Ross Barnett and state Speaker of the House Walter Sillers, combined the Delta district, which was then 65 percent black, with Representative Jamie L. Whitten's Second District to defeat moderate Representative Frank E. Smith, Jr.[8] (see maps 2.2 and 2.3). But this maneuver made Whitten's district the new Delta district, because it preserved the Delta intact, with blacks continuing to outnumber whites in the district by 113,000 persons.

This situation represented no threat to Mississippi's all-white congressional delegation so long as Mississippi's discriminatory voter registration laws prevented blacks from registering to vote in significant numbers. The last black member of Congress from Mississippi had been John R. Lynch in the 1880s; since then, Mississippi's congressional delegation had been all white. The passage of the Voting Rights Act not only threatened Whitten's tenure but also raised the possibility that the district's black majority might elect a black candidate to the House of Representatives.

Ironically, the Mississippi Legislature found the excuse it needed to redraw the congressional district lines in middecade in the Supreme Court's newly announced one-person, one-vote rule[9] and in the MFDP's lawsuit, *Connor v. Johnson*, filed in October 1965, challenging the 1962 plan for unconstitutional malapportionment, described in detail in chapter 3. The basic strategy chosen by the Mississippi Legislature for redrawing congressional district lines was to replace the north-south dividing line between the northernmost two districts with new district lines running east and west, thereby splitting up the majority-black Delta counties among new districts. The state House of Representatives and state Senate deadlocked over competing plans. The House wanted to divide the Delta area among four districts, all of which were majority-white in population. The Senate, on the other hand, wanted to retain a slight, but politically meaningless, black population majority in one district as a defense against a racial gerrymandering claim.

Ultimately, a compromise plan was adopted of the type political scientist Richard Engstrom has termed "equi-populous gerrymandering."[10] The new plan met the one-person, one-vote standard for substantial equality of population among the districts. But it dispersed the Delta counties—which previously were included in the congressional district that was 59 percent black—among three new districts, combining majority-black Delta counties with majority-white counties on the other side of the state. Although one of the new districts had a slight black population majority, all of them were majority white in voting-age population.

The House plan was introduced in the first week of the legislative

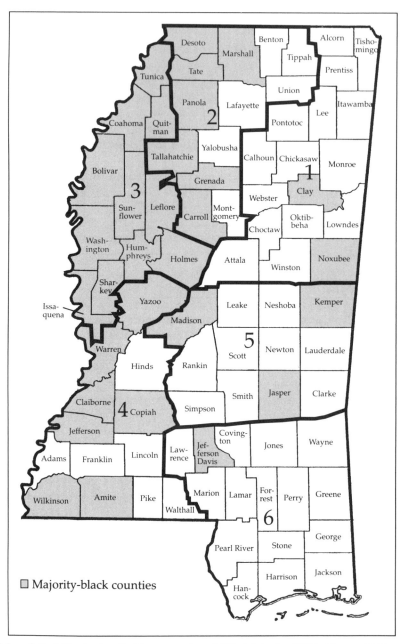

Map 2.2. Mississippi's Congressional Districts in 1956. From 1882 to 1956, the Delta area was preserved intact in a single district (in 1956, the Third Congressional District).

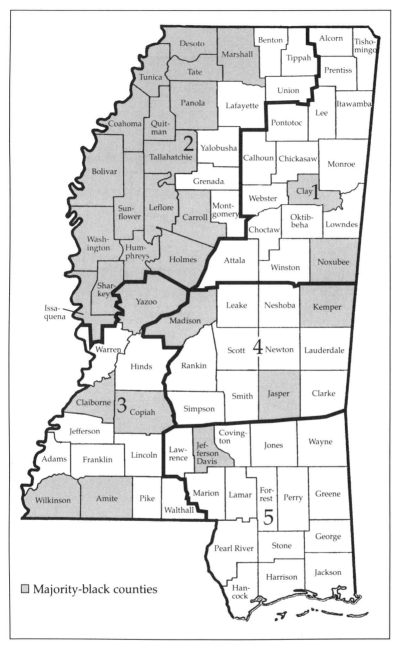

Map 2.3. Congressional Districts Adopted by the State Legislature in 1962. After the 1960 census, as a result of the reapportionment of congressional seats, Mississippi lost a seat in the U.S. House of Representatives. The Second and Third Congressional Districts were simply combined to form a new Second District, which included the Delta area and was almost 60 percent black in population.

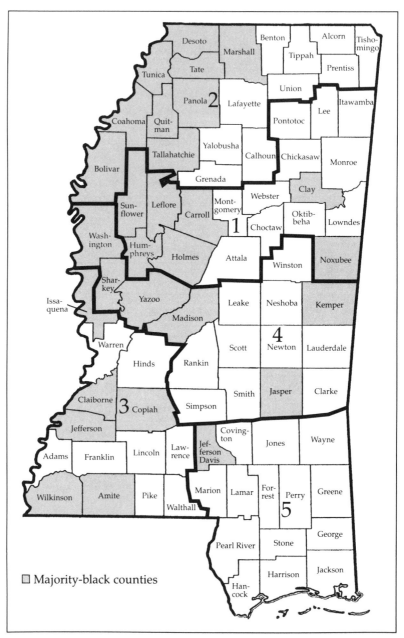

Map 2.4. First Congressional Redistricting Plan Adopted by the State House of Representatives in 1966. The House-passed plan would have divided the Delta among four of the state's five congressional districts, leaving all five districts majority-white in population.

session by Representative Kenneth Williams of majority-black Coahoma County, a Delta county. Williams's bill called for dividing the Delta area among four majority-white districts (see map 2.4). Although Williams justified his plan exclusively on the basis of nonracial criteria (equalizing population; providing compact districts; preserving social, economic, and historical associations; protecting incumbents), the Jackson press reported that the bill reflected "the need for balancing white and negro populations by across-state alignments."[11]

Two opponents of the Williams bill, both of them from the predominantly white First Congressional District in northeast Mississippi, which would have received some majority-black Delta counties for the first time under the proposal, charged that the bill was a racial gerrymander designed to split up the black vote. The Jackson *Clarion-Ledger* reported:

> "Did the Negro situation enter in this redistricting plan?" asked Rep. Odie Trenor [of Chickasaw County]. . . . When he got no answer to his question, he said, "we all know the Negro situation was the main factor."
>
> Rep. Thompson McClellan of Clay [County] said, "When this bill is attacked in the courts they're going to look into what areas were moved, where they were moved and for what purposes they have been moved. They were moved so there shall not be a majority of certain groups in a district. The courts will consider a similar case and they'll throw this out. . . . This patently was drawn in a manner to devalue the vote of a certain group of people."
>
> Backers of the plan did not deny that the Delta area was split up to divide the heavy Negro vote.[12]

The Associated Press account of the debate noted: "Legislators frequently refrain from using the word 'Negro,' and refer to Negroes as 'a certain group.' "[13]

The four-way split of the black population in the Delta "to minimize its influence at the polls" was "an issue proponents had hoped to keep 'under wraps,' " the Memphis *Commercial Appeal* reported.

> Although that was an obvious purpose in the realignment of the counties in the Williams bill proponents had sought to keep it from arising on the floor. They realize once it was brought into the open it would provide the arguments desired by those reportedly planning to challenge it before the United States Supreme Court.
>
> However, the race issue is now out front and opponents of the

Williams proposal have been given the ammunition they had hoped would be supplied from the floor to support their contentions the purpose was to devalue the Negro vote by absorbing it with white majorities in the proposed new districts.[14]

State NAACP field secretary Charles Evers denounced the House-passed bill as "discriminatory and obviously designed to gerrymander districts to split up Negro voting strength." He requested a chance to testify in the state Senate against the bill, but Lieutenant Governor Carroll Gartin announced there would be no hearings and urged anyone with an opinion on the proposal to contact their state senator.[15]

In February the Senate enacted its own version (see map 2.5), sponsored by Senator W. B. Alexander of majority-black Bolivar County, also a Delta county. The Alexander bill split up the Delta region among three districts but left one district with a slight (55.36 percent) black population majority to forestall the anticipated federal court challenge. "Our purpose with this bill," Senator Alexander explained, "is to pass a bill all of us can live with and still pass the scrutiny of the court." He predicted that the Senate bill "will be easy for attorneys to defend in court."[16] An alternative plan that would have established white population majorities in all five districts was defeated by a 25-21 vote after supporters of the Alexander proposal warned that the alternative was too obvious a gerrymander and might result in "the unseating of the entire Mississippi congressional delegation."[17] The Senate also voted down by a narrow 23-21 vote a proposal to elect Mississippi's congressional representatives in statewide, at-large elections.[18]

For six weeks, the House and Senate were deadlocked by the lack of agreement on a congressional redistricting plan.[19] Finally, after an all-night Senate session and just before the April 7 qualifying deadline for congressional candidates, a compromise plan was agreed upon that divided the Delta among three districts, one of which had a razor-thin 51.36 percent black population majority, but which was majority-white in both voting-age population and registered voters (see map 2.6). Again, opponents in the House, led by Representative McClellan, argued that the new plan would not withstand a court challenge: "Any bill that shows discrimination against a certain race . . . they'll knock down. You are trying to take two white counties in northeast Mississippi out of the 2nd District [Congressman Whitten's district] and put a heavy Negro populated county in. They will say this bill is fraught with discrimination."[20]

Racial gerrymandering, the redrawing of district lines to dilute black voting strength, generally is accomplished by one of three tech-

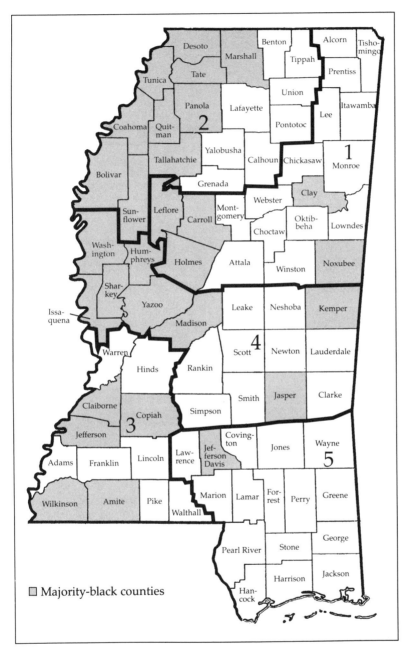

Map 2.5. First Congressional Redistricting Plan Adopted by the State Senate in 1966. The Senate-passed plan would have divided the Delta area among three of the state's five districts, leaving one district with a slight black population majority.

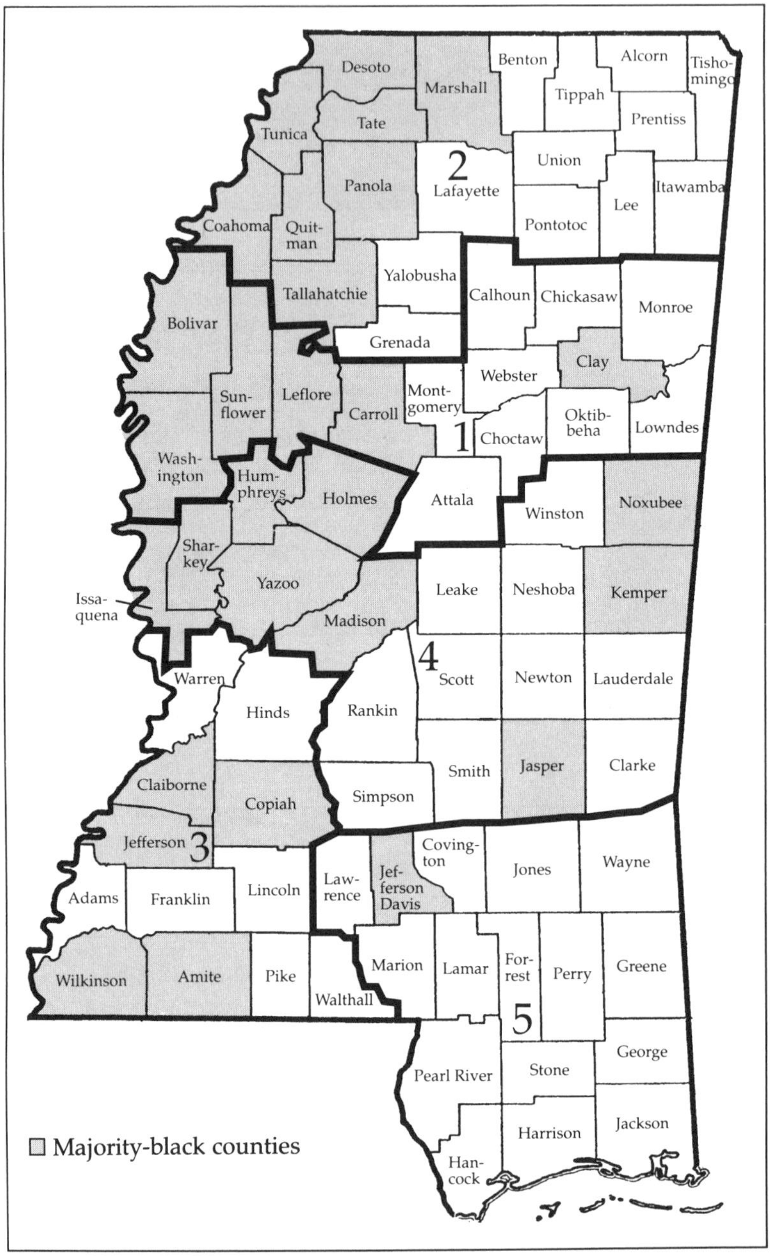

Map 2.6. "Compromise" Congressional Redistricting Plan Adopted by Both Houses of the State Legislature in 1966. The plan divided the Delta area among three of the state's five districts, depriving blacks of a voting majority in any of the districts.

niques—"cracking," "stacking," and "packing."[21] Cracking is the fragmentation of black population concentrations to prevent blacks from having an effective voting majority in any district. Stacking occurs when a heavy black population is diluted by combining it with a more populous white concentration, and packing is overconcentrating blacks in a particular district to prevent them from having a majority or significant influence in adjoining districts. The Mississippi Legislature's 1966 congressional redistricting plan is a classic example of cracking. The majority-black Delta area, which previously had been retained intact, was split three ways, depriving black voters of an effective voting majority in any of the five districts.

An important feature of Mississippi's congressional redistricting gerrymander was the intentional effort to cover up its discriminatory purpose by retaining a "phantom" majority-black district. Based on the population figures alone, the final plan appeared to give blacks a majority in the First Congressional District (see table 2.2). Opponents in the Senate initially opposed it for that reason, albeit the black majority was substantially reduced from the prior plan. Only by looking beyond the total population statistics would anyone realize the political reality of white voting-age population and registered voter majorities. The federal courts, however, would not distinguish between a black population majority and an effective black voting majority until the early 1970s.[22]

Despite a court challenge mounted by the MFDP (described in the next chapter), the essential features of the 1966 plan were preserved intact until 1982, depriving black voters of any opportunity to elect a black representative to Congress.[23] The strategy of cracking black population concentrations was also followed in many county redistricting plans after the 1970 census, a step that further minimized the opportunities for black voters to gain representation in county government.[24]

Changes in Methods of Election and Electoral Rules

Switching from district to at-large, countywide elections. White state legislators were also deeply concerned with the impact of black enfranchisement on elections for county offices. Many of the election districts within counties contained substantial black voting majorities, making it likely that black political influence might soon become a major factor in county government—including the county public school systems. To get around this situation, the legislature enacted four bills providing for at-large, countywide elections for members of the county boards of supervisors and county boards of education, posts that historically had been filled by district elections.

Table 2.2. Racial Composition of Congressional Districts in Mississippi, 1956–1966

Congressional District	Total Population	Black Population		Black Voting-Age Population	
		Number	Percent	Number	Percent
1956 plan					
1	364,963	117,663	32.23		
2	237,879	118,049	49.62		
3	370,554	242,759	65.51		
4	459,186	138,690	30.20		
5	295,072	121,540	41.18		
6	451,565	107,039	23.70		
1962 plan					
1	364,963	117,663	32.24	53,810	25.89
2	608,441	360,780	59.29	159,432	52.09
3	460,100	213,573	46.41	101,790	40.55
4	295,072	121,540	41.19	64,550	39.40
5	449,565	106,652	23.72	50,330	20.54
1966 plan					
1	449,361	230,797	51.36	103,710	44.32
2	427,468	184,424	43.14	82,198	34.72
3	428,447	194,782	45.46	93,071	39.65
4	423,300	203,553	48.09	100,603	44.13
5	449,565	106,652	23.72	55,330	20.54

Source: All population figures from U.S. Bureau of the Census, *1960 Census of Population*.

The technique of switching from district elections to at-large elections had already been adopted for municipal elections in the state in order to dilute black voting strength in urban areas. In 1962, just as the early Mississippi voter registration drives were beginning to get under way, the legislature enacted a bill requiring all code charter municipalities (municipalities organized under the state municipal code) with a mayor–board of aldermen form of government to elect all members of the boards of aldermen on an at-large basis. During the 1962 legislative debate, the bill's sponsor told the legislature that the bill was necessary "to maintain our southern way of life." Many years later, in 1975, a three-judge district court held the 1962 statute unconstitutional, finding that it was racially motivated to prevent the election of black municipal officials.[25]

House Bill 223, passed in May of 1966 by the Mississippi state legislature, authorized county boards of supervisors to switch from district to at-large county supervisor elections.[26] County boards of supervisors are powerful county governmental bodies in Mississippi that levy county taxes; appropriate county funds; supervise the construction and maintenance of county roads and bridges; appoint members of county boards and commissions, such as the county welfare board and county planning board; employ county personnel; and, until 1975, drew up the master jury lists from which state court juries were selected.[27] Beyond their governmental powers, county supervisors have also had considerable political influence in the election of state and other county officials.

Each county in Mississippi is divided into five supervisors' districts, also called "beats," which historically served as election districts for county supervisors as well as other county officials, including county school board members, election commissioners, and until recently, justices of the peace and constables. In most Mississippi counties, the supervisors' districts also served as road districts, and under the "beat system" each supervisor was responsible for the county roads, bridges, and other localized county services within his or her district.

For almost a century, at least since 1869, one member of the county board of supervisors has been elected by the voters of each of the five supervisors' districts. But white legislators feared that this traditional electoral structure might give black voters an opportunity to gain black representation in county government. Countywide elections could submerge the black vote if black voters formed a majority in one supervisors' district but lacked a voting majority countywide. Although the legislation provided that county supervisors would be elected countywide, it still required that candidates must be a resident of and run from each of the five districts, and in "beat system" counties, each county supervisor would still be responsible for road and bridge work within his or her district.

House Bill 223 was introduced by state representative Charles Deaton of Leflore County, scene of some of the strongest and most violent resistance to black registration in the state, joined by eleven other representatives who were mostly from Delta counties or white majority counties that had majority-black county supervisors' districts.

Deaton failed to mention any racial purpose when the bill was introduced. At the time, county one-person, one-vote lawsuits seeking to
equalize the population of the counties' supervisors' districts were
pending in four Mississippi counties, and Deaton stated that the purpose of the measure was to "eliminate the necessity of continuous redistricting, to comply with the one man one vote rule of the federal
courts." If county supervisors were elected countywide, Deaton reasoned, the population of the supervisors' districts would no longer
have to be equal. However, W. F. Minor, Mississippi legislative reporter for the New Orleans *Times-Picayune*, noted that the bill had a
dual purpose as "a hedge against both the threat of electing Negro
supervisors and county redistricting" and reported, "The rising Negro vote, concentrated in particular areas of a number of counties in
the state, has increased the possibility in the next county elections in
1967 that Negroes will be able to win supervisor posts under the district system."[28] During the legislative debates, Senator John Clark
Love of Attala County, a majority-white county that had one majority-black supervisors' district, reiterated Deaton's one-person, one-
vote rationale by saying that the House bill "could answer the one-
man, one-vote requirement of the United States Supreme Court
without the necessity of redistricting the beats on a population
equality basis." Senator Ben Hilbun of Oktibbeha County, however,
was more direct regarding its racial purpose. Hilbun stated that countywide balloting will safeguard "a white board and preserve our way
of doing business." The Memphis *Commercial Appeal* account of the
debate explained, "Under the new Federal Voting Rights Act for registration of Negroes, members of that race outnumber whites in
many county beats."[29] The Jackson *Clarion-Ledger* also reported that
Hilbun "said that Noxubee County, which is in his district, might
have trouble electing a white board because three districts would
vote white and two wouldn't."[30] The bill passed overwhelmingly by a
final vote of 95-4 in the House and 36-8 in the Senate.[31]

Under the authority of this statute and subsequent amendments
enacted in 1968 and 1971 and by court order in lawsuits challenging
the malapportionment of county supervisors' districts for violation of
the one-person, one-vote rule, at least fourteen Mississippi counties
switched from district to at-large elections for county supervisors for
the 1967 county elections and, for some, the 1971 county elections as
well.[32] All but four of these counties had one or more supervisors'
districts that were majority-black.

In order to keep elected county school boards under white control,
the Mississippi state legislature enacted three separate bills in 1966:
Senate Bill 1966, House Bill 275, and House Bill 1074. The segregated

school systems and the poor quality of public education provided to black children were of great concern to the black community in Mississippi. School board elections therefore were an important target for the newly enfranchised black voters. In 1964, the Mississippi Legislature had passed a bill permitting any county to switch from district to at-large county school board elections by countywide referendum. In 1966 the legislature in Senate Bill 1966 amended this statute by requiring at-large school board elections in six Mississippi counties and permitting them at the local option of the county school boards in two more.[33] Although the school board members were to be elected by all the voters of the county, under the new statute one school board member was required to reside in each of the five supervisors' districts. In addition, two separate statutes (House Bill 275 and House Bill 1074), introduced by individual county delegations and applicable only to their counties, mandated at-large school board elections in the Delta counties of Coahoma, Leflore, and Washington.[34] In addition to requiring countywide elections, these statutes also specified a property qualification for school board candidates. School board members were required to own real estate worth at least $5,000 in the district in which they resided, a requirement that far fewer blacks than whites would be able to meet. Of the eleven counties in which countywide school board elections were required or permitted without a referendum, all but two had majority-black supervisors' districts, but none had a countywide black voting majority. Although twenty-eight counties in Mississippi were majority-black in population, fewer were majority-black in voting-age population. Further, although blacks quickly became a majority of the registered voters in numerous supervisors' districts around the state, few counties would become majority-black in registered voters countywide until well into the 1970s.

These statutes had important implications beyond preventing the election of black candidates to county school boards. By 1966 a number of school desegregation lawsuits had been filed in Mississippi, and, under the Civil Rights Act of 1964, the Department of Health, Education, and Welfare was requiring public school desegregation as a condition of the receipt of federal funding. Most Mississippi school boards were vigorously contesting the requirement of desegregation, despite the Supreme Court's desegregation decision of a decade earlier. By enacting these school board election laws in 1966, the legislature hoped to maintain all-white county school boards that would continue to maintain the status quo of segregation.

Abolishing elections for county school superintendents. Another strategy adopted to reduce the impact of the black vote in educational policymaking was the conversion of elective offices into appointed positions. Ever since 1906, county superintendents of education in Mississippi had been elected by the voters of each county. The only exception was Washington County, in the Delta, where prior to 1966 the county school superintendent was appointed by the county board of education. After the June 7, 1966 Democratic primary elections, which demonstrated that blacks might develop sufficient voting strength to influence or win county school superintendent positions in some counties, the Mississippi Legislature enacted a new bill authorizing counties to conduct countywide referendums on the question of abolishing county school superintendent elections and allowing the county school board to fill the position by appointment.[35] However, for eleven counties, all but two of which were majority-black and in three of which (Claiborne, Jefferson, and Holmes) black candidates won countywide majorities or pluralities in the June primary, the statute required that the county school superintendent be appointed by the county school board. Many of these counties were added to the original bill by their county delegations in committee and during the floor debates.

The Mississippi Constitution, like the constitutions of many other states, however, prohibits singling out individual counties by name. House Bill 183 thus described each of the affected counties with surrealistic particularity, making their identification as unmistakable as if their names had been written. For example, the law required the school superintendent to be appointed in "any Class Four county having a land area of six hundred ninety-five (695) square miles, bordering on the State of Alabama, wherein the Treaty of Dancing Rabbit was signed and wherein U.S. Highway 45 and Mississippi Highway 14 intersect." Resorting to an atlas, a road map, and a Mississippi history book, the reader can determine that this description fits no county other than Noxubee, where the 1960 population was less than 5,000 white people to more than 12,000 black people. Table 2.3 shows the counties by their description in the statute and the racial composition of each county in which appointment of the county school superintendent was required.

In 1968 the statute was amended to add another majority-black county (Yazoo County) and a majority-white county (Lafayette County) and to delete another majority-white county (Lincoln County). As a result, ten of the twelve counties in which elections for county school superintendents were abolished by the 1966 and 1968 legislation were majority-black.[36]

Placing the power to consolidate counties in the hands of the state legislature. So concerned were legislators about the possible emergence of countywide black voting majorities, that they adopted House Con-

Table 2.3. Counties Required to Switch from Election to Appointment of County Superintendent of Education

Statutory Language	County	Population
"Any county of the first class lying wholly within a levee district and within which there is situated a city of more than forty thousand (40,000) population according to the last decennial federal census"	Washington	35,239 white 43,097 black 302 other
"In any county of the second class wherein Interstate Highway 55 and State Highway 22 intersect and which is also traversed in whole and in part by U.S. Highways 49 and 51 and State Highways 16, 17, and 43 and the Natchez Trace"	Madison	9,267 white 23,630 black 7 other
"In any Class Four county having a population in excess of twenty-five thousand (25,000) according to the 1960 Federal census, traversed by U.S. Interstate Highway 55 and wherein Mississippi Highways 12 and 17 intersect"	Holmes	7,595 white 19,488 black 13 other
"In any county created after 1916 through which the Yazoo River flows"	Humphreys	5,758 white 13,300 black 35 other
"In any Class Four county having a land area of six hundred ninety-five (695) square miles, bordering on the State of Alabama, wherein the Treaty of Dancing Rabbit was signed and wherein U.S. Highway 45 and Mississippi Highway 14 intersect"	Noxubee	4,724 white 12,064 black 38 other
"In any county bordering on the Mississippi River wherein lies the campus of a land grant institution or lands contiguous thereto owned by the institution"	Claiborne and Jefferson	Claiborne 2,600 white 8,239 black 6 other Jefferson 2,489 white 7,652 black 1 other
"In any county lying within the Yazoo Mississippi Delta Levee dis-	Coahoma	14,630 white 31,440 black

Table 2.3. *(continued)*

Statutory Language	County	Population
trict, bordering upon the Mississippi River, and having a county seat with a population in excess of twenty-one thousand (21,000) according to the Federal census of 1960"		142 other
"In any county having a population of twenty-six thousand, seven hundred fifty-nine (26,759) according to the 1960 Federal census and wherein U.S. Highway 51 and U.S. Highway 84 and the Illinois Central Railroad and the Mississippi Central Railroad intersect"	Lincoln	18,407 white 8,340 black 12 other
"In any Class Three county wherein is partially located a national forest and wherein U.S. Highway 51 and Mississippi Highway 28 intersect, with a 1960 Federal census of twenty-seven thousand fifty-one (27,051) and a 1963 assessed valuation of $16,692,304.00"	Copiah	12,992 white 14,057 black 1 other
"In any county bordering on the Gulf of Mexico or Mississippi Sound having therein a test facility operated by the "National Aeronautics and Space Administration," the Superintendent shall be appointed beginning January 1, 1972"	Hancock	11,784 white 2,246 black 9 other

Sources: Jurisdiction Statement; Appendix C, *Bunton v. Patterson*, decided sub nom. *Allen v. State Board of Elections*, 393 U.S. 544 (1969). Population figures from U.S. Bureau of the Census, *1960 Census of Population*.

current Resolution 36, which amended the state constitution to give the legislature the power to consolidate or combine counties. Previously, Mississippi counties could only be consolidated if a majority of the voters in the affected counties approved the step.[37] But this amendment took the authority away from the counties' voters and authorized the legislature to consolidate counties by a two-thirds vote of both houses of the legislature. The amendment remains part of the Mississippi Constitution (article 14, section 271), although it has never been used. It is nevertheless indicative of the lengths the legislature was willing to go to negate black electoral strength.

The legislative history and timing of legislative action on the measure indicates that its purpose was to eliminate majority-black counties—if they gained countywide black voting majorities—by merging them with majority-white counties. During deliberations in the House of Representatives, efforts to keep its discriminatory intent well in the background were largely successful, except for a hint in an editorial in the hometown newspaper of the proposal's House sponsor indicating that consolidation would be desirable "if voter registration percentages get out of balance,"[38] code words for blacks gaining a majority of registered voters.

Although the measure passed the House in March without difficulty, it was tabled in the Senate in May.[39] Then, on June 7, in the Democratic primary, the Reverend Clifton Whitley—a black candidate for United States senator running with MFDP support—won majorities in two majority-black River counties—Claiborne and Jefferson. The next day, Senator P. M. Watkins of Claiborne County moved to reconsider the tabled resolution.

With this bill, as with the congressional redistricting plan discussed earlier, opponents of the proposal broke ranks to point out its discriminatory intent, not from any solicitude toward black electoral successes, but because they considered the measure more drastic than conditions warranted. "All they're trying to do is avoid a few Negro votes," charged Senator E. K. Collins of predominantly white Jones County in southeast Mississippi. Collins asserted that the bill was being revived "just because a few Niggers voted down there [in Claiborne County]." Similarly, Senator Ben Hilbun of predominantly white Oktibbeha County, in northeast Mississippi, opposed the resolution as meeting the acknowledged danger with a too-drastic weapon: "We get so concerned because some Negroes are voting in a few counties, we are going to disrupt our entire institutions of government."[40]

A supporter of the constitutional amendment, Senator Bill Corr of predominantly black Panola County, in the Delta, announced that he had abandoned his former opposition because "a lot of things have happened," referring to the primary election victory of a black candidate for sheriff in Alabama and to the results of Mississippi's congressional primary elections the day before.[41] These events apparently had changed the minds of others as well, because the proposal then passed the Senate by a vote of 30-13 and was approved in a statewide referendum the following November.

Increasing the qualifying requirements for independent candidates. The 1966 legislature also took steps to make it more difficult for independent candidates to qualify to run for elective office—a measure primarily directed at candidates, mostly black, who were affiliated with the MFDP. The MFDP and its independent candidates had already stumbled against Mississippi's tough qualifying requirements. In 1964, three black candidates seeking to run as independents for Congress, state NAACP president Aaron Henry and MFDP activists Fannie Lou Hamer and Annie Devine, were disqualified from running by state officials because they failed to get the required number of signatures of voters on their nominating petitions, in part because circuit clerks delayed certifying the signatures.[42]

This incident provided the Mississippi Legislature with the inspiration in 1966 to amend the state statute that set out the qualifying requirements for independents in order to make it even more difficult for independent candidates to run for elective office. As passed on June 15, after the results of the June 7 primary became known, the bill (1) increased tenfold or more the number of signatures of registered voters required on independents' nominating petitions (see table 2.4); (2) required each voter "personally" to sign the petition and include his or her voting precinct and county, a requirement that would disqualify most illiterate voters from nominating candidates; (3) required that the number of valid signatures be certified by the county circuit clerks, all of whom were white and generally hostile to black candidates running; (4) required independent candidates to qualify to run by the same qualifying deadline for party candidates in party primaries, rather than forty days before the November general election as prior law permitted; and (5) prohibited anyone who voted in a party primary from running as an independent candidate in the general election.[43]

Although there was little floor debate and no public acknowledgment of the bill's true purpose, a United Press International dispatch in February, after the bill passed the state House of Representatives, reported that the measure was "apparently aimed at the Mississippi Freedom Democratic Party, a civil rights group," and referred to the difficulties experienced by the MFDP candidates in 1964.[44]

Table 2.4. Number of Signatures of Registered Voters Required on Nominating Petitions for Independent Candidates under House Bill 68

Elective Office	Previously	Under H.B. 68
All statewide offices	1,000	10,000
Offices elected by state supreme court district	200	3,500
Offices elected by congressional district	200	2,000
Offices elected by circuit or chancery court district	100	1,000
Offices elected by county, state Senate district, or by municipality with population of 1,000 or more	50	10 percent of the registered voters or 500, whichever is less
Offices elected by supervisors' district with population of 1,000 or more	15	10 percent of the registered voters or 500, whichever is less
Offices elected by supervisors' district or by municipality with population of less than 1,000	15	10 percent of the registered voters

The legislators clearly understood what they were doing. After the MFDP's unsuccessful challenge to the all-white Mississippi delegation at the 1964 Democratic National Convention in Atlantic City, the MFDP decided against running candidates in the state Democratic primaries and announced that its candidates would run as independents. (As described later in this chapter, this was the beginning of an important independent black political movement in Mississippi.) There were also other reasons for black candidates to run as independents. Candidates running in the Democratic primary had to swear allegiance to party principles, which at the time included support for racial segregation.[45] Further, while a majority vote was required to win a party primary, and a primary runoff was required if no candidate won a majority, no majority vote was required to win the general election, and candidates could win with only a plurality. Theoretically at least, this gave black candidates running as independents in the general election an advantage if the white vote was split between white Democratic and Republican candidates.

The open primary bills abolishing party primaries and requiring a majority vote to win office. Apparently believing that increasing the qualifying requirements for independent candidates was not enough, the legislature enacted two additional bills aimed at eliminating any advantages black candidates running as independents might have under the state's existing election system. The so-called open primary bills abolished party primaries, which had been in existence since 1902; established a uniform qualifying deadline for all candidates; and required a majority vote to win the general election. Thus the possibility that a black candidate could win with less than a majority because of a split in the white vote between white candidates was foreclosed. All candidates were required to run in a general election held in October, and if no candidate won a majority, the top two candidates for any office would then compete in a general election runoff in November.[46]

During the floor debates the bills were touted as an effort to eliminate party politics and to emphasize individual qualifications for office, without any mention of their racial implications.[47] Although the bills passed both houses of the legislature with strong majorities, they were vetoed by Governor Johnson—the only veto of election law legislation during the entire massive resistance session. In his veto message, Governor Johnson stated that "this is an inopportune time for radical changes to be made in our election procedures." While expressing sympathy with efforts to eliminate Mississippi's traditional system under which most candidates ran in three elections to win— party primaries, primary runoffs, and the general election—he cautioned that "this can be accomplished without subjecting our entire election procedures to a multiplicity of litigation," an indication that Governor Johnson expected that this legislation would be challenged by civil rights forces in federal court.[48]

Only during the debate on overriding Governor Johnson's veto, an effort that lost in the House by fifteen votes, was the racial purpose of the bills alluded to, and then only in the most veiled terms. A press account reported Representative Irby Turner of majority-black Humphreys County, a supporter of the legislation, raising the threat of black independent candidates winning with less than a majority: "Under present laws, he said, a general election contest could involve more than two candidates—independents as well as nominees run in the general election—and the winner could fail to get a majority. 'In our present state,' he said, 'that is a very dangerous situation. It's a dangerous situation in any state at any time. Since this is the last regular session before next year's general election, this may be the last chance we'll have to do anything.' "[49] Representative Jimmy Walker of Quitman County, an opponent of the bills, contended that the legislation should be defeated because it would strengthen the voting influence of blacks. An Associated Press wire story reported, "[Walker] said the open primary might work in the next elections but afterwards 'it's putting in the hands of minorities to control the elections.' 'You're not going to ever get back where you were. All you can do is outvote them (Negroes).' " The Associated Press dispatch advised, "This was a reference to a growing Negro registration."[50]

This 1966 legislative session was only the beginning of a continuing effort to enact open primary legislation to eliminate the plurality-win feature of the state's general election. The measure sparked renewed interest in the next regular session of the state legislature in 1968 (when it was dubbed the "Charles Evers bill") after Charles Evers won a plurality of the vote in a special election to fill a vacancy in Congress (Evers lost in the runoff). Open primary bills also were passed in 1970, 1975, 1976, and 1979, but in each instance the bills either failed to pass both houses (1968), were vetoed by the governor (1975), or were blocked by Justice Department objections under section 5 of the Voting Rights Act.[51]

Multimember Legislative Districts

The final element in Mississippi's massive resistance to black political participation was the dilution of black voting strength in elections for members of the state legislature. The technique employed involved the creation, under the guise of meeting one-person, one-vote requirements, of large multimember legislative districts that submerged black population concentrations in districtwide white voting majorities.

This discrimination was achieved by using whole counties as the building blocks for framing state House and Senate districts. Legislative districts could be countywide or made up of combinations of two or more counties. Countywide districts diluted black votes where, as in Hinds County (where the city of Jackson is located), whites were in the majority countywide but there were black population concentrations within the county sufficiently large for separate representation. If the county were subdivided, blacks would constitute majorities in several single-member districts, but so long as all the county's voters voted for the entire county legislative delegation, white voters would totally control all the seats. Multicounty legislative districts diluted black votes when smaller counties that were majority-black were combined with majority-white counties to produce a districtwide white majority, or when several majority-black counties were combined in districts that were so large geographically as to make it prohibitively expensive for black candidates to attempt to campaign and mobilize voters throughout the district. Thus, by employing this whole-county strategy, the legislature attempted to satisfy the Supreme Court's 1964 one-person, one-vote rule while minimizing the number of majority-black districts. As long as such a plan was followed, even quite large black population concentrations would have little hope of electing candidates of their choice to the state legislature.

Unlike the previously discussed elements of the state's massive resistance program, the use of multimember legislative districts did not involve a radical revision of the state's election laws. Historically, Mississippi had formed legislative districts out of whole counties, although after 1890 the legislature had created subdistricts within counties when it was convenient to offsetting the voting influence of the Delta counties and to creating majority-white districts in majority-black counties.[52] But after 1965, the Mississippi Legislature turned increasingly to countywide and multicounty legislative districts, raising dramatically the number of legislators elected from multimember districts, while redrawing district lines to avoid any potential black voting majority in legislative districts. Multimember districts thus became the chief impediment to Mississippi's black citizens gaining representation of their choice in the all-white state legislature.

As in the case of congressional redistricting, the MFDP's 1965 lawsuit seeking constitutionally apportioned legislative districts and the desegregation of the state legislature, *Connor v. Johnson*, gave the legislature the opportunity in 1966 to gerrymander the state legislative districts. (The story of this suit and the role of the courts in the Mississippi reapportionment process will be told in chapter 4.) *Connor v. Johnson* challenged state legislative malapportionment as well as malapportionment of congressional district lines. A three-judge district court had warned the legislature in January 1966 that a new legislative apportionment plan had to be adopted, but during the 1966 regular session the Senate and House could not agree. In July the district court ruled that the existing districts violated the Supreme Court's one-person, one-vote rule and warned that if the legislature did not adopt a constitutional plan by December 1, the court would draw its own plan for the 1967 elections.[53] In the end, Governor Johnson called a special session of the legislature to convene November 9 to produce a legislative reapportionment plan.

Some legislators showed unabashed hostility to the Supreme Court's constitutional requirements. One week after the special session began, three representatives introduced a House resolution condemning the Supreme Court's one-person, one-vote rulings as "unconstitutional, unprecedented, novel, and socialistic."[54] After three weeks of wrangling over competing plans, the legislature finally agreed on a new plan that was both racially discriminatory and excessively malapportioned. This plan was destined to be struck down by the district court the following March for violating the one-person, one-vote principle, although the substance of it remained in force during the 1967 statewide elections. Previously, the 122 members of the Mississippi House of Representatives had been elected from 82 districts, mostly single counties, and the 52 members of the state Senate had been elected from 49 districts, mostly single counties or pairs of counties. The new plan aggregated whole counties to construct new legislative districts; it reduced the number of House districts from 82 to 72 and the number of Senate districts from 49 to 41. In selecting members of the House, 80 representatives, or 66 percent of the entire membership, were to be elected from 26 multimember districts.[55]

The legislature's final plan discriminated against black voters in two ways. First, large black population concentrations within counties were submerged in countywide voting. For example, Hinds County had the largest black population concentration of any county in the state—74,750 black persons in the 1960 census—enough to create at least four majority-black single-member House districts and two majority-black single-member Senate districts if the county were subdivided. But countywide, blacks constituted a minority of only 40 percent of the overall population while whites held the majority with 60 percent. The plan thus put the white population of Hinds County in a position to elect all ten representatives and all five senators. Second, the legislature's plan combined a number of majority-black counties—which previously had been given separate legislative representation—with majority-white counties. These alignments, which were brought out in the floor debate, diluted the voting strength of black voters in the majority-black counties by the classic gerrymandering technique of stacking.

As with the other pieces of massive resistance legislation, there was much disingenuousness concerning the racial motivation behind the redistricting effort. During the floor debates, one senator objected to the racial gerrymandering in the new plan. Senator Talmadge Littlejohn, of New Albany in northeast Mississippi, charged that the Senate plan was "taking certain districts and diluting the Negro vote." According to a Jackson *Clarion-Ledger* report: "He said that by linking Hinds [majority-white] with Claiborne County [majority-black], Jefferson [majority-black] to Lincoln [majority-white], and Marshall [majority-black] to Union [majority-white], the superior Negro voting strength in Claiborne, Jefferson, and Marshall would be greatly reduced."[56]

Members of the Senate Rules Committee, which drafted the plan, however, blandly denied the charges of racial discrimination. Two senators from majority-black counties replied that "the racial question was not considered" when the committee drafted the bill and denied "that racial figures were considered." The vice-chair of the committee added, "I'm sorry we injected this. We did the best we could. Let's don't get the racial thing in this." The leadership of the Senate thus avoided a full, on-the-record discussion of the issue of racial discrimination in the reapportionment plan. According to press reports, Lieutenant Governor Carroll Gartin, the presiding officer of the Senate, "repeatedly banged the speaker's gavel for order as controversy rose regarding alleged racial gerrymander."[57]

The 1966 regular and special sessions of the Mississippi Legislature thus represented a massive and comprehensive effort to close the door to effective black electoral participation. The lawmakers employed a wide range of devices—racial gerrymandering, at-large elections, abolishing elective offices, increasing candidate qualifications, and a majority vote requirement—to make it more difficult for Mississippi's newly enfranchised black voters to elect candidates of their choice to office. As described in the next sections, these devices were extremely effective. Despite the enormous efforts of black political organizations to mobilize black voters for the 1967 elections, only a handful of the 108 black candidates who ran were elected.

Black Political Mobilization

In 1967, Early Lott, Sr., a black man who had never run for political office, decided to run for constable in rural, majority-black Jefferson County in southwest Mississippi. Lott, who was elected, described to a reporter for *Ebony* magazine why he decided to run:

> There was a colored man who couldn't walk . . . only got about on his hands and knees. He used to shine shoes to make his way. Well, one day he was up there at the icehouse when a white man—a constable from another county—drove up and had some words with him. That white man shot him there on the icehouse steps, and his blood ran down the street like water. There wasn't no trial, and there ain't *never* been no trial. It was then, when I

saw that, I decided that if the time ever came when I'd have a chance to try and change things, I'd do it.[58]

The 1967 state elections provided Mississippi's black citizens with their first opportunity for massive participation in state electoral politics since the end of Reconstruction in 1875.[59] These elections also tested the extent to which the massive resistance legislation of 1966 would blunt the impact of the newly gained black vote. Enormous numbers of black Mississippians registered to vote for the 1967 elections, and black candidates contested more than 100 offices across the state. But these mobilization efforts stumbled against the new legal obstacles.

In his book *Invisible Politics* political scientist Hanes Walton points out that the study of black political behavior must look outside the black community as well as within it. To be complete, any analysis of black politics must take into account the external forces that shape the black political experience and the structural, systemic, and contextual variables controlling black political participation.[60] Black people in Mississippi in 1967 were not writing on a clean slate, and structural and contextual factors determined to a great extent the successes and failures of the new black politics in Mississippi.

In large part, the white supremacy politics of the white majority have shaped post-1965 black politics. The Mississippi Freedom Democratic Party—the first statewide independent black political party in the South in recent times—was organized in response to the exclusion of blacks from state Democratic party affairs. The racially polarized voting patterns of whites in the state—whites generally refusing to vote for black candidates regardless of qualifications or party affiliation—required majority-black districts for black voters to elect candidates of their choice, usually black candidates. The structural barriers incorporated in the massive resistance legislation of 1966 helped to discourage or defeat large numbers of black candidates in 1967—despite the high black voter registration rates. Discriminatory procedures in the way elections were run—such as locating polling places in locations inconvenient to blacks or limiting assistance to illiterate voters—also undercut black electoral success. Other factors constraining electoral success during this period included continuing disparities in voter registration rates between whites and blacks, and socioeconomic barriers such as disproportionately lower black income and education levels.[61]

The black political mobilization for the 1967 elections had its roots in the Mississippi civil rights movement. The two major black political organizations that led the black political effort, registered voters, fielded slates of candidates, and guided campaign strategy were the NAACP, which had long been active in the voter registration efforts in the state, and the MFDP, which, as described in chapter 1, to a great extent was a product of the organizing efforts and philosophy of the Student Nonviolent Coordinating Committee.[62] Indeed, the early voter registration efforts, the mock "freedom elections" of 1963 and 1964, and the 1964 Freedom Summer campaign, in addition to serving a protest function, were also aimed at preparing black citizens for participation in the electoral process.

Political organizing efforts in Mississippi were given a boost in the summer of 1966 by the James Meredith march. Meredith, who had desegregated the University of Mississippi in 1962, decided to march from Memphis to Jackson in June to encourage black voter registration and to overcome what he called the "all-pervasive and overriding fear that dominates the day-to-day life of the Negro in the United States, especially in the South and particularly in Mississippi."[63] On the second day of his march, he was shot from ambush; a white man was arrested for the crime. Martin Luther King, Jr., of the SCLC, Stokely Carmichael of SNCC, Floyd McKissick of CORE, and their supporters rallied around Meredith and resumed the march for him. The Meredith march spurred the national civil rights groups to take a renewed interest in Mississippi and to sponsor community organizing projects and voter registration drives in cities and towns along the march route. The marchers succeeded in getting between 3,000 and 4,000 black voters registered to vote, and local officials began making long-neglected improvements in black neighborhoods in response to black demands.[64]

Beginning at a rally in Greenwood, SNCC leader Stokely Carmichael began to use the slogan "black power," which had an enormous mass appeal to black audiences along the march route. Although it frightened whites and deepened the divisions among some of the national civil rights organizations, the use of the slogan, as historian Clayborne Carson has noted, "began a new stage in the transformation of Afro-American political consciousness."[65] Sociologist and former Mississippi civil rights worker Joyce Ladner found in a series of interviews in Mississippi that "black power" expressed the "disillusionment that black people have experienced in their intense efforts to become integrated into the mainstream of American society."[66] But she also found that the slogan had a positive impact that led to a renewed commitment to voter registration, running for political office, and political organizing.[67] The use of the slogan cost the civil rights movement dearly in terms of white support and financial assistance. But for black people in Mississippi who, because of racial segregation, were largely uneducated, subsisted on marginal incomes, and had experienced harassment and intimidation from whites, the "black power" slogan was viewed as "a means of combining Negroes into a bond of solidarity" that strengthened their quest for political power.[68]

The 1967 statewide elections provided the first test of the growth in black voting strength in Mississippi since passage of the Voting Rights Act. As many as 2,000 offices were up for election, including all statewide offices and most county and district positions. Estimates of the number of black registered voters vary from contemporary press estimates of about 180,000[69] to estimates of the VEP in Atlanta of more than 260,000.[70]

There were four major candidates for governor, all of whom were white: Congressman John Bell Williams, who decided to run for governor after he was stripped of his congressional seniority for supporting Barry Goldwater for president in 1964, former governor Ross Barnett, state treasurer William F. Winter, and Jimmy Swan, a country music singer and radio broadcaster. Williams would be the victor. Although the appearance of a sizable black electorate may have diminished the strident racial rhetoric which characterized past campaigns, all four candidates nevertheless ran as segregationists.[71]

Blacks did not contest the governor's post or any other statewide positions. A few black candidates ran for the state legislature, but most concentrated on local offices. A total of 108 black candidates qualified to run in the 1967 elections. Table 2.5 shows the offices they ran for and the electoral outcomes.

One or more black candidates ran in twenty-eight of the state's eighty-two counties, mostly in the heavily black, western portion of the state. The prime targets for black candidates were seats on the county boards of supervisors—thirty-six black candidates ran for county supervisor positions. An additional forty-eight black candidates ran for other positions elected by supervisors' district—twenty-three ran for justice of the peace and twenty-five ran for constable. Eight black candidates ran for the state legislature, six ran for sheriff, and ten ran for other countywide positions.[72]

Black candidates pursued two different election strategies, reflecting a split between the two major black political organizations in the state, the NAACP and the MFDP. There were deep ideological and political differences between the two groups. The NAACP, as a long-established organization, was ideologically conservative and looked to the liberal wing of the Democratic party and to the federal government for support. The MFDP, a product of the 1960s civil rights movement, was more militant, although equally committed to change through the political process. The conflict between the NAACP and

Table 2.5. Results for Black Candidates in 1967 Mississippi Primary and General Elections

Office	Both Elections		Democrats in August Primaries				Independents in November General Election		
	Ran	Won	Total	Won	Runoffs	Lost	Total	Won	Lost
Countywide									
Legislator[a]	8	1	5	0	0	5	3	1	2
Sheriff	6	0	5	0	4	5	1	0	1
Superintendent of education	2	0	2	0	1	2	0	0	0
Circuit clerk	4	0	3	0	2	3	1	0	1
Chancery clerk	2	1	2	1	1	1	0	0	0
Tax assessor	1	0	1	0	0	1	0	0	0
Coroner	1	1	1	1	0	0	0	0	0
By supervisors' district									
Supervisor[b]	36	4	21	3	6	18	15	1	14
Justice of the peace	23	9	17	7	2	10	6	2	4
Constable	25	6	19	4	4	15	6	2	4
Total	108	22	76	16	20	60	32	6	26

Source: Mississippi Freedom Information Service, *Mississippi Newsletter*, Aug. 4, Aug. 11, and Nov. 10, 1967, provided courtesy of Jan Hillegas, Freedom Information Library, Jackson, Miss.

[a] Includes multicounty legislative districts.

[b] Includes countywide elections.

the MFDP came to a head during the seating challenge at the Atlantic City convention. Delegates affiliated with the NAACP, including NAACP president Aaron Henry, favored the compromise, but they were outvoted by the MFDP activists. Consequently, in early 1965 the NAACP withdrew from COFO, the Mississippi civil rights coalition, and NAACP leaders formed a new coalition with white Mississippi moderates and liberals, state labor groups, and national Democratic party leaders.[73]

As a result, in the 1967 elections NAACP state field secretary Charles Evers and state president Aaron Henry encouraged candidates to run in the August Democratic primaries. The MFDP, on the other hand, led by Lawrence Guyot, urged its candidates to qualify by petition and to run as independents in the November general election. As explained by Guyot and MFDP leader Mike Thelwell, the decision to pursue an independent political effort outside the Democratic party structure was based on the state Democratic party's exclusion of black voters from party meetings and affairs, the national party's rejection of the MFDP challenges at the Democratic National Convention in Atlantic City in 1964 and in the Democratic-controlled House of Representatives in 1965, and the MFDP's desire to build a democratic, community-based independent political organization that the black community itself could control.[74] In their view the independent route was necessary to build political consciousness in the black community: "Our job now is to establish and entrench in every Negro community the tradition of active participation in politics, in which the people will understand that their involvement and control of *their own* political organization is their strongest weapon."[75] The NAACP, in contrast, remained committed to the national Democratic party and to a biracial political strategy. As Charles Evers stated, "Having fought so hard and so long against segregation, intelligent Negroes don't want any all-Negro party."[76]

Most of the black candidates followed the NAACP strategy—seventy-six black candidates ran in the August Democratic primary in twenty-two counties. The NAACP concentrated its political effort in the predominantly black River counties in southwest Mississippi, where Charles Evers had his political base. Black slates contested most county offices, including sheriff, in majority-black Claiborne, Jefferson, and Wilkinson counties, and blacks ran for district-level posts in Adams (majority-white but with two majority-black districts) and Copiah counties. Thirty-two black candidates followed the MFDP strategy and ran as independents in eight counties, all but one of them in the Delta area. The strongest MFDP effort was in majority-black Holmes County, where a slate of black candidates contested eleven offices. In some MFDP counties, however, such as Madison County, black candidates ran in the Democratic primary.[77]

Both organizations launched extensive voter registration and political organizing efforts preceding the 1967 elections. They held voter registration, voter education, and political organizing meetings almost nightly throughout the state. They encouraged black citizens to register to vote; selected, encouraged, and supported black candidates running for office; instructed voters on the duties of each county official; and showed voters how to mark their ballots or pull the levers on voting machines. As a result of these efforts, black voters gained a new pride in participating in the electoral process. "I've been voting a long time," one black voter told a newspaper reporter. "A year and a half."[78]

Despite this tremendous effort, the election results were disappointing. Only twenty-two blacks won elective office in the 1967 elections—sixteen were elected after winning the Democratic nomination in the August primaries (only one was opposed in the general election), and six black independents were elected in the November general election. One highlight of the election was the victory of Robert G. Clark, a schoolteacher from Holmes County. Clark became Mississippi's first black legislator since the 1890s, defeating J. P. Love, a white Delta planter who had served three terms in the Mississippi Legislature and who was chair of the House Education Committee. Two blacks won countywide offices—chancery clerk in Claiborne County and coroner in Marshall County; four were elected to county supervisor positions in Bolivar, Claiborne, Jefferson, and Wilkinson counties; and fifteen won justice of the peace and constable offices.

The 1967 Electoral Outcome

The election of twenty-two black candidates in the 1967 elections was hailed as a tremendous victory for Mississippi black voters. It marked the first time since Reconstruction that blacks had achieved any significant political representation in the state. As *Ebony* magazine noted, "Their importance is amplified when it is considered that only two years ago, it would have been impossible for even one to be elected."[79] The Greenville *Delta Democrat-Times*, then Mississippi's most liberal paper, hailed the results with the headline "Negro Vote Is Now Potent In The State."[80] The National Committee for Free Elections in Mississippi, a New York–based group formed to send volunteer lawyers and law students to Mississippi to serve as poll watchers for black candidates, reported with enthusiasm:

The victory of 22 black candidates in the 1967 state and county Mississippi elections marks the first time since Reconstruction that Negroes have achieved political representation in that state. These victories stand as monuments to the persistence, bravery and effective organization of black Mississippians because they were wrested from a reactionary white power structure whose methods for oppressing black citizens are notorious. The Mississippi Freedom Democratic Party, which contributed people and time to help all these candidates, has emerged as the significant political instrument of black people in the state.[81]

But from another perspective, the 1967 election results were a substantial victory for Mississippi's massive resistance to black political participation. Black electoral gains had been held to a minimum. Although black voters constituted 28 percent of the Mississippi electorate by the most liberal estimates, black candidates won only about 1 percent of the offices up for election that year. Clearly, the state election law changes enacted in 1966 took a toll on black political successes. The structural elements which had the most significant impact were the increased qualifying requirements for independent candidates, the changes from district to at-large county supervisor elections, multimember legislative districts, and the primary runoff requirement (which predated the 1966 legislative session).

Even before a single Mississippi voter entered the voting booth in 1967, the changes in qualifying requirements for independents mandated by state law in 1966 had disqualified nineteen black candidates—almost as many as won office—in eight counties. Most of these candidates were affiliated with the MFDP, and therefore the legislation succeeded in its goal of curtailing the MFDP's independent political effort. Election officials refused to list these candidates' names on the ballot for such reasons as voting in the Democratic primary, failing to meet the increased signature requirements on their nominating petitions, failing to list the voting precincts of persons who signed the petition, and other technical omissions. The new rules eliminated three candidates for the state legislature, including MFDP leader Fannie Lou Hamer—who was disqualified from running for a seat in the Mississippi Senate because she voted in the August Democratic primary—five candidates for county supervisor, and eleven candidates for justice of the peace and constable offices.[82]

The switch to at-large county supervisor elections caused the defeat of many black candidates and discouraged others from even running. The election results also show that although black candidates were able to win district elections—nineteen of the twenty-two winning candidates won in majority-black supervisors' districts—black candidates had difficulty winning countywide. Of the sixteen candidates who ran for county offices elected countywide, including sheriff positions, only two were successful—Mrs. Geneva Collins, who was elected chancery clerk in Claiborne County, and Osborne Bell, who was elected coroner in Marshall County. In most of the counties that switched to at-large county supervisor elections, black candidates did not even attempt to run for the board of supervisors; in the three counties where blacks did run, all were defeated.[83] The statute authorizing counties to adopt at-large county school board elections did not have an immediate impact in 1967 because county school board positions were not up for election that year. In the county school board elections the previous year, only one black candidate was elected, in majority-black Jefferson County, which retained district elections.[84]

Another structural barrier, one that predated the massive resistance efforts of 1966, was the primary runoff requirement—the statutory requirement for primary elections that stipulated that if no candidate received a majority of the vote, the top two vote-getters had to compete head-to-head in a primary runoff election. Although the efforts of the Mississippi Legislature, in the open primary bill of 1966, to enact a runoff requirement for the general election failed, the runoff feature applicable to party primaries proved an effective barrier to the election of black candidates in 1967. In primaries in which the white vote was split among a number of white candidates, twenty black candidates made it into the Democratic primary runoffs. In the first primaries, eight of these black candidates won pluralities, polling more votes than any of the other candidates, and without the runoff they would have won the party nomination. But in the head-to-head runoff elections against the leading white candidates, all twenty of these black candidates lost.[85]

At least eleven Mississippi counties changed from elected to appointed county superintendents of education as mandated by the 1966 statute. Taking these positions out of the electoral arena certainly undercut the black electoral potential in 1967. But for the change, blacks would probably have run for county school superintendent in several of these counties. Indeed, black candidates ran for other countywide offices in six of the eleven counties that eliminated elections for county school superintendent.[86] Black candidates could have seriously contested the office or even won election in Holmes, Claiborne, and Jefferson counties. As it happened, no black candidates were elected county superintendent of education in 1967.

One black candidate, Robert Clark, actually turned this adverse development to his advantage. When denied the opportunity to run for county superintendent of education, Clark ran for the state legislature against one of the principal supporters of the legislation and won. One year before, in 1966, Clark had met with the Holmes County Board of Education to persuade the board to sponsor an adult education program in the Holmes County schools. When the school board rejected his proposal upon the recommendation of the county superintendent of education, Clark decided to run against the superintendent in the next county election. But then the legislature eliminated elections for the position with the support of a representative from Clark's own district, J. P. Love, who as chair of the House Education Committee reported out the bill and recommended its passage. Frustrated in his desire to run for county school superintendent, Clark determined instead to run for Love's seat in the legislature. Clark's defeat of J. P. Love in the November 1967 general election was the only electoral retribution black voters would gain in 1967 for the legislature's 1966 massive resistance program. For Clark, it was a great personal triumph on several levels.[87]

Clark's victory aside, the system of multimember legislative districts all but devastated black attempts to gain seats in the state legislature. Seven of the eight black candidates for the Mississippi Legislature lost, and all seven losing candidates ran in multimember House or Senate districts. Three of the black candidates for the state House of Representatives ran in Hinds County, where they carried the majority-black precincts but lost countywide.

The discriminatory impact of multimember districts may also be shown by comparison with events in Georgia in the 1965 and 1966 legislative elections held directly after passage of the Voting Rights Act. In that state eight black candidates won election to the Georgia House of Representatives after the legislature, under the pressure of litigation, eliminated a number of multimember legislative districts and drew single-member legislative districts in heavily black areas.[88]

The one black winner in the legislative contests, Robert G. Clark, also ran in a multimember district, a three-member district consisting of Holmes and Yazoo counties. But Clark was able to win because both of the counties in his district were predominantly black (Holmes, 72 percent black; Yazoo, 59 percent black), and his district overall was 65 percent black.

The structural barriers erected by the Mississippi Legislature in 1966 thus had a major impact on blacks' electoral chances in the 1967 state and county elections. However, these were not the only factors that minimized black electoral victories. Additional factors—some of which continue to hamper black efforts to win elective office—also played a role. Other barriers to black electoral success included racial bloc voting by whites, who generally refused to vote for black candidates; control of the electoral machinery by all-white county party committees and election commissions, which resulted in few blacks being appointed polling place managers and clerks; socioeconomic disparities between whites and blacks, which depressed black voter registration and turnout rates; and harassment and abuse of black candidates and voters.[89]

Some of these problems could be addressed by desegregating the electoral process itself by forcing election officials to hire black polling place managers and clerks and by increased political organizing efforts aimed at increasing black registration and turnout. But in many counties and electoral districts, even these efforts would be inadequate if the structural barriers to black political success erected by the Mississippi Legislature in 1966 remained.

The 1967 elections demonstrated that few whites were willing to vote for black candidates. With whites voting as a bloc, the changes in electoral rules and structures designed to dilute black votes would continue to prevent blacks from electing candidates of their choice in most areas of the state even if the black community were to achieve 100 percent registration and turnout.

By the end of 1966, the Mississippi Legislature had set in place some powerful new barriers to black electoral success in the state. Through the actions taken in this massive resistance legislative session, the traditional white leadership of the state had recouped much of the strength it had apparently lost when Congress passed the Voting Rights Act the previous year. If the radical changes in the state's election laws enacted in 1966 could stand up to federal court challenges, Mississippi's segregationist political leaders would have little to fear from the fact that the state's black population was now registering to vote in increasingly large numbers.

Mississippi's legislative white backlash to the Voting Rights Act was not without historical precedent. Historian Morgan Kousser has pointed out that in the post-Reconstruction period, southern legislatures employed a number of similar devices to undermine the impact of the Fifteenth Amendment and federal voting rights legislation. They employed racial gerrymandering of congressional district lines, discriminatory realignment of state legislative districts, switching to at-large elections, and substituting appointment for election of local officials.[90] But never before were so many devices enacted all at the same time to devalue the black vote—and all without denying the federally secured right to register and cast a ballot.

True, the legislature had not accomplished all that it had set out to do, and there had been some bickering along the way. The governor had vetoed the so-called open primary bills, a deadlock over reapportionment tactics had necessitated the calling of a special legislative session in the fall, and in the end the district court had applied the Supreme Court's reapportionment rulings to reject the legislature's reapportionment plan as unconstitutional. Even so, the vast majority of the electoral change measures proposed had been enacted into law, and legislators might have had reason to suspect that the court-ordered reapportionment plan, to be unveiled the following spring, would retain many of the key discriminatory features of the legislature's plan.

In sum, the state legislature's 1966 changes in election laws all but ensured that the new black vote would have little impact on the policies or operations of state and local government in Mississippi. At the end of 1967, then, the massive resistance approach had—at least for the moment—proven quite successful.

3 The Judicial Response to Massive Resistance

Allen v. State Board of Elections

Given the disappointing results of the 1967 elections, it was evident that black leaders and voters in Mississippi would be able to expand their small political gains only if they could eliminate the discriminatory structural barriers imposed by the legislature in 1966. But how could such a reform be accomplished? Obtaining any additional voting rights legislation from Congress so soon after passage of the 1965 Voting Rights Act seemed an unlikely prospect. Moreover, with their voting power so effectively neutralized, Mississippi blacks were powerless to exert the degree of political pressure on the legislative or executive branches of state government necessary to repeal these laws. With these political avenues cut off, Mississippi's civil rights forces turned to litigation and asked the federal courts for relief.

The strategy of seeking judicial relief presented two major problems, however. First, the federal judges of the United States District Court for the Southern District of Mississippi—where any state voting-law challenges had to be filed—were products of Mississippi's segregated system who tended to be hostile to civil rights litigation. Second, the issues presented in these cases involved not outright denial of the right to register and vote but the novel question of dilution of the voting strength of black voters. Apart from some nonbinding statements in the early one-person, one-vote cases, and the Tuskegee, Alabama, municipal deannexation case, which did not present typical gerrymandering issues, the Supreme Court had not yet directly decided whether switching to at-large elections or dividing up black population concentrations among election districts violated the Fourteenth or Fifteenth Amendments.[1] No clear constitutional precedent existed. Nor had the Supreme Court decided what kinds of voting-law changes were subject to the protective provisions of section 5 of the Voting Rights Act.

This chapter describes how the judicial system, specifically the federal district court in Mississippi and the United States Supreme Court, responded to the Mississippi Legislature's bold manipulation of the electoral processes to deprive the state's newly enfranchised black citizens of any real political power. The first section introduces the principal actors in this legal drama, the legal organizations that represented black candidates and voters in their courtroom challenges to Mississippi's massive resistance program, and the federal district judges in Mississippi who initially heard these lawsuits. The second section describes the unsuccessful effort to strike down the gerrymandered congressional districts and the Supreme Court's surprising failure to invalidate the redistricting plan. The ultimate legal victory in the Supreme Court over other elements of the massive resistance program, the statutes changing methods of election and election rules, is examined in the third section.

The Litigators and the Judges

The Litigators: Mississippi's
"Farish Street Crowd"

Since segregated education had excluded blacks from attending law schools in Mississippi and the rest of the Deep South, there were very few black lawyers in the state. During most of the 1960s, there were only four black lawyers in Mississippi who were admitted to practice in the state, and only three of these were willing to take civil rights cases. These black attorneys were extremely courageous and risked their lives to challenge segregation and to defend civil rights workers arrested on trumped-up charges.

However, because of the enormous amount of time and expense involved in complex federal litigation, most of the major civil rights reform litigation after 1965 was handled by three national civil rights legal organizations which maintained offices in Jackson: the Lawyers' Committee for Civil Rights Under Law; the Lawyers' Constitutional Defense Committee (LCDC); and the NAACP Legal Defense and Educational Fund, Inc.[2] Of the three groups, the Lawyers' Committee and LCDC are the least well known. Most accounts of civil rights litigation producing legal change have focused on the school desegregation litigation of the NAACP and the NAACP Legal Defense Fund and have tended to overlook the contributions of other groups. In 1964 both the Lawyers' Committee and LCDC sent more than 100 volunteer lawyers to Mississippi to assist the Freedom Summer project, and these volunteer lawyers represented civil rights workers in hundreds of cases—mostly defense of state criminal prosecutions arising out of civil rights activities and demonstrations. Yet the standard accounts of the Mississippi Freedom Summer Project almost totally neglect the participation of these groups.[3] Similarly, accounts of the legal struggles after the passage of the Voting Rights Act only briefly note or fail to mention these organizations.[4]

In response to the Mississippi Freedom Summer Project of 1964 and the massive civil rights protest and organizing efforts in the state, all three groups opened offices in Jackson in 1964 and 1965. The organizations concluded that a Mississippi presence was needed both to provide continuing representation in cases commenced by summer volunteer lawyers and to more effectively litigate the growing number of Mississippi civil rights cases. As a consequence, in no other southern state did so many national civil rights legal organizations have full-time, staffed offices. The Jackson offices of these organizations initially were staffed mostly by white lawyers who had come to Mississippi from outside the state. National foundations provided the primary funding for these efforts. Because all three of these organizations had their offices along Farish Street, the black business district in Jackson, District Judge Harold Cox dubbed the civil rights lawyers the "Farish Street crowd."

The Lawyers' Committee for Civil Rights Under Law was formed in June 1963. It was nicknamed the "President's Committee," because of its origin at a White House meeting in which President Kennedy urged the leaders of the American Bar Association and the National Bar Association to support the struggle to end racial segregation and to encourage peaceful resolution of civil rights conflicts. Lawyers' Committee attorneys first came to Mississippi, in the view of one observer, "more as missionaries to the Mississippi bar than anything else."[5] After short-term volunteer efforts in the summers of 1963 and 1964 demonstrated the magnitude of the need for legal assistance, the Lawyers' Committee opened an office in Jackson in June 1965 with two full-time lawyers, later increased to four.

Initially the Lawyer's Committee was invited to Mississippi by the National Council of Churches and limited itself to providing legal defense for ministers arrested for civil rights protest activity. Within a short period of time, however, the group gave up its "missionary" stance, broadened its representation role, and began filing a wide range of affirmative civil rights lawsuits, including federal court challenges to exclusion of blacks from state court juries, employment discrimination, and voting rights denials. From 1967 on, the Lawyers' Committee received substantial support from the Ford Foundation and other major foundations.[6]

The second legal organization, LCDC, was formed in the spring of 1964 by a coalition of the chief legal officers of several major New York–based human rights organizations, including CORE, the American Civil Liberties Union, the NAACP Legal Defense Fund, the American Jewish Congress, and the National Council of Churches. During the summer of 1964, LCDC sponsored a legal assistance effort staffed by 130 lawyers who had volunteered their vacation time (two to three weeks) to go south to help meet the legal needs of the civil rights movement.

LCDC established an office in Mississippi in response to a suggestion from Jack Greenberg, head of the NAACP Legal Defense Fund. Greenberg was concerned about the need for additional legal support, given the restrictions on the activities of the Lawyers' Committee at that time. A two-lawyer office was opened in Jackson in January 1965 directed by Alvin J. Bronstein. Funding initially came from a group of small foundations, but in 1966 LCDC became part of the Roger Baldwin Foundation of the ACLU (later renamed the ACLU Foundation). Like the Lawyers' Committee, LCDC in its early days served a largely criminal defense function but then expanded its efforts to challenge antiboycott, antipicketing, and antileafleting statutes passed to curtail civil rights protest activities and to take on voting rights cases.[7]

The NAACP Legal Defense and Educational Fund, Inc. (nicknamed the "Inc. Fund"), the third civil rights legal organization in Jackson, concerned itself primarily with school desegregation litigation, not voting rights, and filed the first school desegregation cases in the state in 1963. The Jackson office was opened in 1964 by the national organization, which was established as an organization separate from the NAACP in 1939 and which had its headquarters in New York City.[8]

The presence of these privately funded outside legal organizations in Mississippi provided a tremendous boost to civil rights litigation in the state. It meant that civil rights litigants had their own lawyers, who were responsible to their civil rights clients, and the black community was no longer dependent upon the Justice Department to vindicate their rights. While the Justice Department had spent an enormous amount of time and money litigating voter registration and harassment cases during the early 1960s, the black community did not control this litigation. The department, whose attorneys did not live in Mississippi and sometimes were not familiar with local conditions in the state, often took conservative positions—frequently the department refused to provide protection to civil rights workers—and agreed to settle cases against the wishes of the individuals involved. Now black plaintiffs had their own lawyers who resided in the state and who developed alliances with their clients; who were familiar with local conditions; who developed a certain level of credibility even with hostile local federal judges by repeatedly getting their decisions reversed on appeal; and who, by repeatedly filing the same kinds of cases and exchanging information and litigation techniques among themselves, developed a high level of expertise in civil rights litigation that gave their clients an advantage.

Given the Inc. Fund's specialization in school-related cases, the lawsuits contesting Mississippi's political massive resistance legislation were handled by either the Lawyers' Committee or LCDC. During the 1960s and early 1970s these two groups litigated almost all of the voting rights cases in Mississippi. The Lawyers' Committee had close ties with the NAACP and Charles Evers and thus generally was retained to handle voting rights cases that originated in southwest and south Mississippi counties where the NAACP was highly organized. LCDC, on the other hand, had a close relationship with the MFDP; MFDP head Lawrence Guyot had an office in the Jackson offices of LCDC for a while. LCDC filed most of its voting rights cases on behalf of black political leaders and voters in the Delta and north Mississippi counties where the MFDP was active. Some cases were handled by both groups; for example, LCDC litigated the legislative reapportionment case from 1966 to 1971 and then, when LCDC's Jackson office closed in 1971, the Lawyers' Committee took over the case.

Lawyers from the Mississippi Attorney General's office defended the voting rights cases. They were always white, and most of them were Mississippi natives who had graduated from the racially segregated University of Mississippi Law School. Sometimes state attorney general Joe T. Patterson or his successor, A. F. Summer, would present arguments in these cases, testifying to the high visibility and political importance of these cases to Mississippi's white establishment.

The District Court Judges

The judges who sat on the U.S. District Court for the Southern District of Mississippi tended to look with disfavor on civil rights lawsuits and generally ruled to preserve the status quo.[9] Mississippi senator James O. Eastland had used his tremendous power as chair of the Senate Judiciary Committee to force the appointment of federal judges who—in the words of southern observers Jack Bass and Walter DeVries—"have tended to join in the resistance to change."[10] Because they were seeking enforcement of their rights secured by the federal constitution and laws, black litigants looked to the federal courts to protect their civil rights. When civil rights plaintiffs were seeking court orders, rather than damages, cases were tried to the federal judge without a jury, with any appeal going first to the court of appeals and then to the Supreme Court. If the constitutionality of a state statute was being challenged, a three-judge federal district court was required, generally composed of one court of appeals judge and two district judges, and the losing party was entitled to a direct appeal to the Supreme Court.

The Mississippi congressional redistricting and legislative reapportionment cases, which were consolidated in the case *Connor v. Johnson*, were heard by a three-judge panel consisting of recently appointed Fifth Circuit Judge J. P. Coleman, District Judge Harold Cox, and District Judge Dan M. Russell, Jr. It is unlikely that a less sympathetic judicial panel could have been assembled anywhere in the South to hear a civil rights lawsuit.[11]

J. P. Coleman, who had served as governor from 1956 to 1960, had been appointed in 1965 to the U.S. Court of Appeals for the Fifth Circuit by President Lyndon B. Johnson. The 51-year-old Coleman was sworn in just two months before the *Connor* case was filed. Coleman's background was that of a strict segregationist. He grew up in Fentress, a small town in the rural hill country of Choctaw County in north-central Mississippi, and before being elected governor had served successively as district attorney, circuit court judge, justice of the Mississippi Supreme Court, and state attorney general. In both of his races for governor (he lost his second bid to Paul B. Johnson, Jr., in 1963), Coleman ran as a "strong segregationist" committed to maintaining, "quietly and successfully," racial segregation in Mississippi's schools and universities.[12] During the 1963 campaign Coleman criticized Paul Johnson's failure, as Ross Barnett's lieutenant governor and stand-in, to block the admission of a black man, James Meredith, to the all-white University of Mississippi. Coleman promised voters that if he were elected "there will be no integration of public institutions, no racial agitation, and no further invasions by U.S. troops and marshalls."[13] At one point in the 1963 campaign he threatened to close the public schools to avoid desegregation: "I'd shut up every school house before we see education by federal bayonet."[14]

When Coleman's appointment to the federal bench was announced two years later, the national NAACP and Mississippi civil rights leaders vigorously opposed his confirmation at the Senate hearings, which were chaired by Senator Eastland. But his confirmation was assured when President Johnson's attorney general, Nicholas Katzenbach, made a rare appearance before the Senate Judiciary Committee and urged Coleman's confirmation. Katzenbach argued that through-out his public career Coleman had never advocated defying the courts to avoid desegregation and that the most "relevant" consider-ation was Coleman's "consistent stand for law and order."[15]

District Judge Harold Cox's hostility to Mississippi civil rights cases is legend.[16] "A master of obstruction and delay, he may well have been the greatest single obstacle to equal justice in the South," one commentator has remarked.[17] Cox, a native of Sunflower County in the Delta and a former college roommate and close friend of Sena-tor Eastland, was the Kennedy administration's first judicial appoint-ment in 1961. Although his racial views may have been known to the Justice Department before his appointment, he won administration support through assurances that if appointed he would enforce the Constitution and laws of the United States.[18]

Judge Cox's views of federal law and the U.S. Constitution were personal and somewhat unique, however, and often ran counter to those of higher federal courts. From 1961 to 1976 an astonishing 76.7 percent of his decisions in civil rights cases were reversed by higher courts on appeal.[19] Racist comments were scattered throughout Cox's opinions and comments from the bench. In a 1962 voter registration discrimination case presenting statistical proof that few blacks were being permitted to pass the literacy test, Judge Cox took judicial no-tice that "the intelligence of the colored people don't [sic] compare ratio-wise to white people."[20] In another voter registration case Judge Cox commented regarding black citizens waiting in line to register: "Who is telling these niggers they can get in line and push people around, acting like a bunch of chimpanzees?"[21] In an employment discrimination case alleging that blacks had been relegated to the most menial and lowest-paying jobs, Judge Cox found in his opinion that these were the jobs for which the black employees "are best suited."[22]

The third member of the panel, District Judge Dan M. Russell, Jr., also regularly decided against civil rights claims, although he was less vocal in his hostility to blacks than Cox was. Russell had been a cor-porate and personal injury lawyer on Mississippi's Gulf Coast before President Johnson appointed him to the federal bench in 1965. His father had been a state chancery court judge and had taught law at the University of Mississippi; Senator Eastland and Harold Cox had been among his students. Russell, active in state Democratic party politics before his appointment, had in 1963 introduced gubernatorial candidate Paul B. Johnson, Jr., to a Gulf Coast political rally. There Johnson delivered a well-worn campaign speech vaunting his own defiance of federal marshalls by standing in the schoolhouse door in a vain attempt to prevent James Meredith from enrolling as the first black student at the University of Mississippi—a speech with the rhetorical tag line, "Was I right in standing up for your beliefs?"

As a federal judge, Russell was notorious for attempting to prevent out-of-state civil rights lawyers from appearing in his court[23] and for his high reversal rate in school desegregation cases.[24] He was reversed so many times that ultimately the Court of Appeals for the Fifth Circuit took the unprecedented step of retaining control of all forty-eight school desegregation cases in the District Court for the Southern District of Mississippi to supervise directly the adoption and implementation of decrees issued by Russell and the two other judges of that district.[25]

The Judicial Response to Congressional Redistricting (*Connor v. Johnson*)

In February 1966, the massive resistance legislative session was just getting under way, and state legislators were anxiously considering various plans to carve up the old Delta congressional district. That month, Dr. Russell H. Barrett, a white political science professor at the University of Mississippi and author of the widely respected book *Integration at Ole Miss*, denounced these plans in a speech at Rust College, a predominantly black school in north Mississippi. Barrett urged Mississippi's white political leadership to stop being "obsessed with race" and predicted that the Supreme Court would strike down current efforts to gerrymander the Delta district: "Even with the prodding of the United States Supreme Court and some sensible comments from some members of the Legislature, the leadership is working diligently to gerrymander the Negro population into the weakest possible position. They must know that the Supreme Court will not accept their grotesque creation, but they persist in a manner similar to that long series of ridiculous and dangerous maneuvers which lasted from 1954 until 1964."[26]

Everyone in Mississippi understood the discriminatory purpose of the congressional redistricting plan. The Jackson newspapers had anticipated an east-west realignment of districts to split the Delta well before 1966. And throughout the spring of 1966, despite legislators' attempts to keep their discriminatory intentions under wraps, the Jackson press, as well as the Memphis and New Orleans newspapers with circulation in Jackson, discussed how the various redistricting plans being considered would split the state's largest concentration of black voting strength.

The MFDP's challenge to the three-way split of the Delta area in the 1966 congressional redistricting plan, part of the marathon case *Connor v. Johnson*, became the first of the anti–massive resistance litigation to reach the Supreme Court. The lawsuit was filed after a statewide mass meeting at the black Masonic Temple in Jackson called by the Mississippi statewide civil rights coalition, COFO, and after meetings between the MFDP state leadership and lawyers associated with LCDC.[27] The plaintiffs were the MFDP and eight black activists affiliated with the MFDP.

The lawsuit reflected the strategic thinking of the MFDP leadership that a major vehicle of political entry into Mississippi's closed political system was federal court litigation.[28] The case was designed to serve both a protest function and a political change function. Lawrence Guyot, state chairperson of the MFDP, advocated "the challenge concept," which he defined as "the underlying concept of challenging the illegal state structure, outside that structure," including lawsuits.[29] The challenge concept had previously been developed and employed by the MFDP in challenging the seating of the all-white Mississippi Democratic party delegation to the Democratic National Convention in Atlantic City in 1964 and in challenging the seating of Mississippi's all-white House of Representatives delegation in Congress in 1965.

In addition, MFDP activists saw "the need for effective and speedy political changes in the State before most of the Negro population had to face the choice of starvation or migration."[30] State government had been unresponsive to the needs of black Mississippians in education, job training, medical facilities, housing, food, employment, and other areas, and had refused to participate in federal programs established to meet the needs of low-income persons in these areas. For the MFDP, the goal of the political movement in Mississippi was "to change the composition and thus policies of the State government."[31]

The initial legal strategy of *Connor v. Johnson* was to take advantage of the Supreme Court's newly declared one-person, one-vote principle[32] to require the restructuring of Mississippi's 5 congressional districts and 131 state legislative districts. The complaint, filed October 19, 1965, challenged the existing congressional and state legislative districts for unconstitutional population malapportionment and for exclusion of black representation from both Mississippi's congressional delegation and the state legislature.[33] The state legislative reapportionment phase of the case, which went on for fourteen years and included nine trips to the Supreme Court before substantial relief was obtained in 1979, is discussed in chapter 4. This chapter will describe the litigation of the congressional redistricting phase of the case, the issue of racial gerrymandering as it was raised in the litigation, and the failure of the Supreme Court to grant relief.

It is important to note that in its earliest stages, *Connor v. Johnson* raised only constitutional claims under the Fourteenth Amendment, which provides that no state shall "deny to any person within its jurisdiction the equal protection of the laws," and the Fifteenth Amendment, which prohibits denial of the right to vote on account of race. Only later—after 1968—would the *Connor* case raise the issue of whether changes in Mississippi's legislative districts were subject to federal preclearance under section 5 of the Voting Rights Act.

The section of the MFDP complaint charging unconstitutional malapportionment in the congressional districts clearly made out a valid claim. The largest district, the Second Congressional District with a population of 608,441, had more than twice the population of the smallest district, the Fourth Congressional District with a population of 295,072.[34] Before any hearing in district court, the Mississippi Legislature, as described in the preceding chapter, redrew the congressional district boundaries and equalized the population among the districts but split up the black population concentration in the Delta among three districts. In response, the MFDP plaintiffs amended their 1965 complaint to allege that the legislature's new plan gerrymandered the heavily black Delta region for the purpose and effect of denying black voters an opportunity to elect black candidates in violation of their Fourteenth and Fifteenth Amendment rights. The MFDP and its LCDC attorneys contested the plan in federal court with the hope that the Supreme Court, which had barred racial segregation in the public schools and enunciated the one-person, one-vote rule to provide equality of representation, would now act to prohibit racial discrimination in congressional redistricting.

After a short trial, the three-judge district court composed of Circuit Judge J. P. Coleman and District Judges Harold Cox and Dan M. Russell, Jr., in September 1966 dismissed for lack of proof the MFDP's claims that the legislature's congressional redistricting plan was unconstitutional. In reaching this conclusion, the court gave short shrift to the MFDP's contention that the new district lines were racially discriminatory. The court treated the issue of whether the new plan apportioned the state into districts of equal population as "the sole question before the Court"[35] and ruled that the plan satisfied that requirement. The judges rejected the MFDP's contentions that black voters were entitled to black representation in Mississippi's congressional delegation and that, because of its heavily black composition, the Delta region should be retained in a single district. The key question then became whether plaintiffs had proved that the plan was enacted for a discriminatory purpose. Here, the judges trapped the plaintiffs in a catch-22 by rejecting as proof the most direct evidence showing discriminatory intent—the newspaper reports of the legislative debates in which state legislators themselves stated that racial discrimination was the main factor behind the plan. The plaintiffs "proved that there were newspaper reports as to what a few legislators 'thought' or said," the court ruled, "but the solemn acts of Congress or of State legislators may not be impeached or invalidated on nothing more than newspaper reports."[36] Of course, the plaintiffs had more than the newspaper reports; they had the timing of the plan and its discriminatory effect. But the court also rejected the evidence of its discriminatory effect because the plan was dissimilar to the one condemned by the Supreme Court in the Tuskegee, Alabama, gerrymandering case, *Gomillion v. Lightfoot*.[37] In *Gomillion*, the Mississippi district court held, the Supreme Court had condemned a revision of the city boundaries that removed all but 4 or 5 of the 400 black residents while not removing a single white voter, and altered the city's boundaries from a square shape to a twenty-eight-sided figure. Because "there are no such facts in this case," the court ruled, "*Gomillion* is simply not apposite."[38]

Thus, the district court held that the Constitution only requires districts that are substantially equal in population, and that had been achieved. Plaintiffs failed to prove that the plan was racially discriminatory in intent or effect because the most direct evidence of discriminatory intent could not be accepted to invalidate the plan and the district boundaries were relatively regular in shape. The other evidence of discrimination—the fact that the plan divided the Delta, which had been maintained intact for more than eighty years, the fact that the plan was enacted immediately after the passage of the Voting Rights Act, and the fact that the plan split up the heaviest black population concentration in the state—was completely ignored.

In its preliminary brief the MFDP put the racial gerrymandering question directly to the Supreme Court. The MFDP contended that the legislature's plan "creates five congressional districts in each of which the white vote will, presently and in the foreseeable future, outweigh the Negro vote, and thus preserves a white majority in all five of the state's congressional districts, despite a 43% Negro population in the state as a whole, which is largely concentrated in one compact and geographically discrete section of the state."[39] In their response, the defendants, who were Governor Johnson, state attorney general Joe T. Patterson, and Secretary of State Heber Ladner, employed two of the primary defense tactics of modern redistricting litigation—the trumped-up nonracial justification for a discriminatory plan and the charge that the black plaintiffs were seeking reverse discrimination. The state officials denied that the plan was enacted for any discriminatory purpose and asserted that it was required to satisfy the one-person, one-vote rule, although undoubtedly equally populated districts could have been drawn without splitting the Delta. In justification for the east-west configuration of the district lines, defendants asserted that the new congressional district lines merely followed the east-west alignments of the three state supreme court districts—a justification that had not, however, been mentioned in the news reports of the legislative debates. The state officials also counterattacked with the charge that the plaintiffs sought not mere racial equality but an unconstitutional racial preference in drawing congressional districts: "Appellants . . . seek a segregated congressional district in favor of the non-white population. Appellants seek inequality in their favor and a segregated district that could not be created without dividing counties and municipalities, along lines tortuously drawn to segregate neighborhoods. The Equal Protection Clause of the constitution does not require that this be done. In fact, the opposite is true and if this were sought to be done to segregate the races, it would be subject to serious constitutional question."[40]

Unexpectedly, the Supreme Court, without full briefs or oral arguments, summarily affirmed the decision of the three-judge district court with a one-line order: "The motion to affirm is granted and the judgment is affirmed."[41] Only Justice Douglas voted to give the case a full hearing. Instead of the strong declaration of constitutional principles they had hoped for, the MFDP plaintiffs received only what might be termed a "nondecision" from the Supreme Court.

Since the Supreme Court gave no reasons for its action, analysts can only speculate on the reasoning behind it. Professor Robert G. Dixon, Jr., in his comprehensive survey of 1960s reapportionment litigation, attributed the Supreme Court's action simply to plaintiffs' failure to fully prove their racial gerrymandering allegation.[42] But this explanation is unsatisfactory. Indeed, it is unlikely that any case could have presented stronger evidence of both the discriminatory intent on the part of the state legislature and the discriminatory impact of the redistricting plan. Neither did the fact that the primary evidence of discriminatory intent came from press accounts of the legislative debate significantly weaken the case. In the absence of official transcripts of the legislative debates, the courts frequently have relied on newspaper reports to document the discriminatory motivation behind southern racial legislation.[43]

A more likely reason may be the Supreme Court's reluctance to address the issue of racial gerrymandering so soon after its highly controversial one-person, one-vote decision in 1964. The justices may also have believed that institutional deference should be given to a plan enacted by a state legislature and approved by a local federal district court. But such deference would seem to be misplaced when the all-white legislature that had enacted the plan was unrepresentative and the district court's opinion failed to address all of the MFDP's extensive evidence of racial discrimination.

The Supreme Court's failure to address black voters' constitutional claims of racial gerrymandering following the passage of the Voting Rights Act—as typified by *Connor v. Johnson*—must be ranked as a major default of the Warren Court, which was otherwise sensitive to civil rights issues. This default exemplifies what Dixon, writing in 1968, termed one of the "remaining thorns in the political thicket" of reapportionment.[44] According to Dixon, the new constitutional mandate of equal-population reapportionment provided a cure for population malapportionment. But, he pointed out, its requirements of regular revision of districts and tight arithmetic equality for all districts actually created "new opportunities for unfairness in representation (gerrymandering)."[45] The failure of the Supreme Court, following the 1964 reapportionment cases, to establish strict guidelines prohibiting racial gerrymandering contradicted the "fair representation" goal of its reapportionment decisions.

Instead of benefiting from the Supreme Court's one-person, one-vote rule, black voters in Mississippi were victimized by it, at least during the years immediately following the passage of the Voting Rights Act. Far from accomplishing a more effective franchise for black voters, the Supreme Court's reapportionment mandate was used by the Mississippi Legislature to debase black voting strength. As a result, constitutionally protected black voters found themselves disfranchised in effect, although technically empowered to cast an equal ballot. The Supreme Court's refusal to address the racial gerrymandering issue in *Connor v. Johnson* had an enduring political impact for black voters in Mississippi. Black voters in Mississippi were effectively prevented from electing a black member of Congress for twenty years, until 1986. In its 1971 congressional redistricting, enacted to compensate for population disparities revealed by the 1970 census, the Mississippi Legislature closely followed the district lines established in its discriminatory 1966 plan. When this plan was submitted to the Justice Department for federal preclearance under section 5 of the Voting Rights Act, the department—following its then-existing policy of deferring to court decisions in redistricting and citing the Supreme Court's *Connor* decision—approved the plan under section 5.

It was not until 1981, when the Justice Department objected under section 5 to a "least change" plan that also split the Delta, that a federal district court restored the Delta district as Mississippi's Second Congressional District.[46] But over this period, the continued outmigration of blacks from the Delta in search of jobs and a better life substantially reduced the black population in that region. Although Mississippi continued to have the largest percentage of blacks of any state, the percentage of black voters was not large enough to win against the solid white bloc vote. In intensely racially polarized voting patterns, white conservative Republican Webb Franklin won the Second District seat over black state legislator Robert Clark in the 1982 and 1984 elections.[47] Finally, in 1986—more than twenty years after the passage of the Voting Rights Act—Mike Espy, a lawyer with roots in the Delta area, turned the situation around in a hard-fought, grassroots campaign and became Mississippi's first black member of Congress in this century.

The 1967 nondecision of the Supreme Court in *Connor v. Johnson* also had disturbing implications beyond the specific issue of congressional redistricting. The failure of the Court to act provided at least a temporary victory for the state's efforts to negate the new black vote. It proved that reasonable voices like Russell Barrett's were wrong and that the Supreme Court in the late 1960s was not willing to reject the legislature's "grotesque creations." It caused great concern among Mississippi's civil rights forces over the fate of the other massive resistance legislation. Unless the Supreme Court's apparent imperviousness to racial vote dilution claims could be reversed, the black political renaissance in Mississippi, and perhaps throughout the South, would be strangled at birth.

The Judicial Response to Discriminatory Electoral Changes (*Allen v. State Board of Elections*)

The next issue to confront the Supreme Court was whether Mississippi's 1966 legislation changing methods of election and election rules, passed in resistance to the Voting Rights Act, was subject to what the Supreme Court termed "an uncommon exercise of congressional power"[48] in section 5 of the Voting Rights Act. Section 5, in effect, freezes the voting laws of every covered jurisdiction that were in effect on November 1, 1964 (later for jurisdictions covered by subsequent extensions of the act). It requires all covered states and localities to obtain federal approval (called "preclearance") *before* implementing any changes in "any voting qualification or prerequisite to voting, or standard, practice or procedure with respect to voting."[49] Jurisdictions covered by section 5 must submit for preclearance any proposed changes in their voting laws to either the United States District Court for the District of Columbia or (the route favored by most states) the United States attorney general. The state or locality has the burden of proving that the proposed change "does not have the purpose and will not have the effect of denying or abridging the right to vote on account of race or color."[50] If the submitting jurisdiction fails to demonstrate that the voting-law change does not have a discriminatory purpose or effect, the district court in Washington must withhold approval of the change, or the attorney general must lodge a section 5 objection, thus prohibiting implementation of the change. Congress in 1965 put this innovative procedure in place for five years, with the option of renewing the act when it expired in 1970. This provision of the act was renewed in 1970, in 1975, and in 1982 for twenty-five years.

As originally passed, section 5 covered any jurisdiction in which literacy or other voter registration tests were suspended by the Voting Rights Act—including seven states and parts of two others, encompassing the entire state of Mississippi and most of the Old South. The question was whether Mississippi's 1966 electoral statutes—none of which directly denied the right to vote itself or affected voter registration procedures—were subject to the preclearance requirement of section 5. The congressional purpose behind section 5 was to prevent evasion of the requirements of the act by covered states through the implementation of new discriminatory voting practices. The voter registration litigation in the early 1960s showed that once the Justice Department had obtained a federal court decree enjoining discriminatory tests that were being used, state and local officials would simply contrive new voter registration tests or rules to perpetuate voting discrimination and to evade the federal court decree.[51] In sustaining the constitutionality of section 5 in 1966, the Supreme Court ruled that "Congress had reason to suppose that these States might try similar maneuvers in the future in order to evade the remedies for voting discrimination contained in the Act itself."[52]

But the language of the Voting Rights Act left open a very important question. What kinds of voting-law changes were covered under section 5? Were the preclearance procedures limited strictly to proposed changes in voter registration laws or balloting procedures? Or should the preclearance requirement be applied more broadly to cover all changes that might affect the impact of a vote? If the federal courts were to take the second, broader position, Mississippi would be obliged to submit all of its 1966 massive resistance legislation for federal preclearance. The state of Mississippi would then have the difficult task of proving that these measures had no discriminatory purpose or effect before they could be implemented.

Black candidates and voters adversely affected by the election-law changes of the Mississippi Legislature's 1966 massive resistance session filed six lawsuits challenging those changes under the Fourteenth and Fifteenth Amendments and section 5 of the Voting Rights Act. The suits were *Whitley v. Johnson, Fairley v. Patterson, Marsaw v. Patterson, Ballard v. Patterson, Bunton v. Patterson,* and *Griffin v. Patterson.*

The first suit, *Whitley v. Johnson,* concerned the Mississippi Legislature's onerous new qualifying requirements for independent candidates. The first black candidates to run afoul of this measure were three MFDP candidates for Congress in 1966, the Reverend Clifton Whitley, Dock Drummond, and Emma Sanders. Whitley and Drummond had run for Congress in the June 1966 Democratic primary and, after losing, had attempted to qualify again to run as independents in the November general election—Whitley for the U.S. Senate and Drummond for the U.S. House of Representatives in the First Congressional District. Mrs. Sanders, who bypassed the primary, attempted to qualify as an independent candidate for the U.S. House of Representatives in the Third Congressional District.

Citing the provisions of the new law, however, the State Board of Election Commissioners refused to place the names of these black candidates on the ballot for the November general election. Whitley and Drummond had run and lost in the Democratic primary, disqualifying them from running as independents in the general election. Moreover, Whitley had failed to collect all 10,000 certified signatures now required to run as an independent for U.S. senator and other statewide offices. Similarly, the petitions of Drummond and Sanders fell short of the 2,000 signatures now required for congressional candidates. All three candidates, however, had more than the number of certified signatures (1,000 and 200) required under the previous statute.

The three MFDP candidates, represented by lawyers with LCDC, then filed *Whitley v. Johnson.* In their complaint, they challenged the new law as racially discriminatory in violation of their Fourteenth and Fifteenth Amendment rights and invalid for lack of federal preclearance under section 5 of the Voting Rights Act. In October, a district court, without reaching the merits of the case, granted a preliminary injunction that provisionally placed the names of all three candidates on the general election ballot as independents.[53]

The preliminary injunction that enabled these MFDP candidates to run in the November general election was the first court victory over Mississippi's massive resistance legislation. It was a limited victory, however. For one thing, all three candidates were soundly defeated in November. Further, the court's decision provided no ruling on the merits of the candidates' legal claims, leaving black candidates in future cases without a precedent on which they could rely.

The next year, when the nineteen black MFDP candidates were disqualified from running as independents for state legislative and county offices in the 1967 statewide election, the *Whitley* plaintiffs sought permanent injunctive relief against the enforcement of the new statute. Because of the impending elections, they needed a speedy ruling on their complaint. Further, the Supreme Court's ruling in the congressional redistricting case, *Connor v. Johnson*, described in the previous section, created doubt as to whether they could succeed on their allegation of Fourteenth and Fifteenth Amendment violations. Consequently, the plaintiffs dropped their Fourteenth and Fifteenth Amendment claims, leaving only the issue of whether the statute establishing the stringent new qualifying requirements was subject to section 5 preclearance.

In October, the three-judge district court rejected the candidates' section 5 claim and denied all relief. The three judges hearing this case were Fifth Circuit Judge Robert Ainsworth, a former Louisiana legislator who had served as president pro tem of the Louisiana Senate, along with District Judges Cox and Russell. The decision drew a distinction between voters and candidates and between voting and elections. The new statute, the judges held, was not a change in voting laws covered by section 5 because it "is directed solely to the qualifications of candidates, whereas Section 5 has reference to the qualifications of voters." "The Act does not deal with voting but deals with elections, and more particularly the candidates; therefore it does not impinge upon Section 5 of the Voting Rights Act of 1965."[54]

Meanwhile, five similar lawsuits were being filed against two other massive resistance statutes: the law that authorized counties to switch from district to at-large elections for county supervisors and the law that turned previously elective county school superintendent positions into appointive offices. Black voters affiliated with the NAACP in Forrest and Adams counties, which had switched to at-large county supervisor elections, brought two lawsuits, *Fairley v. Patterson* and *Marsaw v. Patterson* (which were consolidated as *Fairley v. Patterson*). They charged that the 1966 statute authorizing the change violated black voters' Fourteenth and Fifteenth Amendment rights and demanded that the law be submitted for section 5 preclearance. Seth Ballard, a black community leader who had intended to run for county superintendent of education in Jefferson County, and black voters in Holmes and Claiborne counties filed three additional lawsuits, *Ballard v. Patterson*, *Bunton v. Patterson*, and *Griffin v. Patterson* (which were consolidated as *Bunton v. Patterson*). These three suits challenged the 1966 law that transformed the county superintendent of education position from an elective to an appointive office in eleven counties.

The plaintiffs in all five of these cases were represented by attorneys from the Lawyers' Committee for Civil Rights Under Law. As in the *Whitley* case, the plaintiffs dropped their constitutional claims. The five cases were consolidated into two cases for decision, and the same three judges that had decided the *Whitley* case ruled, for the same reasons, that the changes permitted under the challenged statutes did not directly affect the vote and were therefore not covered under section 5.[55]

All three of these consolidated Mississippi cases—*Whitley v. Johnson*, challenging the new qualifying procedures for independent candidates; *Fairley v. Patterson*, challenging the switch to at-large county supervisor elections; and *Bunton v. Patterson*, challenging the elimination of county school superintendent elections—were appealed to the United States Supreme Court. There they were consolidated for oral argument and decision with a Virginia case, *Allen v. State Board of Elections*, challenging newly instituted state procedures controlling how illiterate voters could vote for write-in candidates.

The future of black political participation in Mississippi and the other states covered by the Voting Rights Act now hinged on how the Supreme Court would interpret the statutory language of section 5. The question before the Supreme Court in the *Allen* cases was not whether the challenged Mississippi statutes should be struck down as racially discriminatory, but whether the Voting Rights Act required that the statutes be submitted to the attorney general or the D.C. district court to determine any possible discriminatory purpose or effect. The issue was solely one of interpreting the statutory language of section 5. How much had Congress intended to cover when it required section 5 preclearance for "any voting qualification or prerequisite to voting, or standard, practice or procedure with respect to voting"? Should section 5 be interpreted narrowly to cover only changes in voter registration laws or statutes regulating the casting of ballots? Or should section 5 be interpreted broadly to cover any change relating to the qualifications of candidates, switches from district to at-large elections, the manner of selecting public officials, or other electoral systems that could influence the outcome of elections? The language of the statute appeared to sustain either interpretation. Both sides could cite legislative history and testimony by Johnson administration officials in support of their positions.

In their brief, the Mississippi state officials argued that the new statutes were not covered by section 5. They quoted in support of their argument a 1965 exchange between Congressman James Corman of California and Assistant Attorney General for civil rights Burke Marshall at the House Judiciary subcommittee hearing. Marshall had helped draft the bill and testified on behalf of the Johnson administration in Congress. Congressman Corman had noted that there had been an issue in some areas of the South of "who can run for public office" and asked Marshall whether the administration had given any consideration in the bill to addressing "the qualifications for running for public office as well as the problem of registration." Marshall had responded that "the problem that the bill was aimed at was the problem of registration" and stated, "If there is a problem of another sort, I would like to see it corrected, but that is not what we were trying to deal with in the bill.[56] The Mississippi officials further argued that a broad reading of section 5 would cause a conflict between the federal courts and the Justice Department in the administration of reapportionment decisions, since any redistricting plan approved by a local district court would also have to be reviewed by the Justice Department or the District Court for the District of Columbia.[57]

The lawyers for the black Mississippi voters, for their part, pointed to an exchange in the Senate hearing between Senator Hiram Fong of Hawaii and Attorney General Nicholas Katzenbach. As originally drafted, the section applied to any "qualification or procedure," and during the Senate hearings Senator Fong voiced concern that the word "procedure" was not broad enough to cover all forms of discrimination. Attorney General Katzenbach suggested that the bill be amended to include "standards, practices, or procedures" because the section "was intended to be all-inclusive of any kind of practice" relating to voting.[58] Katzenbach had also testified before the House Judiciary subcommittee that section 5 was intended to have a broad interpretation because of the past history of evasion of court decrees in voting rights and school desegregation cases.[59] In the House hearings, Katzenbach agreed that certain practices, such as changes from paper ballots to voting machines, could be excluded from section 5 coverage.[60] But Congress in enacting the final bill failed to make any exceptions to section 5, indicating its intent that all voting practices should be covered.

The Justice Department, which previously had not been involved in these cases, filed a friend of the court brief in the Supreme Court in support of the position of the black Mississippi candidates and voters. The Justice Department relied particularly upon the definition of "voting" in section 14 of the Voting Rights Act, which was defined to include "all action necessary to make a vote effective in any primary, special, or general election."[61] Although this wording could have been given a narrow interpretation limited to such practices as ballot box stuffing, the Justice Department interpreted it broadly to include measures that diluted or otherwise abrogated the black vote: "Our position, simply stated, is that the three statutes involved in the instant cases all prescribed practices or procedures which may result in abridging the right of Negro citizens to vote by rendering ineffective their exercise of the franchise so recently achieved. Accordingly, the statutes are plainly within the congressional contemplation in enacting Section 5."[62]

The Supreme Court's decision in *Allen v. State Board of Elections* marked the turning point in the efforts of black Mississippians to overcome the state's political massive resistance program. On March 3, 1969, the Supreme Court ruled in favor of the black Mississippi voter plaintiffs.[63] The vote was 7-2, Justices Black and Harlan dissenting.

In an opinion written by Chief Justice Earl Warren, the Court rejected Mississippi's arguments and ruled that Congress, in passing the Voting Rights Act, intended that it should be given "the broadest possible scope."[64] The Court held that the act was "aimed to the subtle, as well as the obvious" state laws affecting the right to vote.[65] Relying on the broad congressional purpose of eliminating racial discrimination in voting, the definition of "voting" in section 14 of the act, and Attorney General Katzenbach's testimony that the word "procedure" was "intended to be all-inclusive of any kind of practice," the Court ruled that the legislative history "on the whole" showed that "Congress intended to reach any state enactment which altered the election law of a covered State in even a minor way."[66] The Court also considered it "significant" that Congress had refused to specify any exceptions to the kinds of voting-law changes covered by the section, "thus indicating an intention that all changes, no matter how small, be subjected to §5 scrutiny."[67] Once having accepted that section 5 was to have "the broadest possible scope," the Supreme Court then ruled that each of the challenged Mississippi statutes was subject to federal review under the Voting Rights Act because each of them in some way affected the right to vote.

In addition to adopting a broad interpretation of section 5, the Supreme Court also ruled that private parties, in addition to the attorney general, can file private lawsuits to enforce the section 5 preclearance requirement, that section 5 enforcement actions can be filed in the jurisdiction in which the case arose, rather than in the D.C. district court, and that three-judge district courts are required to rule on whether a voting-law change is covered by section 5.[68]

There was only one disappointment. The black voter plaintiffs had asked the Supreme Court to set aside the 1967 Mississippi elections conducted almost a year and a half before under the 1966 electoral statutes and order new elections to be held under the pre-1966 electoral rules. A majority of justices, however, held that the cases involved "complex issues of first impression—issues subject to rational disagreement" and that Mississippi's failure to submit the statutes for section 5 review did not constitute "deliberate defiance" of the Voting Rights Act. The Supreme Court's decision would therefore have only "prospective effect" on future elections.[69] Justices Harlan, Marshall, and Douglas dissented from the refusal to apply the Court's interpretation of section 5 retroactively.

But the Court did instruct the district court to restrain the further enforcement of the 1966 statutes until they had been submitted for section 5 review. The statutes were then submitted to the attorney general, and in May 1969, Assistant Attorney General Jerris Leonard, acting on behalf of Attorney General John Mitchell, lodged a section 5 objection to all three Mississippi massive resistance statutes challenged in the *Allen* cases, citing their racially discriminatory purpose and effect.[70]

Of the three Mississippi cases, the one which resulted in the most far-reaching interpretation of section 5 was *Fairley v. Patterson*, which challenged the switch to at-large county supervisor elections. In the *Fairley* decision, the Supreme Court recognized that racial vote dilution could impinge on the right to vote, a ruling that political scientist Richard Engstrom has noted "was of fundamental importance to the future effectiveness of the new black voting strength."[71]

Each of the other Mississippi cases, as Justice Harlan pointed out in his dissent, more directly involved the right to vote.[72] The switch from elected to appointed county school superintendents denied voters the right to cast a ballot at all for the affected offices. The law increasing the qualifying requirements for independent candidates prohibited voters from voting in party primaries if they wanted to run as independent candidates. In the at-large election case, however, the right to cast a ballot was left unimpaired, although the change had a definite impact on the ability of black voters to elect candidates of their choice. The Supreme Court had recognized in the one-person, one-vote reapportionment cases that the right to vote can be denied "by a debasement or dilution of the weight of a citizen's vote" even though the right to cast a ballot was left intact.[73] In the *Allen* case the Court applied the concept of vote dilution, first recognized in the reapportionment cases, to allegations of racial discrimination affecting the right to cast an effective ballot. The Court held, in a famous passage that has been frequently quoted and relied on in vote-dilution cases since, "The right to vote can be affected by a dilution of voting power as well as by an absolute prohibition on casting a ballot. See *Reynolds v. Sims*, 377 U.S. 533, 555 (1964). Voters who are members of a racial minority might well be in the majority in one district, but in a decided minority in the county as a whole. This type of change could therefore nullify their ability to elect the candidate of their choice just as would prohibiting some of them from voting."[74]

The Supreme Court's 1969 decision in *Allen v. State Board of Elections* was a landmark decision, the *Brown v. Board of Education* of voting rights, critical to continuing black political progress throughout the South. For the first time, although in the context of interpreting the Voting Rights Act rather than applying constitutional principles, the Supreme Court recognized and applied the principle of minority vote dilution—that the black vote can be affected as much by dilution as by an absolute prohibition on casting a ballot. The Court's decision thus established the necessary precedent for challenges to the legality of the entire "second generation" of disfranchisement devices—switching to at-large elections, redistricting, manipulating candidate qualifications, abolishing elective offices, or any other change that alters the state's election laws "in even a minor way."

The decision also established a legal framework under section 5 of the Voting Rights Act that made it easier for minority voters to strike down discriminatory voting laws enacted by covered states in the post-1965 period. Minority voters no longer had to carry the time-consuming and expensive burden of proving that a challenged voting law was unconstitutional. Now, with the requirement of section 5 preclearance of all voting-law changes, the burden of proof lay with the governing bodies in the South that had discriminated in the past, and it was their burden to prove to federal authorities that covered voting-law changes had no racially discriminatory purpose or effect. As a result, the *Allen* decision was an important turning point in the struggle of minority voters for equal political participation, and the decision has had a decisive impact on all contemporary Voting Rights Act litigation.

In addition to its impact on voting rights jurisprudence, the *Allen* decision had critical impacts on national voting rights enforcement policy, which are summarized here and more fully discussed in chapter 6, and on the black political movement in the South. By interpreting the scope of section 5 protections broadly, the decision greatly increased the voting rights enforcement role of the Justice Department, which now had to preclear all voting-law changes in every covered state and locality and, to a lesser extent, the federal district court for the District of Columbia. Equally important, the decision opened the door to private enforcement of section 5 by minority voters themselves, who could now file lawsuits challenging implementation of voting-law changes that had not been submitted for federal preclearance. This portion of the *Allen* case established a private "secondary enforcement system" through private citizen suits that has substantially contributed to the Voting Rights Act's effectiveness.[75]

When the *Allen* case was decided in 1969, the extraordinary enforcement provisions of the Voting Rights Act—including section 5—were scheduled to expire the following year. By demonstrating that southern resistance to equal voting rights for blacks had not ended, the Supreme Court's decision—along with strong proof of voting rights violations in other southern states—all but guaranteed that Congress would extend these protections in 1970, despite the opposition of southern members of Congress and the Nixon administration.

The *Allen* decision also played an important symbolic role in legitimizing black aspirations for full participation in the political process. In the context of the times, this recognition was critical. Mississippi and other southern states had denied blacks the right to vote for almost 100 years with impunity. The Voting Rights Act had established the federally protected right of black citizens to register to vote, but for southern whites the question of whether this meant that blacks also had a federally protected right to hold elective office remained unresolved. When the Supreme Court declared that black voters had a federal right to be free of voting-law changes that would "nullify their ability to elect the candidate of their choice," this meant more than the abstract right to vote. This meant real political power. As the MFDP stated in its press release issued two days after the *Allen* decision: "By the Supreme Court's decision handed down on Monday, the State of Mississippi has been told, again, that it cannot deny black people the right to vote and *exercise political power*."[76]

To be sure, the Supreme Court's decision did not bring an end to legislative efforts to prevent the election of black candidates or to dilute black voting strength. As in the school desegregation area, defiance of Supreme Court decisions remained an element of the southern political strategy, and the Mississippi Legislature and local government bodies have continued to enact discriminatory election laws up to the present. But the Supreme Court's *Allen* decision made clear that these efforts could no longer be viewed as legitimate and immune from judicial scrutiny. This gave the moral high ground to the new black political movement in the South. This movement could now begin to use this moral high ground to mobilize support for black candidates for office, to help win future court decisions protecting black political empowerment, and to influence public opinion to undercut old racial stereotypes about blacks not being fit for public office.

These implications of the *Allen* decision and subsequent voting rights court cases, as well as the impact the *Allen* decision had on the black political movement in Mississippi, are explored in the following two chapters.

4 The Struggle against Discriminatory Legislative Redistricting

The Judicial Response to Discriminatory Legislative Reapportionment

If black voters in Mississippi were to achieve any political progress in post-1965 Mississippi, changing the all-white composition of the state legislature was critical. The state legislature was one of the most powerful, if not the most powerful, of all the institutions dedicated to the preservation of white supremacy and racial segregation in Mississippi. It was the state legislature that passed statute after statute to resist school desegregation, thereby delaying the beginning of compliance with the *Brown* decision for a decade, longer than any other southern state; that led the effort to crush the civil rights movement in Mississippi by establishing the State Sovereignty Commission and passing laws to suppress peaceful civil rights protest activities; and then, when the Voting Rights Act threatened the political status quo, responded by enacting political massive resistance legislation to nullify the new black vote. The 1960 census indicated that Mississippi was 42 percent black, yet the state legislature was all white. Racial progress in all areas depended on substantial changes in the political climate and in the composition of the state legislature.

The Mississippi legislative reapportionment litigation embodied the two elements of the national legislative reapportionment movement that gained momentum in the 1960s with the Supreme Court's one-person, one-vote rulings. As George Bundy Smith has described them, the first element is the one-person, one-vote struggle: the effort to achieve equality of representation by insuring that state legislative districts are substantially equal in population.[1] The one-person, one-vote movement of the 1960s sought to correct the overrepresentation of rural areas and the underrepresentation of both urban and suburban areas that was particularly severe in the South. Thus, it is "population-based" and majoritarian "with the aim of having a true majority of voters select their representation" and "emphasizing and protesting a wrong to the majority of Americans."[2] The second element of the reapportionment movement, as Smith describes it, is the effort to eliminate legislative districts and methods of election that deny minority voters representation. This "racially-based" thrust "emphasizes and protests a wrong to minorities."[3] As such, it "is a continuation of the traditional struggle of Black people for civil and political rights in America."[4]

In the South, the struggle for black political rights in legislative reapportionment after 1965 initially focused on multimember legislative districts as the primary impediment to black voters gaining representation of their choice in the state legislatures. In 1971 the Supreme Court indicated, "The question of the constitutional validity of multi-member districts has been pressed in this Court since the first of the modern reapportionment cases. These questions have focused not on population-based apportionment but on the quality of representation afforded by the multi-member district as compared with single-member districts."[5] In the wake of the first reapportionment cases, legal scholars and social scientists criticized multimember districts as both racially discriminatory and contrary to principles of good government. They objected to the winner-take-all aspect that overrepresented the winning faction and submerged racial and political minorities; to the long "bedsheet" ballots in such districts that listed numerous candidates for multiple seats, depriving voters of the opportunity to make intelligent choices and giving undue influence to slating organizations; and to the disadvantage multimember districts conferred on voters of single-member districts who had only one vote in legislative deliberations versus the superior bloc voting power of the numerically larger legislative delegations from multimember districts.[6]

In the 1960s the national trend was clearly in favor of single-member districts,[7] but in 1965 almost every southern state employed multimember districts in one or both houses of the state legislature. With the black voter registration gains of the 1960s, southern state legislatures—as the discussion of the Mississippi Legislature in chapter 2 shows—increasingly used multimember districts as a racial gerrymandering device to dilute black votes. Thus, the issue of the "quality of representation" afforded by such districts became more focused as growing numbers of legal challenges were filed based on submergence of black voting strength. During the 1970s, reapportionment lawsuits brought by black voters and Justice Department objections under section 5 of the Voting Rights Act eliminated racially discriminatory multimember districts in a majority of the southern states.[8] Once multimember districts were replaced with single-member districts, black representation in southern state legislatures increased dramatically.[9]

In this context, the Mississippi legislative reapportionment litigation was not only important for the political future of black Mississippians but also was on the forefront of the southwide struggle of black Americans against discriminatory legislative districting. As with the other elements of Mississippi's massive resistance campaign, the struggle against multimember districts was a test of whether the Supreme Court's commitment to the principle of "fair and equal representation" that it applied to the white majority in its one-person, one-vote decisions also applied to America's racial minorities. Ultimately, the issue turned on whether the South's historic practice of multimember districting would be struck down to create single-member districts that subdivided counties and broke county lines to give black voters representation in the legislative process. Like the Supreme Court's decision in *Allen v. State Board of Elections*, the Mississippi reapportionment litigation succeeded in establishing new legal principles that strengthened the protections for minority voting rights throughout the South and nationwide.

Writing in 1980, Supreme Court Justice Thurgood Marshall remarked that the Mississippi legislative reapportionment case "has a procedural history that can charitably be described as bizarre."[10] Initially filed as *Connor v. Johnson* in October 1965 by the MFDP and eight black party members, the case was possibly the longest-running legislative reapportionment litigation in the history of American jurisprudence. It was continuously litigated for fourteen years, including nine trips to the Supreme Court, before substantial relief was obtained in 1979. In that year, a single-member district plan enacted by the Mississippi Legislature under the pressure of this litigation resulted in the election of fifteen black House members and two black Senate members. Throughout the case, the black voter plaintiffs struggled with a recalcitrant state legislature and an unsympathetic three-judge federal district court consisting of Fifth Circuit Judge J. P. Coleman and District Judges Harold Cox and Dan M. Russell, Jr., described earlier. As Justice Marshall noted: "Both state officials and the three-judge District Court for the Southern District of Mississippi have shown a firm determination to avoid implementation of an apportionment plan which complies with constitutional and statutory requirements."[11]

In this litigation, the MFDP plaintiffs' allegations of one-person, one-vote violations initially gave the federal district court jurisdiction of their lawsuit, and the one-person, one-vote violations were the basis for district court decisions striking down statewide legislative reapportionment plans adopted by the Mississippi Legislature in 1966 and 1971 and for the Supreme Court decision invalidating a discriminatory plan adopted by the three-judge district court in 1976. Application of this one-person, one-vote rule was relatively easy. It involved merely looking at the population deviation percentages in the districts to determine whether the challenged plan met numerical guidelines established by the Supreme Court. For this reason the three-judge district court in Mississippi frequently struck down plans enacted by the state legislature for failure to provide substantial equality of population among the legislative districts.

The Supreme Court's one-person, one-vote rulings also gave the MFDP plaintiffs the opportunity to pursue their goal of the second element of the reapportionment struggle, the elimination of racially discriminatory districting that excluded black representation. By eliminating a racially discriminatory reapportionment that also violated the one-person, one-vote rule, the MFDP plaintiffs could then seek adoption, either by the legislature or by the district court, of nondiscriminatory districts that gave black voters better opportunities for representation of their choice. But, because of the recalcitrance of the state legislature and the three-judge district court in Mississippi, this goal of racially equitable reapportionment was much more difficult to achieve. It ultimately took fourteen years of litigation for black voters to gain more than token representation in the Mississippi legislature.

The effort to attain nondiscriminatory districting progressed in two phases. The first phase, which lasted from 1965 to 1976, involved challenges to discriminatory multimember districts from which two or more state representatives or senators were elected countywide or from multicounty districts. As described in chapter 2, these multimember districts diluted black voting strength by combining black majority counties with more populous white majority counties to create majority-white multimember districts, and by creating countywide districts in counties with white voting majorities that canceled out the voting strength of black population concentrations large enough for separate representation.

In the earliest reapportionment cases, the Supreme Court had stated that multimember legislative districts are not unconstitutional per se, although they might be unconstitutional if "designedly or otherwise" they "would operate to minimize or cancel out the voting strength of racial or political elements of the voting population."[12] But in the Mississippi case the district court generally ignored the MFDP's plaintiffs' claims of racial discrimination and gave greater weight to the perceived practical difficulties of subdividing counties and to what it characterized as Mississippi's "uniform state governmental policy and tradition" of creating state legislative districts out of whole counties and combinations of counties.[13] The district court in successive decisions followed this "whole county" policy on reapportionment, which had been an element of the state legislature's massive resistance strategy in 1966, until Supreme Court decisions and the attorney general's section 5 objections under the Voting Rights Act made it clear that this policy no longer could be squared either with the one-person, one-vote requirement or the nondiscrimination requirements of the Fourteenth Amendment and the Voting Rights Act.

The second phase of the Mississippi struggle for nondiscriminatory districts, which lasted from 1976 to 1979, involved challenges to racial gerrymandering of single-member district boundaries. During this period, the MFDP plaintiffs challenged legislative single-member district lines that fragmented black population concentrations within particular counties (cracking) and combined black population concentrations with greater white population concentrations (stacking). On this issue, the MFDP plaintiffs ultimately prevailed in the Supreme Court in 1977, and this Supreme Court victory led to the adoption of the statewide, single-member district plan that was used in the 1979 state legislative elections which resulted in the election of seventeen black state legislators.

Phase One: The Challenges to Multimember Legislative Districts

Legislative reapportionment plans enacted by the Mississippi Legislature in 1966 and 1971 that relied heavily on multimember districts were struck down by the three-judge district court for excessive malapportionment, and the legislature's 1975 plan was objected to by the attorney general under section 5 of the Voting Rights Act for racial discrimination. But the state legislative elections of 1967, 1971, and 1975 all were held under court-ordered plans adopted by the district court that were patterned on the legislature's plans. Under these court-ordered plans, a majority of both houses of the state legislature were elected from multimember districts that denied black voters effective representation in the legislature.

As the legislative debates described in chapter 2 reveal, a key element of the massive resistance strategy to prevent blacks from being elected to the state legislature was the creation of large multimember districts that combined majority-black counties with majority-white counties. Previously, each county had elected at least one representative. The state legislature's 1966 reapportionment plan did not survive the MFDP plaintiffs' one-person, one-vote challenge. But for the 1967 elections the district court ordered into effect its own plan that closely followed the legislature's plan and in fact increased the number of legislators elected from multimember districts.

As chapter 2 indicates, the three-judge district court in 1966 sustained the MFDP plaintiffs' claims that the existing legislative reapportionment was unconstitutionally malapportioned in violation of the one-person, one-vote rule.[14] The Mississippi Legislature responded in its 1966 special session by enacting a new plan that increased the number of multimember districts. The MFDP plaintiffs, represented by Alvin J. Bronstein of LCDC and Peter Marcuse of the ACLU, challenged the legislature's plan for unconstitutional malapportionment and racial discrimination. They contended that the plan discriminated against black voters by combining black majority counties with white majority counties in both the Delta area and in southwest Mississippi.

The district court, however, rebuffed plaintiffs' efforts to prove that the plan diluted black voting strength. At the trial, Charles Evers, the NAACP state field secretary who had conducted voter registration drives in six southwest Mississippi counties, attempted to show how the plan submerged black voting strength through testimony about black voting patterns in Jefferson and Claiborne counties, where his activities were concentrated. Both Judge Coleman and Judge Cox objected to his testimony, according to a press account of the trial: " 'You can't possibly testify about how a Negro or white voted unless you went into the voting booth with them and that is prohibited by state law,' Coleman said. Cox continued: 'You seem to be giving conclusions not evidence.' Marcuse said, 'There has been no objection raised.' 'I object to it,' Cox declared."[15] As in the congressional redistricting case, Mississippi Attorney General Joe T. Patterson responded to the plaintiffs' racial discrimination claims by charging that the MFDP wanted reverse gerrymandering. He argued that the thrust of the MFDP arguments was to "compel the Legislature of Mississippi to set up districts to prevent the election of a white candidate and guarantee the election of Negro candidates."[16]

Three months later, in March 1967, the three-judge district court struck down the legislature's 1966 plans for unconstitutional malapportionment, but totally ignored the MFDP plaintiffs' racial discrimination claims.[17] The district court adopted its own court-ordered plan for the 1967 elections that was modeled on the legislature's plan. Forty-four of the state's eighty-two counties were placed in the same districts and given the same representation as in the legislature's plan,[18] and many of the majority-black counties were combined with

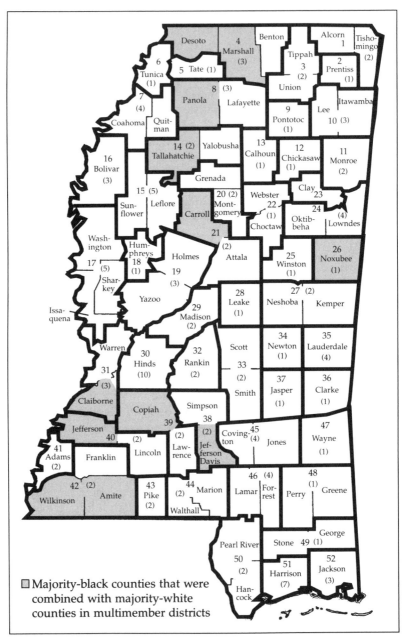

Map 4.1. Court-Ordered Redistricting Plan for the State House of Representatives Adopted by the District Court in 1967. The number of representatives elected appears in parentheses after the district number.

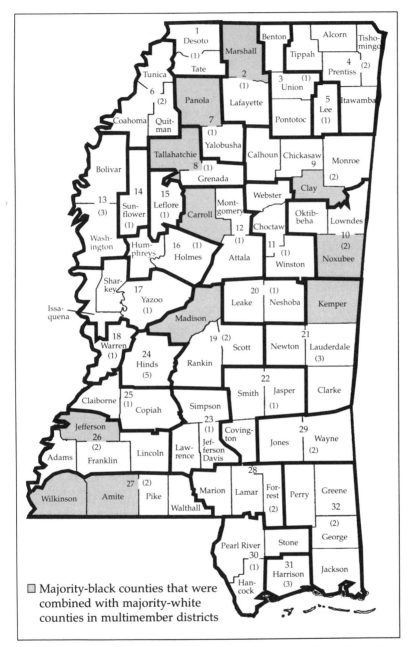

Map 4.2. Court-Ordered Redistricting Plan for the State Senate Adopted by the District Court in 1967. The number of senators elected appears in parentheses after the district number.

Table 4.1. Multimember Districts in Legislative Reapportionment Plans

	Mississippi House of Representatives		
Plan	Number of Districts	Number of Multimember Districts[a]	Number of Representatives from Multimember Districts
1966 legislative plan	72	26 (36%)	80 (66%)
1967 court-ordered plan	52	34 (65%)	104 (85%)
1971 legislative plan	45	35 (78%)	114 (93%)
1971 court-ordered plan	46	33 (72%)	109 (89%)
1975 legislative plan	46	33 (72%)	109 (89%)
1975 court-ordered plan	84	51 (61%)	89 (73%)

	Mississippi Senate		
Plan	Number of Districts	Number of Multimember Districts[a]	Number of Senators from Multimember Districts
1966 legislative plan	41	8 (20%)	19 (37%)
1967 court-ordered plan	36	10 (28%)	26 (50%)
1971 legislative plan	35	14 (40%)	34 (65%)
1971 court-ordered plan	33	14 (42%)	33 (62%)
1975 legislative plan	33	14 (42%)	33 (62%)
1975 court-ordered plan	39	15 (38%)	28 (54%)

Source: Parker and Phillips, *Voting in Mississippi*.

Note: The 1966 and 1971 legislative plans were declared unconstitutional for excessive malapportionment and were never used in state legislative elections. The 1975 legislative plan was objected to under section 5 of the Voting Rights Act. The 1967, 1971, and 1975 Mississippi legislative elections were conducted on the basis of the district court-ordered plans.

[a] Multimember districts include floterial districts, in which one or more legislators are elected from subdistricts and others are elected districtwide.

majority-white counties as in the legislature's plan (see maps 4.1 and 4.2 and table 4.1), although the court disclaimed that "any racial consideration whatsoever" had entered into its deliberations.[19] As in the legislature's plan, the court's legislative districts were based exclusively on whole counties. "Mississippi has no other useful population measuring stick," Judge Coleman declared,[20] despite the fact that the 1960 census published population statistics, not only for counties, but also for subcounty units such as county supervisors' districts and cities. The result was to greatly increase the number of multimember and floterial districts (multimember districts with subdistricts) so that in the court's 1967 plan 85 percent of the House membership was elected from multimember (and floterial) districts (up from 66 percent in the legislature's plan), and 50 percent of the Senate membership (up from 37 percent) (see table 4.1). When Bronstein filed a motion to modify the court's plan to realign four multimember House districts that combined majority-black and majority-white counties, the district court rejected his motion as "tenuous and without factual support."[21]

In 1971 the three-judge district court clashed with the Supreme Court over whether single-member districts could be created by subdividing Hinds County (Jackson), the state's most populous county. Following the publication of the 1970 census, the Mississippi Legislature enacted a new reapportionment plan that, once again, used whole counties and combinations of counties to create legislative districts. This plan, like the legislature's 1966 plan, was ruled unconstitutional for excessive population deviations, so a court-ordered plan had to be devised for the upcoming 1971 legislative elections.[22]

At the district court hearing on the legislature's plan, the attorneys for the MFDP plaintiffs, who were led by George Peach Taylor of the Lawyers' Committee for Civil Rights Under Law (the group that succeeded LCDC in representing the plaintiffs) objected to at-large, countywide election of the entire twelve-member House and five-member Senate delegation from Hinds County. At-large elections in Hinds County had an obvious discriminatory impact. Although Hinds County was 60 percent white countywide, the county contained 84,000 black citizens who were sufficiently concentrated geographically that if the county were subdivided into single-member districts each electing only one legislator, blacks would have majorities in at least four House districts and two Senate districts.

The Lawyers' Committee attorneys filed four plans with the district court, based on 1970 census enumeration districts, to subdivide Hinds County for both House and Senate elections. Alternatively, they asked the district court to appoint a special master, or court-appointed redistricting expert, to subdivide the county. In support of their objections, the plaintiffs' lawyers presented election returns showing evidence of racial bloc voting and minority vote dilution: in the 1967 legislative elections two black candidates had carried the majority-black precincts but had lost countywide.[23]

The district court responded, however, with a plan that made minimal changes from the legislature's formulation. The court plan corrected excessive population deviations but, like the legislature's plan,

Table 4.2. Multimember House Districts in 1967 Court-Ordered
Reapportionment Plan

District	Number of Representatives	Counties	Total Population	Nonwhite Population	Percent Nonwhite
40	2	Jefferson	10,142	7,653	75.46
		Lincoln	26,759	8,352	31.21
		Total	36,901	16,005	43.37
39	2	Copiah	27,051	14,059	52.00
		Lawrence	10,215	3,861	37.80
		Total	37,266	17,920	48.09
31	3	Claiborne	10,845	8,245	76.03
		Warren	42,206	19,759	46.82
		Total	53,051	28,004	52.79
42	2	Wilkinson	13,235	9,428	71.24
		Amite	15,573	8,443	54.22
		Franklin	9,286	3,800	40.92
		Total	38,094	21,671	56.89
38	2	Jeff Davis	13,540	7,414	54.76
		Simpson	20,454	7,200	35.20
		Total	33,994	14,614	43.05
27	2	Kemper	12,277	7,449	60.67
		Neshoba	20,927	5,901	28.20
		Total	33,204	13,350	40.21
21	2	Carroll	11,177	6,500	58.16
		Attala	21,335	9,546	44.74
		Total	32,512	16,046	49.35
14	2	Tallahatchie	24,081	15,501	64.37
		Yalobusha	12,502	5,540	44.31
		Total	36,583	21,041	57.52
8	3	Panola	28,791	16,226	56.36
		Lafayette	21,355	7,245	33.93
		Total	50,146	23,471	46.81
4	3	Marshall	24,503	17,239	70.35
		Desoto	23,891	14,643	61.29
		Benton	7,723	3,609	46.73
		Total	56,117	35,491	63.24

Source: Population Statistics from U.S. Bureau of the Census, *1960 Census of Population.*

continued to rely on multimember districts made up of whole coun-ties and combinations of counties.[24] Nevertheless, the court recog-nized that there was "some merit" to the plaintiffs' objections to at-large elections in Mississippi's three largest counties, Hinds and the Gulf Coast counties of Harrison and Jackson, electing twelve, seven, and five representatives, respectively. The court's opinion was based not on plaintiffs' racial dilution claims but on the potential for "confu-sion of issues and personalities" arising from long ballots listing large numbers of legislative positions to be filled and many candidates run-ning for those seats. The court determined that it would be "ideal" if counties electing four or more representatives could be divided into districts. But the court refused to subdivide those counties for the 1971 elections, calling it a "sheer impossibility" to obtain dependable population statistics and boundary locations, despite evidence to the contrary supplied by the plaintiffs' sample plans. The court promised to appoint a special master by January 1, 1972—after the 1971 legisla-tive elections—to explore the feasibility of subdividing those counties for the 1975 and 1979 legislative elections.[25]

The plaintiffs appealed to the Supreme Court and filed an applica-tion for a stay pending appeal, seeking interim relief before full briefs could be prepared and the case argued on its merits. Plaintiffs ob-jected to the district court's failure to subdivide Hinds County and argued that the 1970 census maps and population statistics currently available provided sufficient data to subdivide the county, as demon-strated by the plans they already had filed with the district court. For relief, they asked the Supreme Court to order the district court either to submit its plan for section 5 preclearance or to create single-mem-ber districts for Hinds County for the 1971 elections.

The Supreme Court denied the plaintiffs' request for section 5 pre-clearance of the court's plan, ruling, "A decree of the United States District Court is not within the reach of Section 5 of the Voting Rights Act."[26] But the Court agreed with the district court's view that sub-dividing Hinds County into single-member districts would be "ideal" and accepted the plaintiffs' argument that sufficient time and census data existed to accomplish the task. For the first time in any case, the Supreme Court adopted a rule requiring single-member districts in court-ordered plans: "We agree that when district courts are forced to fashion apportionment plans, single-member districts are preferable to large multi-member districts as a general matter."[27] The Supreme Court ordered the district court to extend the June 4 qualifying dead-line for legislative candidates and instructed the district court "absent insurmountable difficulties, to devise and put into effect a single-member district plan for Hinds County" by June 14.

The Supreme Court's decision in *Connor v. Johnson* was a break-through of momentous proportions in the struggle against multi-member districts. Throughout the 1960s a number of cases had been filed challenging multimember districts on constitutional grounds, but in a string of seven successive cases the Supreme Court consistently had rejected such challenges.[28] Four days after its decision in *Connor v. Johnson*, the Court, in the Indiana legislative reapportionment case, *Whitcomb v. Chavis*, recognized the numerous objections to multimember districts and their potential for discrimination but reversed a district court decision striking down multimember districts in Marion County (Indianapolis) for submerging black votes and held, "We have not yet sustained such an attack."[29] However, those cases were Fourteenth Amendment challenges to legislative redistricting plans enacted by state legislatures, while the *Connor* case involved a plan devised and ordered into effect by a district court. In the case of a court-ordered plan, the Supreme Court's jurisdiction to order a revision of the plan is based on its general power to supervise proceedings in lower courts. Thus, the Court does not have to decide the issue of whether there is a Fourteenth Amendment violation, the proof of which imposes a heavy burden on minority voter plaintiffs. Further, as Justice Harry Blackmun explained the distinction in a subsequent case, when the plan is a court-ordered plan, rather than a legislatively enacted plan, the Supreme Court is free of the usual constraints imposed by the requirement of deference to state policies.[30]

The *Connor v. Johnson* victory therefore owes much to the context in which the case reached the Supreme Court. The lawyers for the MFDP plaintiffs had made a strong case that multimember districts in Hinds County were racially discriminatory. Although the district court did not accept the plaintiffs' argument, its comment that single-member districts would be "ideal" to avoid voter confusion gave the Supreme Court—which was aware of the numerous objections to multimember districts—an opening to require single-member districts in court-ordered plans. In this context, the Supreme Court could order single-member districts without departing from its repeatedly expressed position that multimember districts are not per se unconstitutional or from the line of precedent rejecting Fourteenth Amendment challenges to such districts. This decision represents the first instance in which the Supreme Court ruled against multimember districts, although their discriminatory effect was not made an explicit basis for the Court's decision.

In Supreme Court jurisprudence, the *Connor v. Johnson* decision marks the beginning of the elimination of discriminatory multimember districts through judicial action. The decision had an immediate impact, as described later, in other southern reapportionment cases —particularly the Alabama, Louisiana, and Texas cases—in which the district courts replaced multimember districting with court-ordered single-member district plans. Two years later, in *White v. Regester*, the Texas legislative reapportionment case, the Supreme Court for the first time sustained a Fourteenth Amendment challenge to multi-member districts adopted by a state legislature for diluting black and Mexican-American voting strength. The *Connor* decision also had a broad national impact. The Supreme Court has applied the "*Connor* rule," as it became known, requiring single-member districts in court-ordered plans, as a nationwide rule of general application whether or not there are claims that multimember districts dilute minority voting strength.[31]

While the *Connor v. Johnson* decision led to the implementation of single-member districts outside Mississippi, it had no immediate impact in the state in which the case arose. In response to the Supreme Court's order, the recalcitrant district court stood its ground, asserted once again that there were no accurate or reliable population statistics to subdivide Hinds County into legislative districts using existing voting precincts or county supervisors' districts, and thus concluded that the task was prevented by "insurmountable difficulties."[32] (This was wrong. With the same census data that existed in 1971, the district court in 1975 approved a plan that subdivided Hinds County into single-member districts.) When the plaintiffs returned to the Supreme Court, the Court pushed no further and refused the plaintiffs' request for further relief.[33]

The district court's plan for the 1971 elections required 89 percent of the House members and 62 percent of the senators to run in multimember districts, many of which again submerged black voting strength in white countywide and districtwide majorities. Twenty-nine black candidates ran for the legislature in those elections, most of them from multimember districts, and all of them were defeated, except for Robert Clark. Clark, the lone black state legislator, was reelected from a reconstituted two-member House district consisting of two majority-black counties, Holmes and Humphreys, that was 67 percent black.

The Supreme Court's 1971 decision had only been an interim order and did not decide the merits of the MFPD plaintiffs' appeal. But when the plaintiffs' appeal on the merits was finally considered by the Supreme Court—after the 1971 legislative elections had taken place—the Supreme Court declined to consider the merits of the district court's 1971 plan because of its promise to appoint a special master to explore subdividing Hinds, Harrison, and Jackson counties. Repeating its admonition that in court-ordered plans, single-member districts are preferred, the Supreme Court merely vacated the district court's 1971 plan and remanded the case back to the district court for further proceedings.[34] However, on remand the district court failed to appoint a special master and failed to order any further proceedings to subdivide those counties.

Both the impact of the Supreme Court's *Connor v. Johnson* decision and the continued resistance of the Mississippi Legislature and the three-judge district court to the MFDP's pleas for nondiscriminatory legislative reapportionment are highlighted by a comparison with litigation against multimember districts in nearby southern states, particularly in Georgia, Alabama, and Texas. Beginning in Georgia in 1964 the continued use of at-large voting in legislative elections came under increasing challenge throughout the South. Between 1971 and 1975 discriminatory multimember legislative redistricting plans were struck down by section 5 objections and/or court decisions in Alabama, Georgia, Louisiana, South Carolina (state House of Representatives), and Texas, and the single-member districting plans that superseded them resulted in dramatic increases in the number of black legislators.[35] Events in Georgia, Alabama, and Texas illustrate this process.

In Georgia, in a lawsuit filed by black and Republican political leaders, a district court in 1964 struck down multimember districts for the election of state senators in two counties, not for racial discrimination, but because voters in single-member districts could elect their own senator, while voters in "subdistricts" within multimember districts had their senators elected by the voters countywide, despite the preferences of the voters of the subdistrict.[36] The Supreme Court reversed the district court's decision, holding that this rationale failed to state a constitutional violation but nevertheless stated that under some circumstances multimember districts might be subject to constitutional challenge where "designedly or otherwise" they "would operate to minimize or cancel out the voting strength of racial or political elements of the voting population."[37] Since no racial dilution claims had been presented, the Court's admonition was not binding precedent. But the Court's statement was sufficient to persuade the Georgia Legislature in 1965 to establish some single-member state House of Representatives districts in Fulton County (Atlanta) and other counties with black concentrations. As a result, eight black candidates won seats in the 1965 Georgia legislative elections.[38] By 1971 the number of black representatives had increased to thirteen.[39] In 1971 and 1972, following the 1970 census, the Georgia Legislature enacted new House reapportionment plans that employed multimember districts—including shifts from single-member districts to multi-member districts—that diluted black concentrations, and when they were submitted for section 5 preclearance the attorney general lodged two section 5 objections to successive plans. When the Georgia Legislature refused to take any further action, the Justice Department filed suit and obtained a district court injunction against further use of those plans. In the 1973 appeal of that case, the Supreme Court in *Georgia v. United States* followed the *Allen* decision, held that the legislative reapportionment plans were covered by section 5, and sustained the attorney general's objections.[40] These section 5 objections forced the Georgia Legislature to create single-member districts in counties with heavy black concentrations, and by 1976 Georgia had twenty black House members, more than any other state.[41]

In Alabama in 1965 a three-judge district court sustained a discrimination claim that was almost identical to the one rejected by the three-judge district court in Mississippi in 1967. Under court order to reapportion itself to comply with the Supreme Court's one-person, one-vote ruling, the Alabama Legislature in 1965—six weeks after the passage of the Voting Rights Act—adopted the same strategy subsequently followed by the Mississippi Legislature. In the redistricting plan for the state House of Representatives the legislature devised large, multicounty, multimember districts that combined heavily black counties in the Black Belt region of east-central Alabama with adjoining predominantly white counties to dilute black votes. The three-judge district court in the Alabama case was composed of Circuit Judge Richard T. Rives and District Judge Frank M. Johnson, Jr., who were notable during this period for their sensitivity to racial discrimination claims, along with District Judge Daniel H. Thomas. In contrast to the ruling of the Mississippi district court which rejected such a claim, the Alabama court held multimember districts that combined predominantly black counties with predominantly white counties unconstitutional for racial gerrymandering: "Historically, counties have been the voting unit, but suddenly we find without any apparent reason a number of counties that are entitled to their own representatives on a population basis aggregated, turning Negro majorities into minorities. It would be unfortunate if Alabama's Negroes were to find, just as they were about to achieve the right to vote, that that right had been abridged by racial gerrymandering."[42] While the district court's decision invalidated two large multimember districts that combined majority-black and majority-white counties, it did not invalidate other multimember districts that submerged black voting strength, particularly in Alabama's three largest cities, Birmingham, Montgomery, and Mobile.

In 1972, however, the district court eliminated all multimember districts and ordered into effect a plan that contained single-member districts statewide for both the state House of Representatives and the state Senate.[43] Following the 1970 census the Alabama Legislature failed to adopt a new reapportionment plan, and the district court ordered into effect a court-ordered plan devised by the plaintiffs in the lawsuit. The district court thought single-member districts statewide were required because plans proposed by state officials that used multimember districts were excessively malapportioned and because of the Supreme Court's decision in the Mississippi case, *Connor v. Johnson*, holding that single-member districts were preferable in court-ordered plans.[44] Thus, the Alabama district court was more responsive to the Supreme Court's decision in the *Connor* case than was the Mississippi district court. The district court's single-member district plan went into effect in the 1974 legislative elections, and as a result of the elimination of multimember districts, fifteen black candidates won seats in the legislature, two in the state Senate and thirteen in the state House of Representatives.[45]

In Texas, black and Mexican-American voters filed suit challenging at-large elections for the Texas House of Representatives in Dallas and Bexar (San Antonio) counties for unconstitutional dilution of minority voting strength. At the time, Texas was not covered by section 5 of the Voting Rights Act. In 1972 a three-judge district court, consisting of Circuit Judge Irving Goldberg and District Judges William Wayne Justice and John H. Wood, Jr., held that countywide voting in both Dallas and Bexar counties violated the Fourteenth Amendment rights of minority voters. The court cited a number of evidentiary factors that supported the plaintiffs' constitutional claim that countywide voting denied minority voters equal access to the political process, including the past history of racial discrimination against both blacks and Mexican-Americans in Texas; racially polarized voting that resulted in the defeat of minority candidates; electoral rules, such as a majority vote requirement, a "place" system that limited candidates to a specified "place" or post on the ballot, and the lack of any district residency requirement, which made it difficult for minority candidates to win office. The court found that few minority candidates had won legislative seats in the challenged districts; that minority candidates had been excluded from winning slates fielded by local slating organizations; that racial campaign tactics had been used to defeat minority candidates; and that minority registration and turnout was depressed by socioeconomic conditions and (for Mexican-Americans) language and cultural barriers. For relief, the district court, citing the Supreme Court's decision in *Connor v. Johnson*, adopted single-member districts for both Dallas and Bexar counties.[46] On appeal, the Supreme Court in 1973 affirmed the district court's decision invalidating at-large legislative elections in the two counties and ordering single-member districts.[47] In further proceedings the district court struck down multimember legislative districts in several additional counties, and the Texas Legislature responded by adopting single-member districts in the challenged counties.[48]

These developments left Mississippi, by 1975, alone among the Deep South states in retaining racially discriminatory multimember legislative districts in both houses of the state legislature. When attorneys for the plaintiffs in the Mississippi case pointed out these developments to the district court in a 1975 hearing, Circuit Judge J. P. Coleman responded, "What they have done in other states and so forth is really of no help."[49]

On the eve of the 1975 state legislative elections in Mississippi, the *Connor* litigation confronted a rather convoluted maneuver by the Mississippi Legislature. Up to this point, Mississippi officials had refused to submit any of the legislature's plans for section 5 approval as the *Allen* decision, described earlier, appeared to require. But the state officials were being boxed in by recent developments. In 1973, the Supreme Court in *Georgia v. United States* had specifically ruled that reapportionment plans passed by a state legislature were indeed subject to section 5 preclearance. In addition, the Justice Department in the Georgia case had lodged a section 5 objection to multimember districts that diluted black voting strength. Thus, it seemed unlikely that the reapportionment plan the Mississippi state legislature was devising for the 1975 elections could escape section 5 scrutiny. Neither, as the Supreme Court had made clear in its 1971 *Connor* decision, would multimember districts be permitted in court-ordered plans. With these safeguards in place, it appeared that the 1975 legislative elections would have to be carried out under a nondiscriminatory, single-member district plan.

But Mississippi state officials apparently hoped they could maintain the status quo by taking advantage of a possible loophole created by the Supreme Court's 1971 ruling that "a decree of the United States District Court is not within reach of Section 5." Thus, in 1975 the Mississippi Legislature adopted the tactic of enacting the district court's own 1971 court-ordered plan as a legislative plan and submitting it to the district court for approval in the hope of bypassing the section 5 preclearance process. The 1975 plan modified the 1971 plan only in Hinds, Harrison, and Jackson counties, where the legislature proposed that county supervisors' districts be used as legislative districts, with leftover seats that could not be apportioned among supervisors' districts elected countywide.

In challenging the legislature's 1975 plan, the attorneys for the MFDP plaintiffs adopted a broader strategy than they had employed in the past. In the prior stages of the litigation, they had sought adjustments in the court-ordered plans that realigned counties to eliminate combinations of majority-black and majority-white counties (1967) and to subdistrict only the most populous counties (1971). This time, for the first time in the litigation, the plaintiffs' attorneys presented the court with two complete alternative plans that subdivided the entire state into single-member districts for both House and Senate seats.

These statewide single-member district plans were drafted by Dr. David Valinsky, professor of statistics at Baruch College of the City University of New York, who had developed plans and testified as an expert witness in the successful Alabama reapportionment case, and Henry J. Kirksey, one of the original MFDP plaintiffs in this case and one of Mississippi's leading civil rights activists.[50] The Valinsky and Kirksey plans showed not only that it was possible to subdivide the entire state into single-member districts using 1970 census data, but also that multimember districts across the state submerged black majorities that showed up in single-member district plans. As shown on table 4.3, the Valinsky plan contained twenty-three House districts that were majority-black in voting-age population; the Kirksey plan included twenty-six such districts. In contrast, the legislature's plan contained only fourteen. The Valinsky and Kirksey plans contained seven Senate districts that were majority-black in voting-age population, as opposed to only five in the legislature's plan. In addition, the Justice Department, which intervened in the case after the Supreme Court's decision, developed a plan that contained twenty-nine districts with black voting-age population majorities in the House and eleven in the Senate.

Over plaintiffs' objections that the legislature's plan was malapportioned and diluted black voting strength across the state, the three-judge district court approved the legislature's 1975 plan.[51] Moreover, for the first time the judges discussed, but rejected, plaintiffs' racial dilution claims. The court ruled that it was the one-person, one-vote rule that deprived majority-black counties of their own representation because those counties lacked sufficient population to retain their own legislative seats, and that the historic use of whole counties and multiple-county districts was not motivated by a racial purpose.[52] No sooner was the plaintiffs' appeal docketed in the Supreme Court, when the Supreme Court, in a highly unusual order, requested the

Table 4.3. Number of Majority-Black Voting-Age Population Districts
in Court-Ordered and Alternative Reapportionment Plans

	House Districts	Senate Districts
1975 court plan	14	5
Valinsky plan	23	7
Kirksey plan	26	7
Justice Department plan	29	11

parties to file briefs on the issue of whether Mississippi's 1975 plan
was subject to the preclearance requirement of section 5 of the Voting
Rights Act. In their brief, the Mississippi officials argued the loophole: that the Mississippi Legislature's plan actually was a court-
adopted plan and thus "not within reach of Section 5."

Two weeks after the appeal was filed, the Supreme Court—acting
unanimously and without oral argument—in *Connor v. Waller* (as the
case was now called) summarily reversed the district court's approval
of the legislature's plan.[53] The Court ruled that the district court erred
in even considering the MFDP plaintiffs' constitutional objections to
the plan prior to section 5 review: "The District Court erred in holding that [the legislature's House and Senate plans] are not legislative
enactments required to be submitted pursuant to §5 of the Voting
Rights Act of 1965 [citation omitted]. Those Acts are not now and will
not be effective as laws until and unless cleared pursuant to §5. The
District Court accordingly also erred in deciding the constitutional
challenges to the Acts based upon claims of racial discrimination."[54]
The Court indicated, however, that its reversal was "without prejudice to the authority of the District Court, if it should become appropriate" to adopt a court-ordered plan for the 1975 elections, but the
Court clearly indicated that any court-ordered plan would have to
comply with the Court's prior decisions requiring single-member districts in court-ordered plans. The Supreme Court thus closed a poten-
tially dangerous loophole in section 5 coverage, a loophole that had
been created by its 1971 ruling that court-ordered plans are not covered by section 5.[55]

Compelled by the Supreme Court's 1975 decision, Mississippi submitted its reapportionment plan to the Justice Department for section
5 review. The Justice Department already had declared the plan racially discriminatory in its friend of the court brief filed in the Supreme Court in support of the Mississippi plaintiffs' appeal. In that

brief, the Justice Department had indicated that a racially discriminatory purpose could be inferred from the fact that "where black majority counties were combined with white majority counties, white majority districts were produced wherever possible" and from the continuation of at-large voting in countywide districts, as in Hinds County, where black population concentrations large enough to create majority-black single-member districts were submerged in countywide voting.[56] Responding quickly then, on June 10 U.S. assistant attorney general J. Stanley Pottinger telegrammed his section 5 objection to Mississippi attorney general A. F. Summer: "We are unable to conclude, as we must under the Voting Rights Act of 1965, that the implementation of H.B. 1290 and [S.B.] 2976 does not have the purpose and will not have the effect of denying or abridging the right to vote on account of race or color."[57]

The Justice Department's section 5 objection to the plan should have barred its use as a matter of law. Nonetheless, the district court in July 1975—ruling once again that there was not enough time available to devise a permanent plan for the August primaries and the November general election—ordered the legislature's plan into effect as a "temporary" plan "for the year 1975 only."[58] But the task which, according to the district court's 1971 ruling, had posed "unsurmountable difficulties" now became feasible. For the 1975 elections, the district court subdivided Hinds County into five single-member Senate districts and twelve single-member House districts, using existing voting precincts.[59] In addition, the court created single-member districts in two counties adjoining Hinds—Madison and Rankin—and in the Gulf Coast counties of Harrison and Jackson by using existing supervisors' districts from adjoining counties. The plaintiffs' attorneys filed objections to the court's plan, criticizing its failure to adopt single-member districts across the state. The court responded that this was merely a temporary plan and announced its "firm determination" to adopt a permanent court-ordered plan by February 1, 1976. Any dilution of black voting strength in the 1975 plan, the court ruled, could be corrected by ordering special elections prior to 1979.[60]

However limited the relief, the 1975 court-ordered plan was the first meaningful success in the effort to eliminate discriminatory multimember districts in Mississippi. The switch to single-member districts gave black voters in Hinds County their first opportunity to elect black legislators since the passage of the Voting Rights Act. In the 1975 elections, three additional black legislators joined Robert Clark in the state House of Representatives, all elected from majority black single-member districts in Jackson's central city area. As a result of subdividing Hinds County into single-member districts, Douglas

L. Anderson, a mathematics instructor at Jackson State University, was elected from a 91.4 percent black district; Rev. Horace L. Buckley, a minister and assistant principal in the Jackson public schools, was elected from an 83.8 percent black district; and Fred L. Banks, Jr., a Jackson civil rights attorney, was elected from a 70 percent black district.[61] But no blacks won seats in the state Senate because the Hinds County supervisors' districts, which were used as Senate districts in the court's plan, were racially gerrymandered to split up the black population concentration in Jackson.[62] After ten years of continuous litigation, black voters in Mississippi finally won a meaningful court victory in the Supreme Court. But, as in the case of the election-law changes involved in the *Allen* case, it was not a constitutional victory—the Supreme Court did not declare the legislature's 1975 plan unconstitutional for racial discrimination. But it was an important statutory victory; the enforcement mechanism of the Voting Rights Act had been upheld and the Justice Department lodged a section 5 objection to the plan.

For black voters in Mississippi, however, the Supreme Court's decision provided less than complete relief. The district court found excuses for not implementing a statewide single-member district plan for the 1975 elections, and as a result the legislative elections in most areas of the state once again were conducted in discriminatory multimember districts. The results of the 1975 legislative elections showed that the Mississippi Legislature's massive resistance strategy still worked ten years after passage of the Voting Rights Act, and black voters statewide were still being denied effective representation in the state legislature.

In spite of the district court's patent noncompliance with the Supreme Court's mandate requiring single-member districts, the plaintiffs did not appeal the district court's July 1975 decision to implement the legislature's plan as a temporary plan for the 1975 elections. Another appeal would have further delayed adoption of a statewide single-member district plan at the district court level and would have given the district court an excuse to renege on its announced "firm determination" to adopt a permanent court-ordered plan by February 1, 1976. But the plaintiffs and their attorneys failed to anticipate that the district court would find its own reasons for further delay. As the court's deadline approached in January 1976, the district court postponed all further proceedings in the case for the stated reason that there were three voting rights cases from Louisiana and New York awaiting decision in the Supreme Court that might provide guidance in the Mississippi case. Their patience with the district court's failure to comply with legal requirements and its own promises long since exhausted, the MFDP plaintiffs filed an extraordinary petition for a writ of mandamus in the Supreme Court.

Despite the almost total lack of precedent for a Supreme Court mandamus order against a district court, the High Court, with only Justice Rehnquist dissenting, ruled that there was no justification for delaying a final decision on this "long-pending case" and directed the district court to "bring this case to trial forthwith" and enter a final judgment. "Ten years of litigation," the Supreme Court said, "have not yet resulted in a constitutionally apportioned Mississippi Legislature."[63]

Three months later—for the first time in this extended litigation—the district court adopted a statewide plan for the House and Senate under which all 174 state legislators were to be elected from single-member districts.[64] The plan, like single-member district reapportionment plans in other states, involved extensive subdividing of counties and combining portions of one county with another county. As we have seen, it was an important break with tradition in Mississippi. "For 159 years," Circuit Judge J. P. Coleman remarked in his opinion, "no legislative district has been formed by combining fractions of counties (fracturing county boundaries)."[65]

Phase Two: The Challenge to Racial Gerrymandering of Single-Member Districts

The *Connor* litigation now entered a second phase, typical of other challenges to racially discriminatory at-large elections. The first phase, sometimes referred to as the liability phase, was the challenge to at-large voting, that is, the attack on multimember districts, which covered the period 1965 to 1976. The second phase, which might be referred to as the remedy phase, involved disputes over district lines. Having won adoption of single-member districts, the plaintiffs were now required to enter a new round of litigation to contest racial gerrymandering in the new districts. This phase in the *Connor* case lasted from 1976 to 1979.

Once again, in November 1976, the *Connor* case went to the Supreme Court as a Fourteenth Amendment challenge to a district court-ordered plan. Both the MFDP plaintiffs and the Justice Department, which had intervened in the case following the 1975 Supreme Court decision, filed extensive objections to the court-ordered plan. They objected to both excessive malapportionment of population among districts and racial gerrymandering of black population concentrations. Once again, the Supreme Court acted quickly and set an expedited briefing schedule and expedited oral argument.

In May 1977, the Supreme Court, in what was now called *Connor v. Finch*, in a 7-1 decision written by Justice Potter Stewart, with only Justice Lewis Powell dissenting, reversed the district court's decision and in a critically important ruling with broad implications established new legal principles governing legislative reapportionment plans.[66] First, the Supreme Court struck down the court-ordered plan for excessive population deviations in voting districts for both the Mississippi Senate and House. Applying the rule that court-ordered plans must achieve population equality among districts with no more than "de minimis" deviations, the Court established a new one-person, one-vote standard by ruling that the total deviations from the ideal sized district of 16.5 percent in the Senate plan and 19.3 percent in the House plan failed to meet Fourteenth Amendment requirements and that these deviations were not justified by the state policy of maintaining the integrity of county lines.[67]

Second, although the Court noted that the plan's excessive malapportionment was sufficient to invalidate it, the Court took the unusual step of providing "further guidance" to the district court on plaintiffs' racial gerrymandering claims.[68] The Court discussed two examples of what it termed "unexplained departures from the neutral guidelines the district court adopted . . . which have the apparent effect of scattering Negro voting concentrations among a number of white majority districts." In the first example, the Court disapproved what is known in the redistricting jargon as cracking: fragmentation and dispersal of black concentrations large enough for separate representation.[69] The Court condemned the district court's use as Senate districts of Hinds County's five "oddly shaped" supervisors' districts "that extend from the far corners of the county in long corridors that fragment the city of Jackson, where much of the Negro population is concentrated."[70]

In the second example, the Court disapproved what is known as stacking: combining black concentrations with greater white concentrations into districts that submerge the black vote.[71] The Court cited two Senate districts in southwest Mississippi: one that combined heavily black Claiborne County with majority-white Lincoln County and Supervisors' District 3 of Copiah County to make a majority-white district, and another that combined heavily black Jefferson County with four supervisors' districts in majority-white Adams County to create an irregularly shaped district with only a slight black voting-age population majority. Although the Supreme Court did not directly charge the district court with purposeful discrimination, it did say, with regard to both sets of examples, that such "unexplained departures from . . . the district court's own neutral guidelines can lead . . . to a charge that the departures are explicable only in terms of a purpose to minimize the voting strength of a minority group."[72]

Thus, for the first time in a case challenging discriminatory line drawing, as opposed to challenges to at-large elections, the Supreme Court gave content to its general prohibition against racial gerrymandering in legislative reapportionment. Although the Supreme Court specifically disclaimed reliance on the Fourteenth Amendment in addressing plaintiffs' racial dilution claims and stated that it was only addressing "the District Court's appropriate exercise of its discretion in remedying the Mississippi Legislature's failure to enact a valid apportionment,"[73] the Court's decision strongly suggested the types of racially discriminatory districting the Court could invalidate on constitutional or statutory grounds in future cases.

The series of Supreme Court decisions from 1971 to 1977 requiring single-member districts and condemning discriminatory districting, coupled with the Justice Department's section 5 objection to discriminatory multimember districts, had a cumulative effect on the state legislature's perception of its ability to maintain its multimember district strategy. During its next session, in April 1978, the Mississippi Legislature enacted another legislative reapportionment plan. Seeing few alternatives, the legislature abandoned its historic practice of multimember districting and adopted a plan containing single-member districts statewide for both the House and the Senate. The Justice Department objected under section 5 to some of the districts, but the United States District Court for the District of Columbia cleared the plan.[74] The D.C. district court found that there were only minimal differences between the legislature's plan and a new district court plan adopted in 1979 that parties to the litigation had already agreed upon.

But before the legislature's plan was precleared by the D.C. district court, the three-judge district court in Mississippi ordered special elections in January 1979 to fill vacancies in several legislative districts. The court ordered that the vacancies should be filled from single-member districts, and two additional black legislators were elected. Arthur Tate, from Madison County, became Mississippi's first black state senator since Reconstruction, but only for one year (he lost in the November election). Edward Blackmon, also from Madison County, joined the four other black representatives in the House.

In the regularly scheduled 1979 legislative elections, which were carried out under the legislature's new single-member district plan, seventeen blacks were elected to the Mississippi Legislature: fifteen to the House and two to the Senate. As Jackson State University historian E. C. Foster has noted, the 1979 reapportionment was "seen as a victory by blacks. It culminated many years of dedicated struggle by many individuals; it was a 'victory' won at the expense of much hard work, especially work by the Lawyers' Committee and black activist Henry Kirksey."[75] Henry J. Kirksey won a seat in the state Senate from a majority-black district in Jackson. Senator Kirksey—who had been an original plaintiff in the case since 1965 and a driving force as a legal strategist, plan drafter, and expert witness since 1971—was elected with the campaign slogan He Made It Happen.

The Litigation Victory over Massive Resistance

By 1979 the victory over the Mississippi Legislature's 1966 massive resistance program was all but complete; the racial gerrymandering of congressional district lines was not corrected until 1982. As of July 1980 the Joint Center for Political Studies reported in its *National Roster of Black Elected Officials* that there were 387 black elected officials in Mississippi, including the 17 black legislators elected in 1979, 27 black county supervisors and 38 county school board members elected from supervisors' districts, and 7 black county school superintendents. Black elected officials still constituted less than 10 percent of the total number of elected officials in the state; but the wall of massive resistance had been breached, and the gains achieved in the 1970s formed a solid basis for further progress in the 1980s.

As noted in chapter 1, Mississippi became the testing ground for whether the goals of the 1965 Voting Rights Act could ever be fulfilled, and the Voting Rights Act played a critical role in overcoming Mississippi's political massive resistance strategy. The Supreme Court in the early 1960s was unwilling to establish firm constitutional guidelines against minority vote dilution, as the defeat in the congressional redistricting phase of *Connor v. Johnson* indicates. Nevertheless, the Supreme Court, in its 1969 decision in *Allen v. State Board of Elections,* was willing to adopt an expansive interpretation of section 5 of the Voting Rights Act that required federal preclearance of all voting-law changes in covered states, and this decision was critical to striking down newly erected barriers to black political progress. The Supreme Court's application of the *Allen* decision to the Mississippi Legislature's reapportionment plan in *Connor v. Waller* in 1975, plus its 1971 decision in *Connor v. Johnson* requiring single-member districts in court-ordered reapportionment plans, had the effect of ending the state legislature's reliance on multimember districting as a means of diluting black voting strength in state legislative elections.

Requiring section 5 preclearance of Mississippi's massive resistance legislation shifted the responsibility to the Justice Department for making the ultimate determination whether a voting-law change was discriminatory. Thus, the Justice Department's 1969 section 5 objection to Mississippi's new laws changing methods of election and election rules and its 1975 objection to the legislature's multimember district reapportionment plan also were critical to blocking the legislature's efforts to negate the black vote.

But the success in overcoming Mississippi's political massive resistance was not solely the result of the operation of such outside forces as the Voting Rights Act, Supreme Court decisions, and Justice Department section 5 enforcement. As this account demonstrates, the structural barriers enacted by the state legislature in 1966 had a "real-life" impact on the opportunities of black voters in Mississippi to elect representatives of their choice. None of the lawsuits that were filed that ultimately resulted in the elimination of these barriers were Justice Department lawsuits, although the Justice Department substantially contributed to the successes by filing friend of the court briefs and intervened in the private litigation at critical times. To the extent that the litigation struggle over political massive resistance was successful, that success was due to the diligence and perseverance of black Mississippians, the black candidates and black voters, who filed these lawsuits to vindicate their rights, and to the civil rights legal organizations located in Mississippi whose attorneys ultimately persuaded the Supreme Court and the Justice Department to make favorable rulings. The black Mississippians' litigation struggle over massive resistance established a number of important legal precedents that had an impact on national voting rights policy and on court cases elsewhere in the country and in the South. The impact of these important decisions is explored in chapter 6.

Although the massive resistance strategy was ultimately unsuccessful, the litigation required to overcome it took years to complete, and this delay had attendant costs. The legislature's resistance to fair and nondiscriminatory legislative districts alone cost the taxpayers of the state well over a million dollars. In addition to the expenses of litigating the legislative reapportionment case for fourteen years, the state was required to spend $1.2 million in 1977–78 just to develop a single-member district plan that finally met the requirements of Supreme Court rulings and section 5 of the Voting Rights Act. In addition, the district court ordered the state to pay $127,687 to the Lawyers' Committee attorneys to compensate them for their time and expenses in litigating the case.[76] Beyond the financial cost, this delay meant that black voters were denied representation of their choice in government until their litigation was successful: black voters in

Mississippi were denied black representation in Congress until 1986, were denied all but token representation in the state legislature until 1979, and were denied effective representation in policymaking positions in county government through the early 1970s.

This was one of the costs and limitations of reliance on the judicial process to achieve political and social change. Although the judicial process ultimately vindicated black voters' rights to fair representation in Mississippi's political process, the changes that occurred were incremental, with long delays between court decisions and appeals and in obtaining court-ordered relief. Further, the court decisions were always prospective, never in these Mississippi cases invalidating elections that had been held under racially discriminatory structures or rules. This in effect defeated one of the purposes of the Voting Rights Act by giving the benefit of nonaction and inertia to those seeking to exclude blacks from meaningful political participation.

Throughout these periods of litigation and delay, political power remained in the hands of hostile whites, who generally were free to disregard black interests. At the state government level particularly, this meant that numerous lawsuits had to be filed to strike down racially discriminatory state legislation aimed at impeding black registration, diluting black voting strength, providing state funding for racially segregated private schools, and the like. Altogether, approximately twenty discriminatory state laws enacted from 1966 to 1979 were struck down by the federal courts as unconstitutional or voided by Justice Department section 5 objections.[77] In addition, civil rights litigation was required to remedy pervasive racial discrimination in state employment and to eliminate brutally unconstitutional conditions of confinement at the state penitentiary.[78] Black people, denied opportunities to improve the quality of their lives in Mississippi, continued to leave the state at an alarming rate in search of better jobs, better housing, and better educational opportunities.

Has the victory over Mississippi's massive resistance to black political participation made any difference? This is the question that will be addressed in chapter 5.

5 The Impact of the Struggle for Black Political Participation on Mississippi Politics

On March 26, 1987, Speaker C. B. "Buddie" Newman of the Mississippi House of Representatives announced that he was stepping down as Speaker, a position he had held since 1976. "I just think it's best for Mississippi if I get out of the way," Newman commented.[1]

Newman's retirement marks the end of an era in Mississippi politics. A sixty-six-year-old Delta planter from rural Issaquena County, the smallest county in the state (population 2,513), and a member of the House since 1952, Newman was one of the most powerful forces, if not the most powerful force, in state government. For more than a decade, the Speaker ruled the House with an iron grip. Through his power to appoint committee chairs, make committee assignments, and control the House calendar, Newman single-handedly determined the fate of bills by manipulating their assignment to particular committees, determining their position on the House calendar, and timing floor actions. Once an avowed segregationist who cheered on Governor Ross Barnett's 1962 effort to keep James Meredith out of the University of Mississippi, in more recent times Newman frequently blocked efforts at progressive change in Mississippi. In 1982, for example, Newman abruptly adjourned the House, over the protests of lawmakers, to kill for that legislative session a bill—supported by Governor William Winter and a majority of the House members—that would have established public kindergartens.[2]

Newman's tenure as Speaker was the last prominent vestige of the white Delta planter elite's control of state politics. From the turn of the century until the legislative reapportionment of the 1970s, conservative white politicians from the Delta exercised a disproportionate influence in state affairs. Since 1944, except for a brief ten-year interregnum from 1966 to 1976, two powerful Speakers from the Delta, Walter Sillers and Newman, dominated the House. As veteran political observer Bill Minor noted of Newman's resignation, "Historically, it is more than the Newman era that is coming to an end. It could be said that it will be the end of the Delta Dynasty in the House."[3]

The end of Newman's reign symbolizes the changes in Mississippi politics brought about by the struggle for black political participation in the state. His departure was the result of a successful revolt against the House leadership spearheaded by a "New South generation" of young white legislators together with the members of the House Black Caucus who succeeded in enacting a change in the House rules at the beginning of the 1987 session that diminished the Speaker's power. The members of both groups were elected mostly from single-member House districts in 1979 or later, and neither of these two political forces would have existed in the Mississippi House but for the reapportionment victories of the late 1970s. Thus, the struggle of blacks for political participation has substantially affected the alignment of power in the state legislature. First, as with other types of elective office in the state, blacks now hold a significant number of seats in the formerly all-white state legislature. Second, the same electoral reform, the adoption of single-member districts that made it possible for blacks to win those seats, loosened the iron grip of the old political establishment and enabled significant numbers of younger, better-educated, and relatively moderate whites to win seats in the legislature as well.

This chapter will assess the impact of the black struggle for political participation upon Mississippi politics. The first section will discuss the political impact of state legislative reapportionment. The next section will describe the increasing influence of black voters in party politics and how black voters' demands for inclusion in the state Democratic party produced a merged state party organization. The chapter will then show how the continuing struggle against racially discriminatory electoral structures, such as racial gerrymandering and at-large elections, produced continued increases in black elected officials at the county and local levels through the 1970s and well into the 1980s. Finally, the chapter will address the impact of increases in black representation in government at the local level.

Earl and Merle Black, two widely regarded southern political scientists, in their book *Politics and Society in the South* contend that while giving southern blacks the vote was important, nevertheless blacks overall remain "tangential" to southern politics because there are so few jurisdictions where blacks comprise a majority of the voters.[4] The question is an important one: Do Mississippi's black voters remain tangential, or do they wield real political power now?

The Political Impact of the Legislative
Reapportionment Litigation

During the 1970s, several students of legislative reapportionment concluded that although reapportionment was a significant advance in providing more population-based equality among districts, nevertheless it had not resulted in any significant changes in state policies.[5] The negative conclusions of scholars in the 1970s may have been premature. In Mississippi, as indicated in chapter 4, some of the most important changes accomplished by the reapportionment litigation, including the switch to single-member districts statewide, did not occur until the end of the 1970s. Moreover, in general the policy changes resulting from legislative reapportionment probably take a substantial period of time to be realized because the new legislators elected as a result of redistricting need time to learn the rules and to work themselves into positions of influence. In addition, the policy changes are generally incremental, and most southern states lack the economic resources to implement major, expensive changes.

In Mississippi, a decade after the successful conclusion of the 1970s reapportionment litigation and the conversion to single-member districts, there are indications that legislative reapportionment has influenced state politics and state policy in a progressive direction. First, the elimination of multimember legislative districts and the adoption of single-member districts statewide significantly increased black membership in the Mississippi Legislature, especially in the House of Representatives. This change in the racial composition of the legislature has had a decisive impact on some legislative bills and votes of particular concern to the black community. Second, the 1979 conversion to single-member districts increased turnover in the legislature as a whole, but particularly in the House. This turnover in turn has increased the numbers of what has been termed a New South generation of white legislators, who are increasingly willing to challenge the Old Guard. This political realignment has produced a leadership change in the House, as indicated by Speaker Newman's retirement, and opens up new possibilities for progressive legislation. Third, although some analysts predicted that population-based reapportionment, by taking seats from the rural districts and giving more seats to the urban and suburban areas, would increase Republican strength in state legislatures, this has not occurred in Mississippi. Despite the radical change in the method of electing state legislators, the Mississippi Legislature remains essentially a one-party, Democratic state legislature.

The most obvious change in Mississippi resulting from legislative

Figure 5.1. Black Legislators in Mississippi, 1968–1988

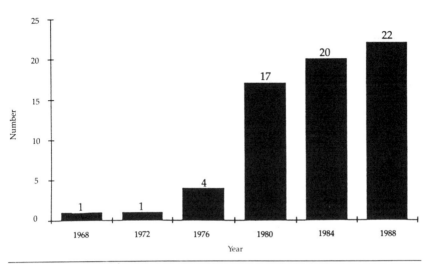

Source: Joint Center for Political Studies, *Black Elected Officials*, 1970, 1972, 1976, 1980, 1984, 1988.

reapportionment has been the significant increase in black membership in the Mississippi Legislature, as shown in figure 5.1. As Black
and Black have observed, state legislative positions "are among the
most important elective positions won by blacks"[6] because of the key
role of state legislatures in statewide policymaking, distribution of
state tax dollars, and allocation of state-provided services. Further,
the increase in black legislators has enormous symbolic importance
for state politics. The formerly all-white state legislature that was in
the forefront of massive resistance to black gains in education and
politics now has twenty blacks in the state House of Representatives
and two blacks in the state Senate. The integration of the Mississippi
state legislature—one of the last bastions of virulent racism in the
South—is one of the great triumphs of the Voting Rights Act and the
black political movement in Mississippi.

Yet, the number of black representatives remains relatively small.
With only 20 votes in the 122-member House and only 2 votes in the
52-member Senate, have black legislators had any impact on legislation and state policy? Black and Black concluded (based on 1982 data)
that because blacks remained severely underrepresented and com-
prised such small percentages of the total membership in state legislatures in the South, they had little influence on state policy.[7] But

more recent evidence from Mississippi indicates a contrary conclusion. A complete answer to this question would require an analysis of votes on critical bills in each session of the legislature since 1979, a study which is beyond the scope of this book. However, at the perceptual level, there is a consensus among both House Black Caucus members and veteran white legislators that when the black members of the House are in agreement on an issue and vote as a bloc, they can determine the fate of major legislation. Representative Tyrone Ellis of Starkville, a black representative, reported in a 1986 interview (when there were only 18 black representatives): "When it gets down to a revenue bill that needs a three-fifths vote for passage, 18 votes are very pivotal." A white legislator, Representative Fred Dobbins of Leakesville, agreed: "When it gets down to suspension bills that take a two-thirds vote or revenue bills, their bloc vote definitely is a determining factor then."[8] In addition, black House members have sufficient numbers to invoke certain procedures that do not require a majority vote, such as removing a bill from the noncontroversial House calendar (on which floor debate and amendments are limited) and requiring full floor debate on bills. Black members also have had influential committee appointments. Since 1980 black House members also have served as chairpersons of a number of House committees: Education (Robert G. Clark), Ethics (Fred L. Banks, Jr., Clark), Judiciary A (Percy W. Watson), Judiciary B (Banks), Universities and Colleges (Charles B. Sheppard), Municipalities (Charles L. Young), and Library (Hillman T. Frazier). Black members also have served on critical House committees, such as Ways and Means, Rules, and Appropriations.

Both black legislators and interested observers believe that the black membership of the Mississippi Legislature has made the legislature more responsive to black needs in the enactment of legislation for educational reform, the establishment of state-financed kindergartens for the first time in the history of the state, improvements in the state education financing system, the enactment of salary increases for public schoolteachers, improvements in the provision of health care under Medicaid, and the blocking of an increase in the state sales tax.[9] Both black and white legislators credit the black members of the House with an important role—they form coalitions with white allies to pass major legislation that serves black interests and to defeat some measures opposed by black legislators, and, on occasion, they employ the tactics traditionally used by strong minority legislative factions, such as filibustering. Members of the Black Caucus are particularly pleased with their role in the enactment in 1982 of a new state Education Reform Act aimed at improving education in the public schools through better teacher certification procedures, performance-based school accreditation, the adoption for the first time of publicly funded kindergarten programs in every district, statewide competency testing, and other reforms. As black representative Barney Schoby has commented: "Do you think we would have passed the Education Reform Act if it hadn't been for the Black Caucus?"[10] Although they did not lead the effort, black House members also provided the critical margin of victory in the successful 1987 effort to change the operating rules of the House of Representatives that resulted in Speaker Newman's decision to retire.

In 1986 the Black Caucus provided the crucial votes that killed a bill reducing the size of the state legislature. The bill was defeated on a 59-62 House vote with all 18 Black Caucus members voting against it. Black House members regarded the bill as an effort to reduce black representation in the legislature. Further, in 1988 Black Caucus members joined conservative factions of the legislature in defeating a bill calling for a state constitutional convention to rewrite Mississippi's 1890 constitution. The call for a constitutional convention had been a centerpiece of the legislative programs of Governor Bill Allain and his successor, Governor Ray Mabus, who contended that a new constitution was needed to eliminate inefficiency in state government. Black lawmakers were concerned, however, that the constitutional convention, whose delegates would be selected from House districts, might be dominated by white delegates insensitive to black concerns and would have the power to undo some of the progressive changes accomplished by civil rights litigation since the 1960s. As black representative Percy Watson put it: "A new constitution—that's an unknown. We know what we've got with this constitution. It's been cleaned up by the federal courts." The unlikely coalition that defeated the constitutional convention bill included, in addition to most of the House Black Caucus, legislators who represented antiunion positions—who were concerned that the present constitution's right-to-work section would be repealed—and conservative white Delta lawmakers. The bill was defeated in the House by a 74-48 vote after a House-Senate negotiating team had recommended a compromise bill to resolve conflicts between separate bills passed by both houses and after it had passed the Senate.[11]

The House Black Caucus had shown its power in other ways as well. In 1986, outraged by the defeat in committee of a Martin Luther King state holiday bill, black legislators maintained a week-long filibuster during the deadline week for legislation by invoking a seldom-used rule that required the clerk to read all bills on the floor of the House before every vote. This tactic resulted in the death by inaction of almost 120 House bills.[12]

Certainly the power of black legislators is limited in that they lack the votes to pass anything on their own and have difficulty forming coalitions with white legislators on measures identified as black issues. Many bills identified with black House sponsors have failed to pass, and divisions within the Black Caucus have prevented a unified vote on some issues. Black Caucus members initially were split on whether to oppose Speaker Newman on the rules change, and five black House members were in favor of the constitutional convention bill. In addition, black legislators were unable to persuade Speaker Newman to replace Representative Fred L. Banks, Jr., with another black member on the House Ways and Means Committee in 1985 when Banks resigned to take a state court judgeship, and they could do nothing to counter several other adverse committee assignments made by Newman when he was Speaker.

However, when white legislators take the lead on progressive legislation, such as the 1982 Education Reform Act, or other progressive measures, such as the 1987 House rules change that ultimately toppled Newman, the black legislators can provide the necessary votes to win. In addition, black legislators have the power to prevent the passage of measures that would adversely affect black interests. Because of its limited size, the first generation of black legislators can be successful in achieving its legislative goals only to the extent to which it can maintain unity and cohesion within its ranks and form coalitions with white legislators toward the accomplishment of common goals.

The switch to single-member districts produced by the *Connor* case increased the number of black legislators by increasing the number of heavily black districts, and this has important policy implications for future reapportionment efforts and for remedies in redistricting litigation. Racial voting patterns in Mississippi indicate strong preferences among black voters for black representatives, and those preferences are defeated when blacks constitute a voting minority and their favored candidates are constantly defeated by racially polarized voting by white voters for white candidates.[13] This has two important consequences: because of continued white bloc voting, black candidates in Mississippi generally cannot get elected in white majority districts, and in order for black voters to gain representatives of their choice, black majority districts must be established.

In the 1979 legislative elections and subsequently, black candidates in Mississippi have had to rely for the most part on black voters to get elected. As tables 5.1 and 5.2 show, all seventeen legislative districts in which black candidates won in 1979 were majority-black in both population and voting-age population. Sixteen of the seventeen districts were 60 percent black or more in voting-age population, with a

Table 5.1. Characteristics of Districts Electing Black Legislators in Mississippi in 1979

Characteristic	Number of Legislators	Percent of All Black Legislators ($n = 17$)
Type of district		
Urban (cities of 10,000 or more)	13	76.5
Rural	4	23.5
Region		
Jackson	6	35.3
Delta	4	23.5
Southwest	3	17.6
Piney Woods	1	5.9
Gulf Coast	1	5.9
Northeast	1	5.9
East Central	1	5.9
Percent black population		
51–60	1	5.9
61–70	5	29.4
71–80	6	35.3
81–90	4	23.5
91–100	1	5.9
Median = 73.0		
Average = 75.4		
Percent black voting-age population		
51–60	2	11.8
61–70	8	47.1
71–80	3	17.6
81–90	3	17.6
91–100	1	5.9
Median = 69.4		
Average = 71.9		

Sources: Mississippi Secretary of State, *Mississippi Official and Statistical Register*, 1980–84; data in table 5.2; population statistics from U.S. Bureau of the Census, *1980 Census of Population*.

median of 73.0 percent black in population and 69.4 percent black in voting-age population, and an average of 75.4 percent black in population and 71.9 percent black in voting-age population. The racial composition of each district that elected a black legislator in 1979 is shown on table 5.2.

Table 5.2. Black Legislators Elected in Mississippi in 1979
and Their Districts

Legislator	Percent Black Population in District	Percent Black Voting-Age Population in District
Rep. Horace L. Buckley	94.46	92.41
Rep. Credell Calhoun	88.66	85.53
Rep. Fred L. Banks, Jr.	87.92	84.83
Rep. Hillman Frazier	86.09	82.09
Sen. Douglas Anderson	81.99	77.35
Rep. Leslie King	80.25	75.89
Rep. Charles Sheppard	78.61	76.76
Rep. Aaron E. Henry	73.82	69.83
Rep. Percy Watson	72.99	68.19
Sen. Henry J. Kirksey	71.85	69.44
Rep. Charles Young	71.06	67.18
Rep. Robert G. Clark	69.93	65.91
Rep. Clayton Henderson	69.80	66.41
Rep. Barney J. Schoby	67.85	61.97
Rep. Tyrone Ellis	67.56	64.71
Rep. David Green	60.96	60.00
Rep. Isiah Fredericks	58.72	53.68

Source: Mississippi's submission to the United States Department of Justice for section 5 review of 1981 plan enacted by the Mississippi Legislature.

Note: Districts as of 1979; population figures from 1980 census.

These statistics confirm that not only must districts be majority-black for black voters to elect candidates of their choice, but generally the districts must be at least 65 percent black in population and 60 percent black in voting-age population, a standard recognized in the redistricting cases as the "65 percent rule."[14] This figure reflects the realities of black political participation that, because of socioeconomic differences and past discrimination, blacks generally constitute a smaller proportion of the voting-age population than of the total population, are registered to vote at lower rates than whites, and turn out to vote at lower rates than whites. Consequently, the black population percentage of a given election district must be augmented 5 percent for voting-age population disparities, 5 percent for registration disparities, and 5 percent for turnout disparities, so that at 65 percent, black voters will have a chance of electing candidates of their choice. This rule of thumb was developed in the Mississippi redistricting cases when black voters, although they had bare population majorities in certain districts, nevertheless were unable to elect candidates of their choice because they lacked a black voting majority, and the standard has been widely accepted by the federal courts and the Justice Department.[15] However, the 65 percent rule is only a rough guide or rule of thumb, and the threshold for black electoral success may be higher or lower, depending upon the local population characteristics and registration and turnout rates. In some parts of Mississippi, particularly in the Delta area where black registration and turnout is particularly low, the threshold for a winnable black district may be much higher, even as high as 80 percent. Where black registration and turnout rates are closer to white rates, the threshold for black electoral success may be lower. Nevertheless, the data from the 1979 legislative elections shown on table 5.2 support the 65 percent rule; fifteen of the seventeen districts from which black legislators were elected were more than 65 percent black in population and sixteen of the seventeen were 60 percent black or more in voting-age population.

Since 1979 the black membership in the Mississippi Legislature has increased from seventeen to twenty-two. Five additional black House members have been elected, all in majority-black districts, but the black Senate membership remains at two. In 1987 Senator Henry J. Kirksey was replaced by a black woman, Senator Alice Harden, when Kirksey left his Senate seat to run unsuccessfully for lieutenant governor. As table 5.3 shows, all twenty-two current black legislators are from majority-black legislative districts, although one district, from which state representative Alfred Walker, Jr., was elected in 1987, is only barely majority-black in population (50.60 percent) and majority-white in voting-age population. As of 1988, nine years after single-member districts were first instituted on a statewide basis, the vast majority of black legislators are from districts that are more than 65 percent black. Sixteen of the twenty-two districts electing black legislators are more than 65 percent black in population and more than 60 percent black in voting-age population. Six of the districts with black representatives are less than 65 percent black (five of them are 60 percent black or more). Assuming the continued accuracy of the census statistics, this indicates that, on occasion, a few black candidates can get elected from districts with black percentages as low as 60 percent (and very rarely, lower than 60 percent), although 65 percent or more continues to be the norm.

The adoption of majority-black single-member districts has not guaranteed the election of black candidates in every such district, however. In the 1982 reapportionment, which followed the 1979 plan and which governed legislative elections in the 1980s, there were ten Senate districts that were more than 50 percent black and four that were more than 60 percent black in voting-age population. Yet, there are still only two blacks in the state Senate; eight of these ten majority-black Senate districts are still represented by whites. In the House, the 1982 plan had twenty-three House districts that were more than 50 percent black and fifteen that were more than 60 percent black in voting-age population. Although five additional black House members have been elected, including two in the 1987 elections, there are still three majority-black House districts represented by white legislators.

In the 1986 congressional elections, Representative Mike Espy was elected to the U.S. House of Representatives from a large congressional district, the reconstituted Second District, that according to 1980 census data was only 58 percent black in population and 53 percent black in voting-age population. Espy's election, the election of state supreme court justice Reuben Anderson from a district that was 45 percent black, and the election of a handful of other black officials from districts that were less than 65 percent black has led some observers to conclude that the 65 percent threshold no longer has any validity and that a simple black voting-age population majority, or slightly more than that, is all that is necessary to allow black voters to elect candidates of their choice. Is this enough to indicate a trend at this time? Probably not. As of 1988, of Mississippi's approximately 600 black elected officials, only 4 were elected from white majority districts and, in the western part of the state where the vast majority of the black elected officials are concentrated, only 17 were elected from majority-black districts that are less than 65 percent black.[16]

In addition, there are indications that Espy's and Anderson's elections are aberrational, do not indicate a trend, and were due to contextual factors peculiar to their individual elections. Espy, a lawyer, had worked for the state attorney general and the state secretary of state before running for Congress, had the support of the governor and state Democratic party officials, and presented a clean-cut and articulate public image. Despite all this, in 1986, running against two-term Republican incumbent Webb Franklin, Espy won by only a slim 4,800-vote margin (out of over 141,000 votes cast) and was unable to win more than 12 percent of the white vote.[17] The critical factor ap-

Table 5.3. Black Legislators Elected in Mississippi in 1987
and Their Districts

Legislator	Percent Black Population in District	Percent Black Voting-Age Population in District
Rep. Horace L. Buckley	96.72	96.17
Rep. Hillman T. Frazier	82.30	77.28
Rep. Leslie D. King	82.06	78.14
Rep. Aaron E. Henry	78.85	75.43
Rep. Charles B. Sheppard	78.61	75.82
Rep. Alyce Clarke	77.69	74.51
Sen. Douglas Anderson	76.25	70.98
Rep. Credell Calhoun	75.70	70.28
Rep. Walter Robinson, Jr.	71.25	65.86
Sen. Alice Harden	71.14	68.55
Rep. Tyrone Ellis	69.42	64.98
Rep. Edward Blackmon, Jr.	68.89	63.06
Rep. Percy W. Watson	68.35	63.49
Rep. Barney Schoby	67.45	62.99
Rep. Charles L. Young	66.47	62.72
Rep. Robert G. Clark	66.29	62.91
Rep. Mitchell Ellerby	64.12	57.88
Rep. Clayton Henderson	63.98	58.22
Rep. George Flaggs, Jr.	63.69	58.42
Rep. Isiah Fredericks	60.67	54.72
Rep. David Green	60.36	57.38
Rep. Alfred Walker, Jr.	50.60	43.31

Source: Mississippi's section 5 submission to the United States Department of Justice.

Note: Districts as of 1983; population figures from 1980 census.

pears to have been a drop-off of white turnout from the 1984 election, in which Franklin defeated black state representative Robert Clark. In 1984, 63 percent of the voting-age whites turned out to support Franklin against Clark; in 1986 only 51 percent of the voting-age whites voted.[18] Disenchantment among Delta farmers with the Reagan administration's farm policies and an increasing number of mortgage foreclosures appear to have persuaded many whites to protest these policies, not by voting for Espy against Franklin, but simply by going fishing on election day. Anderson, also a clean-cut and articulate attorney, had served on the Hinds County circuit court and had been appointed to the Mississippi Supreme Court by Governor Bill Allain to fill a vacancy—Anderson was the first black person to serve in that position—before he was required to run for election to his supreme court seat in 1986. Anderson was elected with an astonishing 58 percent of the white vote because he had the endorsement of the white political and legal establishment and also because he had no politically credible white opposition. His only opponent was Richard Barrett, who had never held elective office and who ran as an avowed segregationist of the Ross Barnett variety, expressing segregationist views that are no longer fashionable for most white political and legal leaders publicly to espouse.

For these elections to indicate a trend, there will have to be an increase in the number of black officials elected from districts that are less than 65 percent black. The test will occur in the legislative reapportionment and the elections that take place after the 1990 census. There may still be some opportunities to increase the black membership of the state legislature in the remaining majority-black districts without black representation (if these are retained after 1990). However, so long as white voters generally continue to refuse to vote for black candidates, the number of majority-black districts provides a limitation on further increases in black representation. The number of majority-black districts without black representatives has begun to run out, particularly in the state House of Representatives, although there are opportunities to make additional gains in the state Senate as the districts are presently constituted. The challenge for Mississippi's black political leaders will be to increase black representation in the state Senate.

What are the characteristics and backgrounds of Mississippi's black legislators? Mississippi's black legislators resemble their counterparts nationally in most ways. Nationwide, black people who hold elective office are primarily college-educated, middle-aged males who hold a professional degree and are employed in middle-class, white-collar or professional occupations,[19] although the percentage of black officeholders who are women, now at 12 percent, has more than tripled since 1975.[20] All of the black Mississippi legislators elected in 1979 (see table 5.2) were college-educated black males. The first black woman legislator, Representative Alyce Clarke, was not elected until a special election in 1985 to fill a vacancy in Representative Fred L.

Banks's district. Mississippi then became one of the first Deep South states to have a black woman in the state Senate when Senator Alice Harden was elected to replace Kirksey in the 1987 elections.

Mississippi's black legislators tend to be younger than black elected officials nationally. All but five of the black legislators elected in 1979 were under the age of forty-five when they first took office and seven of the seventeen were under thirty-five years of age. Most black legislators in Mississippi also are from urban areas, defined in Mississippi as cities of 10,000 or more, suggesting that urban areas in Mississippi provide a freer environment for successful black political participation than the rural areas.

Political scientist Abigail Thernstrom has contended that the creation of single-member districts, while increasing black representation, may overall be counterproductive to black interests because "as blacks are drained from white districts, the latter become fertile ground for conservative candidates."[21] Thernstrom may be able to cite a few examples where this has occurred. But overall in Mississippi, the creation of single-member districts has led in a number of instances to the election of more moderate white legislators who are willing to form coalitions with black legislators on matters of common concern, contradicting what Thernstrom and others have argued would happen under single-member district plans.

Earl Black has identified what he calls a New South generation of southern politicians first elected to office after the passage of the Voting Rights Act of 1965 and composed of individuals who "reached political maturity after the principle of desegregation had been settled."[22] In Mississippi, the switch to single-member districts statewide, which radically altered the method by which state legislators are elected, resulted in a substantial turnover of the membership of the state legislature and the election of a number of younger, less wealthy, better-educated, and more moderate New South white candidates who lack the strong ties their predecessors had with Mississippi's segregationist traditions. The switch to geographically smaller single-member districts with fewer voters eroded the power bases of many of the veteran, Old Guard legislators and made it easier for challengers to win office because the smaller districts reduced campaign expenses and made it easier to run door-to-door campaigns.[23]

As shown on table 5.4, turnover of members for both houses of the Mississippi Legislature generally has been high, with an average of 43 percent (House) and 44 percent (Senate) new members after each new legislative election. After the switch to single-member districts in 1979, the number of new members in the Senate increased from nineteen (1976) to twenty-six (1980), while the number of new mem-

Table 5.4. Age and Race of New Members of the Mississippi House and Senate, 1979–1984

	1968	1972	1976	1980	1984
House					
Number of new members	57	49	56	56	46
Number of black members	1	1	4	15	18
Average age of members	46	45	42	41	44
Median age of members	44.5	43	40.5	38	42
Average age of new members	43	45	38	37	43
Senate					
Number of new members	24	28	19	26	17
Number of black members	0	0	0	2	2
Average age of members	45	45	47	47	47
Median age of members	44	44	48	46.5	46
Average age of new members	41	42	44	43	41

Source: Mississippi Secretary of State, *Mississippi Official and Statistical Register*, 1968–72, 1972–76, 1976–80, 1980–84, 1984–88.

bers in the House remained relatively high at fifty-six. The redistricting litigation of the 1970s is associated with declines in both the average age of all House members and the average age of new members, both reaching their lowest points in 1980, when the average age of all House members was forty-one years and the average age of new members was thirty-seven years. The impact of single-member districting on the average age of Senate members is less evident, although the average age of new members in 1980 declined slightly from 1976.

The battle over changing the House rules, which led to Speaker Newman's stepping down, noted at the beginning of this chapter, exemplified the eagerness of this new generation of white legislators to challenge the Old Guard leadership. The first, but unsuccessful, challenge to the House rules that gave the Speaker strong control was mounted on the opening day of the 1984 session of the legislature. The chief spokesperson for this effort was Representative Eric C. Clark, a white, thirty-three-year-old part-time college professor who was first elected to the House from a largely rural, east-central Mississippi single-member district in 1979. The effort failed by a vote of 95-26,[24] but the vote clearly was a generational revolt—twenty-three of the twenty-six House members who voted for the change were first elected in either 1979 or 1983.

Black House members were in conflict on whether or not to join this rules battle in 1984. Although they were aware of Newman's record and his use of power to block such measures as the kindergarten bill, only seven black House members voted for the change. Most were concerned that a vote for the change would be a vote against the Speaker, and this would inevitably result in reprisals, such as loss of committee chairs or poor committee assignments. Indeed, the 1984 rules battle splintered the House Black Caucus and created some feelings of distrust among its members.[25]

Three years later, during the first week of the 1987 session, however, the rules change effort carried by a vote of 75-45, with new members joining legislators elected in 1979 and 1983 to break the Speaker's power, and with the House Black Caucus becoming more unified on the issue. The Speaker was limited to two terms in office; a new position of Speaker pro tempore was created; the Speaker was denied the power to appoint the Management Committee, which handles House business such as hiring of House staff and interim committee work; and the House membership gained the power to elect the Rules Committee, which controls the House calendar. In addition, neutral criteria, such as seniority and geography, were adopted for committee assignments, and a new timetable for reporting bills out of committee was adopted to prevent committee chairpersons from killing bills by inaction. Although opponents of the new rules warned that they would hurt the black members because it was unlikely that blacks would be elected to the Rules or Management committees, sixteen of the eighteen Black Caucus members voted for the new rules, providing the necessary margin of victory to carry the change by a three-fifths vote.[26]

A year earlier, an unsuccessful generational battle over procedural rules against the Old Guard leadership was begun in the Senate. In January 1986 two young white senators, Senator Gene Taylor, thirty-three, and Senator Steve Hale, thirty-five, both elected from Gulf Coast districts in 1983, lacking the votes for a successful floor battle filed a state court lawsuit against Lieutenant Governor Brad Dye, who presided over the Senate. Their complaint charged that Dye's exercise of legislative functions in appointing committee chairs and standing committees and assigning bills to committees violated the separation of powers doctrine of the Mississippi Constitution because the lieutenant governor is a member of the executive branch of state government. The Hinds County circuit court ruled in favor of the two senators' lawsuit, but the Mississippi Supreme Court ruled against their challenge.[27]

During the 1980s, this New South generation of state legislators provided the core of legislative support for some progressive measures, particularly in the area of public education. They helped pass the 1982 Education Reform Act and in 1988 a teacher salary increase to match the southeastern states' average and increases in appropriations for the state's public colleges and universities. Also in 1988 this new generation of white members helped pass—for the first time in the House—a landlord-tenant bill long supported by the House Black Caucus, but the bill died in Senate committee.[28]

Contrary to Thernstrom's argument, the switch to single-member districts also does not appear to have resulted in significant Republican representation in the state legislature. Statewide, for at least the past twenty years, the majority of Mississippi's votes in presidential elections have gone Republican in all but one election (Jimmy Carter in 1976), and Mississippi, which historically had a solid Democratic delegation in Congress, now has two Republican U.S. senators. But Republicans have made only limited gains in the Mississippi Legislature. Table 5.5 shows the number and percentage of Republicans for 1979 and 1989 in state legislatures of southern states covered in whole or in part by the Voting Rights Act. As this table shows, despite the adoption of single-member legislative districts in 1979, Mississippi continues to have the lowest percentage of Republicans of any southern state legislature. During this ten-year period, Republican representation has increased substantially in southern state legislatures. However, these gains cannot be attributed exclusively to single-member districting, but rather are more indicative of the resurgence of the Republican party throughout the South in recent years. Further, for all nine states, Republicans currently constitute only 25.7 percent of all state legislators. Since according to a 1988 *New York Times*/CBS poll, 35 percent of all southern voters call themselves Republicans,[29] these figures show that despite the adoption of single-member districts the Republican party remains significantly under-represented in southern state legislatures.

To summarize, the successful black struggle for legislative representation has had a significant influence on the politics of Mississippi. Although whites retain a majority of the votes in the state legislature, the level of black representation has gone beyond token representation, particularly in the House. Despite the fact that black legislators remain a distinct minority, they are able to have significant influence by forming coalitions with white allies, through committee membership, and by using tactics such as filibustering. Although black membership has been increasing since 1979, it is unlikely—if past racially polarized voting patterns continue to prevail—that black representation will approximate the percentage of blacks in the state's

Table 5.5. Republicans in Southern State Legislatures, 1979 and 1989

		1979		1989	
State	Total Number of Legislators	Republican Legislators	Percent Republican	Republican Legislators	Percent Republican
Alabama	140	4	3.8	22	15.7
Florida	160	42	26.2	64	40.0
Georgia	236	26	11.0	47	19.9
Louisiana	144	9	6.2	23	16.0
Mississippi	174	4	2.3	17	9.8
North Carolina	170	20	11.8	59	34.7
South Carolina	170	18	10.6	48	28.2
Texas	181	26	14.4	65	35.9
Virginia	140	27	19.3	45	32.1
Totals	1,515	176	11.6	390	25.7

Source: Southern Legislative Conference, "Results of Elections for the State Legislatures in the South" (December 1988).

population because black representation remains limited by the number of majority-black legislative districts.

But increases in black representation are not the only measure of political change since 1979. The change to single-member districts also produced a substantial increase of younger, New South white legislators less tied to Mississippi's segregationist traditions than their predecessors and more willing to ally themselves with black legislators on matters of common concern. This has resulted in legislative decision making that is more representative of the state's racial and political diversity.

Black Participation in Party Politics

The black political mobilization for the 1967 statewide elections—the first since passage of the Voting Rights Act—was described in chapter 3. After 1967, black political organizing in Mississippi reached higher levels, and blacks gained greater influence within the Democratic party. The black political movement, excluded from state Democratic party affairs, was accorded official recognition by the national Democratic party as its official Democratic party organization in Mississippi; increased numbers of black candidates ran for elective office; and the number of black elected officials continued to multiply, although structural barriers such as racial gerrymandering and at-large elections continue to limit black gains.

As described in chapter 3, in the immediate post-Voting Rights Act period the organizational bases of black political mobilization in Mississippi reflected the preceding civil rights organizing efforts. Statewide, black politics was split between the NAACP, which was committed to Democratic party politics and whose candidates ran in the state Democratic party primaries, and the MFDP, which pursued the establishment of a statewide independent political base outside the national party organizations. After 1968, however, the MFDP began to lose its identity as a statewide organization, although county organizations continued to exist into the 1970s. The statewide black political movement was brought into the national Democratic party, was recognized as a separate state party for eight years, and then, succumbing to the demands of state leaders and the national Democratic party, merged with the white state Democratic party organization to create a united, biracial state Democratic party.

The 1964 Democratic National Convention, although it refused to seat the MFDP delegation, adopted a nondiscrimination requirement to be included in the call to the 1968 convention. Then, in 1967, the party's Special Equal Rights Committee, called the Hughes commission, warned state party officials that failure to comply with the national party's nondiscrimination guidelines would result in the unseating of that state's delegation at the next national convention.[30] In 1968 a biracial coalition, led by state NAACP president Aaron Henry and composed of the major black organizations and a number of white liberals, including Hodding Carter III and Patt Derian, mounted a new challenge to the seating of Mississippi's predominantly white delegation to the Democratic National Convention in Chicago. This coalition eventually was joined by the MFDP, which had planned its own challenge at the 1968 convention. With little controversy, the Democratic National Convention in Chicago sustained this group's challenge to the seating of the predominantly white Mississippi delegation. The predominantly black but biracial group, termed the "Loyalist" Democrats by the press, was seated as the Mississippi delegation to the Democratic National Convention and was recognized by the national party as the Democratic party in Mississippi.[31]

This resulted in Mississippi having two Democratic party organizations, both claiming to be the Democratic party of Mississippi. The Loyalists, chaired by Aaron Henry, were the nationally recognized party organization and held Mississippi's seats on the Democratic National Committee, while the Regulars, as the predominantly white state organization was called, retained control of the state's party primary election machinery and remained the state party organization under state law.

The political alignments of the 1967 election thus went in opposite directions and switched sides. The MFDP, which in 1967 asserted its independence from the Democratic party as it attempted to build an independent political base, was in effect swallowed up by the Loyalist faction of the state Democratic party. On the other hand, Charles Evers, who in 1967 led the move to stay within the Democratic party and urged black candidates to run in the Democratic primaries, began running as an independent candidate for statewide office. In 1971 Evers ran as an independent candidate for governor, receiving 172,762 votes, and subsequently became the spoiler in the 1978 United States Senate race to replace Senator James O. Eastland. Evers, by running as an independent, drained black votes away from the Democratic nominee, Maurice Danton, to insure the election of current Senator Thad Cochran, the first Republican senator from Mississippi since Reconstruction.

In 1972 the Regulars, at the instigation of Governor Bill Waller, filed an abortive lawsuit against the Loyalists, seeking to deny the predominantly black group seats at the 1972 Democratic National Convention in Miami and the use of the Democratic party label. But the Loyalist faction once again won the national party convention seats and the U.S. Court of Appeals for the Fifth Circuit sustained the Loyalists' right to use the party name.[32] By the time of the 1976 presidential primaries, however, national party leaders and Mississippi governor Cliff Finch were successful in persuading the two factions to merge to unite Mississippi's Democratic votes for the 1976 presidential election. Under the terms of the merger, the leaders of the two factions, Henry for the Loyalists and Tom Riddell for the Regulars, became the co-chairs of the merged state Democratic party organization; the state Democratic executive committee was expanded from 35 to 100 members to include members from both factions; and all state party offices were to be rotated among members of different races and genders. Four years later the county Democratic executive committees, which run the county party primary elections, were merged and were required to reflect the racial composition of their respective counties.[33]

For blacks, the merger ended their isolation from state Democratic party affairs and increased their influence in the state party, which controlled the state party primary elections. Increased black participation on the merged county Democratic executive committees meant that blacks had a greater role in appointing managers and clerks to supervise the balloting and deciding election contests growing out of party primaries. By 1986, twenty-two of Mississippi's eighty-two county Democratic executive committees had black chairpersons.[34] The merger also ended the role of the state Democratic party as the party of Mississippi's white population, although for conservative whites this increased the attractiveness of the state's Republican organization, which remained predominantly white. The merger also aided the national Democratic party in the 1976 presidential election. That year both the Regulars and the Loyalists supported the national party candidate, Jimmy Carter of Georgia, who became the first Democratic party nominee for president to carry Mississippi since 1956. Black voters, who supported Carter overwhelmingly, provided his margin of victory in Mississippi,[35] and as reports of the national balloting came in on election night, Mississippi's electoral votes gave Carter the presidency.

The disadvantage of the merger for the black political movement was that blacks gave up their ability to pursue their goals through an independent party organization. In addition, blacks within the merged party were forced to make concessions to the whites for party unity. For example, after William Winter was elected governor in 1979, he insisted that the biracial co-chairpersonship, which had been an element of the 1976 merger, be abolished and that the party be headed by "a white man" to prevent further white defections to the state Republican party.[36]

Despite the fact that the black political movement in Mississippi by 1968 had been officially recognized by the national Democratic party as its state affiliate and despite the merger in 1976, large numbers of black candidates continued to run for office as independents outside the Democratic primaries. In this regard, Mississippi was perhaps unique among the southern states. The MFDP policy of black candidates running as independents, commenced in 1967 in part because of the MFDP's disaffection from the national party, continued even after the black political movement was incorporated into the national party and merged with the state Democratic party organization. In the 1971 statewide elections, almost two-thirds of the black candidates who ran—195 of the 309 black candidates—followed Charles Evers's lead and ran as independents. In the 1975 elections 126 black candidates ran as independents, and in the 1983–85 elections (including some county elections delayed by redistricting litigation) 194 black candidates ran as independents. Most of the black candidates who ran as independents lost, however. In 1975 only 31 of the 126 black independents won, and in 1983–85 only 21 of the 194 black independents won office.[37]

The continuation of this independent candidate practice appears to be based on two considerations. One factor is the continued disaffection with national party politics among blacks; some national and state black leaders continue to be critical of both national party organizations for not being sufficiently responsive to the needs and interests of black voters. Another factor is more pragmatic—state election law continues to appear to give some advantage to independent candidates. Some black candidates believe that their chances of getting elected are better if they bypass the party primaries, in which a majority vote is required to win, and qualify and run as independents in the general election, in which they can possibly take advantage of a split in the white vote and win with only a plurality of the vote.

Black Representation in County and Local Government

After 1967 there were steady increases in the number of black candidates elected to office. In the 1971 statewide elections the number of black officeholders more than doubled—fifty black candidates were elected in 1971 as compared with twenty-two in 1967. As in 1967, the 1971 elections were marked by widespread complaints of election irregularities as white election officials attempted to prevent the election of black candidates.[38] But structural barriers, such as racial gerrymandering of district lines and at-large elections, continued to be a major factor in impeding black electoral successes through the 1970s and into the 1980s, despite black voters' court victories over the state legislature's 1966 massive resistance program.

The Supreme Court victory over elements of the state legislature's 1966 massive resistance program in *Allen v. State Board of Elections* did not end efforts by the white political establishments at the state and local levels to dilute black voting strength. As described in chapter 4, the struggle to eliminate discriminatory multimember districts in the state legislature continued through the 1970s until 1979. At the county level, the state legislature's unsuccessful effort to switch to at-large election of county officials historically elected by district, blocked by the Supreme Court in the *Allen* decision and by the Justice Department's section 5 objection, was superseded by racial gerrymandering of supervisors' district lines to prevent the election of black county officials. At the municipal level, white city councils retained at-large election systems put in place prior to the passage of the Voting Rights Act, under which city council members were elected citywide rather than from wards, which limited the opportunities of black voters to elect city council members of their choice.

An analysis of increases in the number of black elected officials in succeeding state elections after 1965 shows that these discriminatory devices—multimember legislative districts, racial gerrymandering of district lines, and at-large city council elections—constituted substantial barriers to the election of black elected officials. Once these barriers were struck down in voting rights litigation, the numbers of black elected officials in the state legislature and at the county and local levels increased dramatically. This evidence strongly supports the view that in the post–Voting Rights Act period electoral structures were a key determinant of black electoral success or failure and that voting rights litigation to eliminate these barriers remained a critical component of black political progress.

The success achieved after the elimination of multimember districts in the state legislature was described in chapter 4. The results of the efforts to eliminate structural barriers to black political success at the county and local levels are discussed in the following section.

The struggle over county redistricting in Mississippi shows the persistence of the white political massive resistance strategy after passage of the Voting Rights Act at every level of government. The white political leadership was prepared to use every means at its disposal to prevent any power-sharing with the newly enfranchised black voters. Deprived of the opportunity to dilute black voting strength through the state statutes providing for at-large elections that were blocked in *Allen v. State Board of Elections*, white county officials turned to racial gerrymandering of district lines. In this sense, the county gerrymandering litigation was the sequel to the massive resistance cases decided in *Allen*. Black voters, having won a major victory by striking down the state statutes allowing at-large election of county supervisors and county school board members, then had to challenge, on a county-by-county basis, these new efforts to negate the black vote through county redistricting.

Although racial gerrymandering at the county level occurred throughout the South after 1965,[39] it was most pervasive in Mississippi. From 1970 to 1987 the Justice Department lodged a record forty-eight section 5 objections to Mississippi county redistricting plans in twenty-eight counties,[40] and more than thirty county redistricting lawsuits were filed (including many in counties in which section 5 objections were entered).

As described previously, each county in Mississippi is divided into five supervisors' districts. In addition to being administrative units for county services, these county supervisors' districts also serve as election districts for county officials, including members of the county board of supervisors, county school board members, and, for most of the period under discussion, county election commissioners, justices of the peace, and constables. Under state law, the county boards of supervisors themselves are given the responsibility for setting the boundaries of these supervisors' districts.

Beginning in 1969—the year *Allen v. State Board of Elections* was decided—at least half of the counties in the state hired a Mississippi firm, Comprehensive Planners, Inc. (CPI) of West Point, Mississippi, to devise their new county redistricting plans, some before, but most after, the 1970 census. CPI became notorious for its supposedly racially neutral system of redistricting. Because under the "beat" system of county government each county supervisor was responsible for maintaining the county roads and bridges in his or her own supervisors' district, CPI hit upon the notion of dividing the supervisors' responsibilities by equalizing the county road mileage, the number of county bridges, and in some instances, land area among each of the five supervisors' districts. Although this equalization formula sounded logical, the approach in fact was racial gerrymandering in disguise. The county-maintained roads and bridges usually were in the sparsely populated rural areas, and, in many counties, the black population was concentrated in the largest municipality, usually the county seat. To equalize the road mileage and bridges, and to draw districts of equal population as well, CPI generally drew districts that started in the rural areas of the county and then converged on the major municipality, dividing up the municipality and placing portions of it in several, sometimes all, of the supervisors' districts. The stated justification for splitting up the municipality was to equalize the population among the districts, but the usual result of CPI's road-and-bridge approach was to carve up the largest black population concentration in each county like an apple pie and split it up among several majority-white supervisors' districts. Although not every CPI plan drew a Justice Department section 5 objection or was voided by the federal courts, and some plans were struck down that were not devised by CPI, a high proportion of the CPI plans were challenged for racial discrimination.

Hinds County, where the state capital of Jackson is located, provides a good example of this approach. Prior to redistricting, blacks—who constituted 39 percent of the total county population (1970 census)—were in the majority in two of the county's five supervisors' districts. In 1969 the Hinds County board of supervisors employed CPI to redraw the five supervisors' district boundaries according to its road-and-bridge equalization formula. As a result, the county board of supervisors adopted a new CPI plan under which all five districts crossed the county in long, narrow corridors and split up the city of Jackson, which contained 69 percent of the county's black population, among all five districts. The two majority-black districts were eliminated, and under the new plan all five districts were majority-white in both population and voting-age population, denying Hinds County black voters the opportunity to elect candidates of their choice in any of the districts.[41]

Voting rights activist and later Mississippi state senator Henry J. Kirksey exposed the CPI approach in a booklet, "County Redistricting in Mississippi." After graphically describing in maps and text the discriminatory impact of this redistricting formula on black population concentrations in counties throughout the state, Kirksey concluded: "Blacks concerned about racial composition of most newly drawn districts are convinced that the new *equal road mileage criterion* is only an excuse for dilution of black voting strength by politically destroying cognizable concentrations of blacks and, thus, minimize, if not void, opportunities for blacks to be elected to county and state government offices."[42]

The history of the Hinds County redistricting litigation is indicative of the difficulty Mississippi blacks experienced in overcoming this gerrymandering. After the county redistricting plan described above was adopted, county officials submitted it for section 5 review, and in 1971 the Justice Department objected to it under section 5.[43] However, county officials ignored this section 5 objection and implemented the plan in the 1971 county elections,[44] resulting in the defeat of all the black candidates for county offices. In a lawsuit filed by Kirksey and other black Hinds County voters, styled *Kirksey v. Board of Supervisors of Hinds County*, the district court after the 1971 election invalidated this plan, not for racial discrimination, but because it was unconstitutionally malapportioned on the basis of 1970 census data. However, in 1973 the still all-white county board of supervisors adopted a revised plan that equalized the county's population among the districts, but continued to fragment the black population concentration in Jackson. Two of the districts had slight black population majorities, but all five were majority-white in both voting-age population and registered voters. The district court conceded that the result of running long corridors into the Jackson urban area did "create rather unusual looking supervisors' districts," including a district that looked like a "turkey" and another that resembled a "baby elephant."[45] Nevertheless, District Judge Walter L. Nixon, Jr., of the Southern District of Mississippi upheld this new plan on the ground that equalizing population and county-maintained road mileage and bridges was a complete defense to a claim of intentional discrimination, and a panel of the United States Court of Appeals for the Fifth

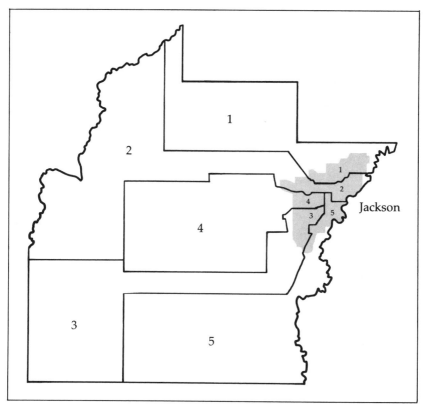

Map 5.1. Hinds County Supervisors' Districts Adopted by the County Board of Supervisors in 1973. This districting plan was ruled unconstitutional by the U.S. Court of Appeals for the Fifth Circuit in 1977. The district court, which upheld the plan, stated that District Three looked like a turkey and District Four resembled a baby elephant. The districts split up the black population concentration in the city of Jackson, as parts of the city were assigned to each of the five districts.

Circuit affirmed.[46] However, in 1977 the entire Fifth Circuit, sitting *en banc*, by a vote of 10-3 in an opinion by Circuit Judge John Godbold held the plan unconstitutional because, by fragmenting a geographically concentrated minority voting community in the context of racially polarized voting, it perpetuated a past history of racial discrimination against Hinds County black citizens.[47]

The Fifth Circuit's *en banc* decision in *Kirksey v. Board of Supervisors of Hinds County* was a landmark decision of critical importance in the campaign against gerrymandering. For the first time the court re-

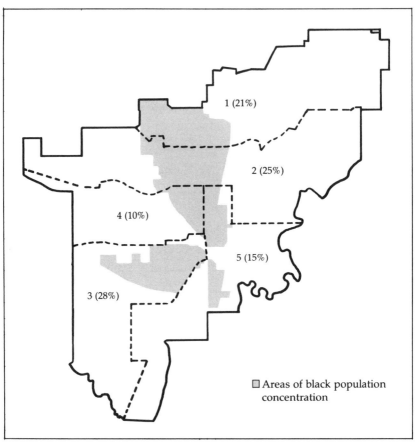

Map 5.2. Division of Jackson's Black Population Concentration in 1973 Board of Supervisors Districts. Figures in parentheses show the percentage of Jackson's black population concentration that was included in each district.

jected the road-and-bridge equalization defense to a gerrymandering claim and held that cracking a black population concentration constituted unconstitutional racial gerrymandering. On remand from the Fifth Circuit's ruling, the board of supervisors was forced to adopt a new plan that contained two districts that were over 65 percent black. In the 1979 county elections—after eight years of litigation—two black county supervisors, Bennie G. Thompson and George Smith, were elected as the first black county supervisors in Hinds County since Reconstruction, along with black justices of the peace and black constables.

An analysis of the rate of increase in the number of black elected officials at the county level after 1965 shows that the greatest increases occurred after section 5 objections and voting rights lawsuits challenging racial discrimination in county redistricting. Successful legal challenges to those discriminatory redistricting plans between 1970 and 1980 produced an increase in the number of majority-black districts, resulting in steady increases in the number of black county supervisors from eight in 1971 to sixteen in 1975 to twenty-seven in 1979. (See table 5.5 and figure 5.2.) Although most of the black county supervisors elected in 1979 were from heavily black counties in the Delta and southwest Mississippi, eight of them—including Thompson and Smith—were elected as a result of section 5 objections and successful court challenges to discriminatory plans. The increase in majority-black districts also led to the near doubling of black justices of the peace and constables, from fifty-one in 1971 to ninety-three in 1979, since those offices are also elected by supervisors' districts.

In the county redistricting that followed the 1980 census, black voters were forced to counter a new wave of gerrymandering. Many of the plans adopted after 1980 were modifications of discriminatory plans that had gone unchallenged in the prior decade. Civil rights legal organizations, private attorneys, and black community groups were successful in persuading the Justice Department to object to a record thirty-six Mississippi county redistricting plans for racial discrimination, most of them handed down after Assistant Attorney General William Bradford Reynolds's highly publicized trip to Mississippi in the summer of 1983 at the invitation of the Reverend Jesse Jackson. Taking advantage of the legal precedents established in the 1970s litigation, county redistricting lawsuits were filed in twenty-eight counties. This effort was successful in striking down a large number of discriminatory districting plans and led to a great increase in the number of majority-black districts which were winnable by black candidates. In the county supervisor elections of 1983–84,[48] the number of black county supervisors nearly doubled, from twenty-seven to fifty. By 1988 there were sixty-eight black county supervisors in Mississippi, more than two and a half times the number of black county supervisors elected after the 1979 statewide elections.

The increase in the number of black county elected officials, particularly the dramatic growth in the number of blacks on county governing boards, has important implications for Mississippi politics. Traditionally, county supervisors have exercised great influence over state and county politics, and black county supervisors and other black county officials are in a position to remedy the decades of ne-

Table 5.6. Number of Black Elected County Officials
in Mississippi, 1968–1988

Office	1968	1972	1976	1980	1984[a]	1988
Elected countywide						
Sheriff				3	2	3
Chancery clerk	1		1	2	2	3
Circuit clerk		1	2	2	3	4
Tax assessor-collector		1	2	2	1	1
Coroner-ranger	1	3	4	4	2	3
Superintendent of education			4	7	7	8
County attorney			1	2	1	2
Elected by district						
County supervisor	4	8	16	27	47	68
Justice of the peace	9	18	19	27	19[b]	25
Constable	6	22	28	39	44	40
School board[c]	1	20	44	59	73	95
Election commissioner		15	13	19	33	47
Total	22	88	134	193	234	299

Sources: United States Commission on Civil Rights, *Political Participation*, app. VI (1968); Joint Center for Political Studies, *Black Elected Officials*, 1972, 1976, 1980, 1984, 1985, 1988 (with some corrections supplied by author).

[a] In a number of counties, district elections scheduled to be held in 1983 (with officials taking office in 1984) were postponed by court order in county redistricting lawsuits and not held until 1984. The 1984 data for county officials elected by district therefore include some officials elected in 1984 who were not reported until subsequent years.

[b] Prior to the 1984 elections, justices of the peace were renamed justice court judges and the number of positions was reduced in most counties to two or three justice court judges.

[c] Includes members of consolidated school boards who are not necessarily elected from supervisors' districts.

glect of black needs in the delivery of local services in such areas as law enforcement, health care, housing, county road maintenance, and water and sewer services. By 1988, 43 of Mississippi's 82 counties had one or more black members on their county board of supervisors. Blacks constituted a majority of the board of supervisors in 5 counties—Claiborne (4), Holmes (3), Humphreys (3), Jefferson (4), and Wilkinson (3), 2 of the 5 supervisors in 13 counties, and 1 out of five in 25 counties.[49]

Figure 5.2. Black County Supervisors in Mississippi, 1968–1988

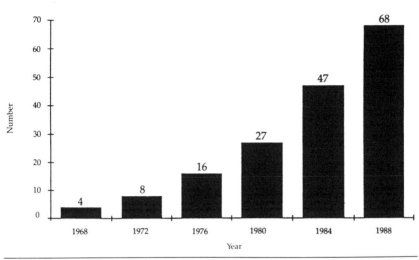

Source: Joint Center for Political Studies, *Black Elected Officials*, 1970, 1972, 1976, 1980, 1984, 1988 (with some corrections for 1988 supplied by author).

Nevertheless, while these increases have been dramatic, particularly since 1980, black county supervisors still constitute only 17 percent of Mississippi's 410 county supervisors in a state that is 35 percent black. Black gains in many rural areas remain limited, including some majority-black counties in the Delta area such as Bolivar (62 percent black, 1 black county supervisor), Coahoma (64 percent black, 1 black supervisor), Sunflower (62 percent black, 1 black supervisor), and Washington (55.6 percent black, 1 black supervisor). In addition, while these successes have resulted in integrated county boards of supervisors, they have not yet achieved true integrated politics. All of the black county supervisors who have won office have been elected from majority-black districts, most of them 65 percent black or more. This means that so long as the vast majority of whites continue to refuse to vote for black candidates, successful black political efforts will remain confined to black majority districts, imposing a severe constraint on future gains.

While Voting Rights Act litigation was successful in preventing switches to at-large election of county officials, at-large city council elections remained a barrier to the election of black city council members after 1965. A principal reason is that most municipal at-large election systems in Mississippi were immune from the section 5 preclearance requirement because they were put into place prior to the passage of the Voting Rights Act.

Our high school civics book taught us that at-large voting systems were first adopted in the early 1900s as an antidote to municipal corruption and bossism that characterized ward systems in some of America's largest cities. However, more recent in-depth research has provided a more complex explanation of the at-large movement. Bradley Rice in *Progressive Cities* shows that the at-large movement was used by business and upper-class professional interests to gain control of city governments, and that part of the motivation behind at-large voting was to cancel out the political influence of racial and ethnic minorities whose political power was based on ward voting.[50] Most of Mississippi's major cities adopted commission forms of government with citywide voting during this period, including Jackson (1912), Gulfport (1912), Meridian (1913), Vicksburg (1913), Hattiesburg (1911), and Laurel (1912), as well as Clarksdale (1910), Charleston (1912), and Greenwood (1915).[51]

At first glance, there would appear to be a contradiction between an ascribed racial motivation for at-large elections and the fact that Mississippi's black population was all but totally disfranchised as a result of the Mississippi disfranchising constitution of 1890. But further analysis reveals that there was no aversion to redundancy in disfranchising mechanisms during this period. After all, the state constitutional convention that adopted the literacy and constitutional understanding tests also adopted the poll tax, the durational residency requirement, and the disfranchising crimes section, all for the same purpose, and this was closely followed by the adoption of the white primary in the early 1900s, for good measure.

In fact, one of the strongest pieces of direct evidence of the racially discriminatory purpose behind at-large municipal elections in the early 1900s comes from Greenville, Mississippi. In 1906, Greenville conducted a municipal referendum on whether to retain at-large city council elections under its special charter from the state legislature or to go under Mississippi's municipal code, which provided for ward voting. One of the chief opponents of the change was state senator J. L. Hebron, a prominent Delta legislator, who told an opposition meeting, "I oppose the bringing of the negro back into politics, which going under the Code and allowing the wards to select their Aldermen, will surely do."[52]

The next wave of interest in at-large municipal elections hit Mississippi more than 50 years later as a result of black voter registration efforts that began in the late 1950s and early 1960s. In response to these voter registration drives, the Mississippi Legislature in 1962 passed a new law requiring all municipalities operating under the municipal code with mayor–board of aldermen forms of government —which covered most cities and towns in the state—to elect their city council members on an at-large basis. Previously, all mayor-aldermen cities over 10,000 in population were required to elect six aldermen by ward and one at-large, while all municipalities under 10,000 had the option of electing four by ward and one at-large or five aldermen at large. The author of the bill stated during the floor debate that the statute—with its obvious purpose of diluting the potential voting power of blacks in majority-black wards—was necessary "to maintain our southern way of life."[53]

Stewart v. Waller, the first lawsuit challenging at-large municipal elections in Mississippi—and one of the first in the nation—was filed in 1973 by black candidates and black voters from four Mississippi cities alleging that this statute violated the Fourteenth and Fifteenth Amendments.[54] Because this lawsuit involved cities in northern Mississippi, it was filed in the U.S. District Court for the Northern District of Mississippi and received a more sympathetic hearing than the lawsuits challenging the 1966 massive resistance legislation, which were filed in the District Court for the Southern District. The case was assigned to a three-judge district court consisting of Circuit Judge Charles Clark of the U.S. Court of Appeals for the Fifth Circuit, who was more of a moderate than J. P. Coleman, his Mississippi colleague on the Fifth Circuit, and District Judges William Keady and Orma Smith. Keady and Smith, in contrast to their Southern District brethren, were strongly committed to upholding constitutional principles of equal civil rights, and much of the racial progress that has occurred in Mississippi stems from their judicial rulings.[55]

The evidence in Stewart v. Waller showed that in five of the cities that switched from ward to at-large elections, twenty-two black candidates ran for the boards of aldermen in the 1969 and 1973 municipal elections, and all of them were defeated in at-large balloting, although they carried one or more of the majority-black wards.[56] The district court held the statute unconstitutional because of its "intent to thwart the election of minority candidates to the office of alderman" and its discriminatory effect of making "election of black aldermen a virtual impossibility in cities in which blacks do not constitute a clear majority of the qualified electorate."[57] The district court's injunction against the 1962 statute required forty-seven cities to revert to the method of election they had prior to the 1962 law, and thirty of these cities were required to adopt ward voting plans (the remaining seventeen were allowed to retain the at-large systems they had before the 1962 law was passed).

However, the district court refused to void all at-large municipal voting in Mississippi, holding that each factual situation was different and would have to be litigated on a case-by-case basis. Between 1973 and 1977 twelve separate lawsuits were filed seeking court orders against at-large city council elections in cities not covered by the *Stewart v. Waller* decree, and several of them were settled for ward voting systems before the 1977 city council elections. The litigation successes in challenging at-large municipal elections in the 1970s not only made it possible for more blacks to be elected to municipal office but also encouraged more black candidates to run and win city council positions. The numbers of black city council members grew from 61 in 1974 to 143 in 1979, an increase of 134 percent. Twenty-four of the 82 new city council members elected after 1975 won office in municipalities that had been forced to revert to ward voting plans under the *Stewart v. Waller* court order.

Despite the impressive evidence of the discriminatory impact of at-large municipal voting, a number of cities resisted any efforts to change their methods of election. The leader of this resistance was the city government of Jackson, which opposed any change through seven years of bitterly contested litigation. *Kirksey v. City of Jackson,* the first lawsuit seeking to eliminate at-large city council voting in Jackson, was filed in 1977 by the Lawyers' Committee on behalf of Henry J. Kirksey and sixteen other black Jackson voters following the defeat of a municipal referendum proposing a change to ward voting. The Jackson city council consisted of a mayor and two city commissioners who exercised both legislative and executive functions and who were all elected citywide. Although Jackson was 40 percent black (1970 census), the city council had been all white, and no black had ever been elected since at-large voting was adopted in 1912. District Judge Walter Nixon, Jr., of the Southern District, in two separate opinions in 1978 and 1981 ruled that the Fourteenth Amendment required proof of discriminatory intent and rejected the testimony of plaintiffs' expert witnesses and other proof that discriminatory intent was a factor in the adoption and maintenance of at-large voting in Jackson, and the Court of Appeals for the Fifth Circuit affirmed.[58] In 1982 Congress amended section 2 of the Voting Rights Act to eliminate the requirement of proving discriminatory intent in Voting Rights Act cases and to prohibit any voting law that had a discriminatory result. The plaintiffs then filed a new lawsuit in 1983, *Kirksey v. Danks,* alleging that at-large Jackson voting violated the new section 2 standard. In 1984, the handwriting on the wall, the city council approved putting another referendum to the voters on the question of whether to change the city's government to a mayor-council form of government with seven city council members elected from wards. The referendum passed by a 65 percent vote after supporters contended that if the voters didn't vote in the change, it would be imposed by the federal court.[59] In the 1985 city election, for the first time in this century three blacks and three women were elected in ward voting to the seven-member city council.

The Jackson city government's resistance to dismantling the at-large election system had enormous political consequences in Mississippi's most populous city. It meant that until 1985, twenty years after the passage of the Voting Rights Act, Jackson's growing black population (which had reached 47 percent of the city's population by 1980)— the largest black population concentration in the state—was denied any black representation in the city government of the capital city. Ironically, beginning in 1979 Jackson's black voters were able to elect two black state senators and five black state representatives from single-member legislative districts in Jackson, and two black county supervisors from majority-black supervisors' districts that included the black sections of Jackson, but they were denied representation of their choice on the city council until 1985 because of the council's refusal to accept a ward voting plan.

The statewide effort by black candidates and voters, supported by the state's civil rights legal organizations, particularly the Lawyers' Committee for Civil Rights Under Law; attorneys Victor McTeer and Margaret Carey of Greenville, associated with the New York–based Center for Constitutional Rights; legal services groups; and individual black attorneys, including Carroll Rhodes of Hazlehurst, Ellis Turnage of Cleveland, and Willie Perkins of Greenwood, radically altered the structure of municipal government in Mississippi. After 1982, as a result of the liberalization of the proof requirements in the 1982 amendment to section 2 of the Voting Rights Act, lawsuits were filed challenging citywide voting in thirty-two municipalities. The result was that while in 1965 the majority of Mississippi cities and towns had at-large city council elections, by 1988 most cities and towns elected their city council members in ward voting. As a consequence, by January 1989 the state had 282 black city council members, by far the largest number of black elected officials in any category of elective office in the state.[60]

As yet, there are no statistical studies available showing the impact of Mississippi's black elected officials on local policies or on the quality of governmental services provided to black citizens. These factors are difficult to measure and the data that would support such studies are difficult to collect. We do know that prior to black voting

Figure 5.3. Black City Council Members in Mississippi, 1968–1988

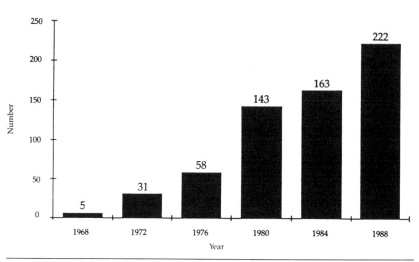

Source: Joint Center for Political Studies, *Black Elected Officials*, 1970, 1972, 1976, 1980, 1984, 1988.

and the election of significant numbers of black elected officials, state and local policies were hostile to blacks in important areas and black needs and interests were neglected in the provision of governmental services, and that black voting and the election of black elected officials have resulted in significant changes. The assumption of those who support the black political movement and the election of black candidates is that when black voters can hold black officials electorally accountable, those black officials will support policies and work for the provision of governmental services that are favorable to blacks.

Studies of black representation have pointed out that policy and services issues are not the only measures of the significance of the election of black officials. The election of black officials benefits the black community by promoting knowledge and awareness of state and local government, by providing symbolic reassurance of blacks' capability to serve in public office, by stimulating more black participation in government, and by decreasing the alienation of blacks toward government and political participation.[61] A 1974 study of black voting in Mississippi showed that black candidates' running for office does have a positive impact on black political participation; the study found a significant positive relationship between the number of black candidates running for office and levels of black electoral turnout.[62]

Black elected officials face special problems and limitations, as studies have shown.[63] Often they cannot fulfill the high expectations of black voters seeking immediate and dramatic changes in their lives as a result of the election of blacks to office. In most instances, as the preceding discussion indicates, black officeholders constitute a minority of representatives on governing bodies and thus do not have the power to enact legislation, change policies, or reorder the provision of governmental services on their own. When they do gain a majority on a governing body, it may be a hollow victory because that jurisdiction may lack the financial resources or tax base necessary to provide services at the high level expected by their black constituents. Similarly, black officials may be criticized for not making dramatic improvements in the levels of income and employment of blacks. Thus, in Mississippi, despite the election of a large number of black officials and although substantial progress has been made, black income and employment levels remain disproportionately lower than white income and employment levels, and black poverty has not been eliminated. But these socioeconomic disparities are the result of economic factors that are beyond the power of black elected officials to influence or control, and black officials cannot be criticized for failing to achieve total racial equality in the economic sphere.

However, studies of the impact of black elected officials show that they can make a difference in policy and service areas.[64] Black officials in jurisdictions studied have made increased efforts to gain federal and other funding to meet educational, housing, employment, social service and other important needs. They have increased minority municipal employment and have increased spending on police and fire protection and other municipal services in which black needs have been neglected. In localities in which blacks control local government, their policies can result in increased black employment and black personal income.

The election of black officials at the local level has also resulted in improvements in the provision of municipal services to black voters. An outstanding example, although not necessarily a typical one, is the extent to which the all-black town government in Bolton, Mississippi, has been able to make changes in services provided by the municipal government. Bolton is a small (population about 800), majority-black town west of Jackson in rural Hinds County. In 1973 an all-black slate, led by Mayor Bennie G. Thompson (who subsequently was elected county supervisor), won all the positions in city government.[65] Upon taking office, the black mayor and board of aldermen found the city's water and sewer systems were in shambles, there was no city fire protection, the one garbage truck the town had was repossessed by the county government, the lease on the city garbage dump that was on land owned by a white man was revoked, the entire membership of the predominantly white police force resigned, and the white former city clerk refused to turn over the town's municipal records to the new government. In addition, Bolton had an unemployment rate of 40 percent, and 75 percent of the town's housing—mostly occupied by blacks—was dilapidated or beyond repair.

With a small tax base and very little municipal revenue, Thompson and the board of aldermen were successful in winning federal grants and extensive outside assistance from national organizations that turned Bolton around. They obtained donations of a fire truck and a garbage truck. As a result of successful applications for federal discretionary funds, they improved the water and sewer systems, built the first combined city hall and fire station, built a day care center, and constructed forty units of new housing and rehabilitated twenty-two additional units, thereby completely eliminating substandard housing in Bolton.[66]

In sum, the struggle for fair representation in Mississippi did not end with the *Allen* decision or even with the legislative reapportionment victory in 1979. At the county and city levels, black voters struggled to overcome gerrymandered county redistricting plans and at-large municipal elections through the 1970s and into the 1980s. The result has been dramatic increases in black representation in county and city government, making local government more nearly reflective of the state's racial diversity and more responsive to the needs of black Mississippians.

6 The Impact of Mississippi Litigation on National Voting Rights Law

Today the Voting Rights Act is widely viewed as the most successful piece of civil rights legislation ever enacted by Congress. This is true not only because it enfranchised millions of black voters throughout the South who previously were denied the right to vote and subsequently was extended to protect non-English-speaking Americans,[1] but also because it has become the chief vehicle for blocking voting-law changes that adversely affect minorities' voting power and for affirmative lawsuits challenging election systems that dilute minority voting strength.

Since 1965, under section 5—which requires federal preclearance of all voting-law changes in covered states—the Justice Department through section 5 objections has blocked the implementation of over 2,000 discriminatory voting-law changes.[2] In 1982 Congress extended section 5 for another twenty-five years and also adopted an important amendment to section 2 of the act—a provision that applies nationwide—to eliminate the requirement of proving discriminatory intent in minority vote dilution lawsuits.[3] This new section 2 "results" test, which prohibits any voting practice or procedure that results in discrimination, for the first time incorporates in a federal statute the minority vote dilution principle that prohibits any voting law under which minority voters "have less opportunity than other members of the electorate to participate in the political process and to elect representatives of their choice."[4] The Justice Department estimates that since section 2 was amended in 1982, more than 1,300 jurisdictions have changed their methods of electing officials in response to section 2 litigation or the threat of litigation.[5] Section 2 has been applied in the South and throughout the nation to strike down discriminatory congressional redistricting and legislative reapportionment plans, at-large election systems, and voter registration procedures that limit black citizens' opportunities to register to vote.

The laws and legal principles that today govern national voting rights policy and litigation were forged in the post-1965 struggle of black voters in the South to overcome the structural barriers to equal participation in the political process. In particular, the struggle of black voters in Mississippi to overcome the state's political massive resistance strategies had an especially profound influence on voting rights law nationally, the effects of which are still being felt today. The Mississippi cases first established the principle of minority vote dilution in Supreme Court jurisprudence; helped secure extensions of the Voting Rights Act, especially over the opposition of the Nixon administration in 1970; and strengthened section 5's federal preclearance requirement and the Justice Department enforcement role.

This chapter explores the impact of these developments on national voting rights policy and examines the criticisms that have been made against this expansion of federal power to protect the right to vote. To understand the contribution of these Mississippi cases to federal voting rights law, we must ask several questions: Precisely what legal principles of general application were established by the cases described in the previous chapters? How did those principles fit into the developing body of modern voting rights law? How should we evaluate the statutory and constitutional safeguards for black political participation today? How valid are current critiques of this body of law? What contemporary implications do these developments have for future challenges to discriminatory electoral structures?

The Principle of Minority Vote Dilution

The Supreme Court's refusal in 1967 to hear the black voters' appeal in the Mississippi congressional redistricting case, *Connor v. Johnson*, described in chapter 3, was symptomatic of the insensitivity of national institutions in the immediate post-1965 period to the legitimate claims of black voters who were being victimized by new forms of voting discrimination. The national movement that produced the Voting Rights Act had identified the denial of the franchise as the central issue of discrimination, and many assumed that once the Voting Rights Act had remedied this problem nothing more needed to be done. As a consequence, the federal courts, with some notable exceptions that included District Judge Frank M. Johnson, Jr., of Alabama,[6] initially were resistant to black voters' claims that their voting power was being diluted by discriminatory electoral mechanisms such as at-large elections and racial gerrymandering.

This problem was compounded by the lack of direct Supreme Court precedent holding that such forms of dilution of minority voting strength violated federal constitutional or statutory guarantees. Historically, there were parallels between the efforts to dilute black

votes after 1965 and the devices employed during the Reconstruction and post-Reconstruction periods. Historian Morgan Kousser has
documented that "Reconstruction and Post-Reconstruction southern
Democrats used at least sixteen different techniques to hamper black
political power without actually denying the franchise to sufficient
numbers of voters to invite a strengthening of federal intervention."
These dilution techniques included racial gerrymandering, at-large
elections, white primaries, voter registration requirements, poll taxes,
secret ballots, multiple box laws, petty crimes disfranchising requirements, and municipal annexations and deannexations.[7] The Supreme
Court held that there was a constitutionally protected right to vote
without discrimination in decisions striking down such devices as
ballot-box stuffing, grandfather clauses, and the white primary,[8] but
these decisions failed to provide any direct judicial precedent against
the use of vote-dilution devices such as at-large elections or racial
gerrymandering. In the one-person, one-vote reapportionment case,
Reynolds v. Sims, the Supreme Court explicitly endorsed the use of
at-large voting and multimember districts in state legislative reapportionment.[9] In subsequent one-person, one-vote cases, the Court
warned that multimember districts might not pass constitutional muster if "under the circumstances of a particular case, [multimember
districts] would operate to minimize or cancel out the voting strength
of racial or political elements of the voting population."[10] But the issue of minority vote dilution was not directly presented in those
cases, and the Court's admonition did not constitute binding precedent.[11]

   In the Tuskegee gerrymandering case, *Gomillion v. Lightfoot*, the Supreme Court held that plaintiffs' allegations that an odd-shaped revision of the municipal boundaries that excluded all but a few black
voters established a Fifteenth Amendment violation.[12] But the majority opinion by Justice Felix Frankfurter was based not on a dilution
of the effectiveness of black votes (Justice Frankfurter was opposed to
courts being involved in what he called the "political thicket" of vote-
dilution adjudication[13]) but on the fact that the boundary change actually denied black voters who were left outside the city limits the
right to vote in municipal elections. Further, the boundary change
in that case was not a typical legislative redistricting gerrymander of
the cracking, stacking, and packing variety but a municipal deannexation.[14] Finally, the Supreme Court in *Wright v. Rockefeller* in 1964 rejected the Fourteenth and Fifteenth Amendment claims of minority
voters in New York City who complained that they were packed into
gerrymandered, irregularly shaped districts, ruling that plaintiffs had
failed to prove either that the redistricting was racially motivated or
that the districts were drawn along racial lines.[15]

The relative absence of any clear judicial precedent prohibiting minority vote denial by dilution was radically altered in 1969 when the Supreme Court handed down its decision in *Allen v. State Board of Elections* and held, in the *Fairley* case, that the switch to at-large elections could nullify black voters' "ability to elect the candidate of their choice just as would prohibiting some of them from voting."[16] The *Allen* decision, while based in part on the vote-dilution principle of the reapportionment cases, nevertheless constitutes a major doctrinal development directly responsive to black voters' quest for political and electoral equality. The Supreme Court's decision provides a textbook example of how Supreme Court decision making can respond to historical events and societal needs, and several factors may have contributed to this judicial about-face. First, the Mississippi vote-dilution statutes and the allegations concerning their impact in the *Allen* cases revealed that the black vote dilution of the 1966 congressional gerrymander presented in *Connor v. Johnson* was not an isolated aberration but was part of a comprehensive program of the Mississippi Legislature to negate the voting strength of newly enfranchised black voters. All three Mississippi cases—*Fairley v. Patterson*, involving a switch from district to at-large elections for county supervisors; *Bunton v. Patterson*, eliminating elections for county school superintendents and making the office appointive; and *Whitley v. Williams*, drastically increasing the qualifying requirements for independent candidates for office—challenged statutes enacted by the same legislature that had adopted the congressional district gerrymander. All three statutes involved different election-law changes, but they all had the same potential impact—depriving black voters of the opportunity to elect candidates of their choice.

Second, by March 1969, when *Allen* was decided, it was apparent that the problem of minority vote dilution was not confined to Mississippi but was occurring in other southern states in which literacy tests and poll taxes had been struck down by the act. In May 1968 the United States Commission on Civil Rights had issued a comprehensive report, *Political Participation*, describing in detail state and local laws adopted after the Voting Rights Act became law that had a discriminatory impact upon black voters and candidates.[17] Although the report disavowed that the hostile reaction to black enfranchisement under the Voting Rights Act was as organized or as massive as the resistance to school desegregation, the commission concluded that there had been "resistance to change in varying degrees in the Deep South States of Mississippi, Alabama, Louisiana, Georgia, and South Carolina and isolated incidents in other Southern States."[18] This indicated that the issues presented in the Mississippi cases were not indigenous only to Mississippi but were regional in scope.

Third, the *Allen* cases did not require the Supreme Court to adopt any new constitutional principles or to expand any established ones. As previously described, for reasons of litigation strategy the plaintiffs' lawyers in the Mississippi cases dropped all their constitutional claims that the challenged statutes violated black voters' rights secured by the Fourteenth and Fifteenth Amendments. Instead, when these cases reached the Supreme Court they presented only an issue of statutory interpretation—did section 5 of the Voting Rights Act cover these changes in election procedures? In an institutional sense, this made it easier for the Supreme Court to sustain the black voters' claims since historically the Court has been more reluctant to adopt new constitutional principles than to engage in statutory interpretation of federal laws.[19] The minority vote dilution principle embodied in the *Allen* decision was not judge-made law, but simply the Court's interpretation of the will of Congress.

The Supreme Court in the *Allen* decision held that each of the three challenged voting-law changes had a potential adverse impact on black voting strength. In so deciding, the Court was not making a final determination whether the changes had a racially discriminatory purpose or effect that was prohibited by section 5—that decision was reserved under section 5 for the attorney general or the U.S. District Court for the District of Columbia. But the challenged statutes' potential for discrimination was relevant to the question of whether these changes were the kind that Congress in enacting section 5 intended to be covered by the preclearance requirement. The change from election of county school superintendents to appointment had a direct impact on the right to vote, the Court ruled. "The power of a citizen's vote is affected by this amendment; after the change, he is prohibited from electing an officer formerly subject to the approval of the voters."[20] Similarly, the increases in the qualifying requirements for independent candidates would prevent voters from being able to vote for candidates who could not satisfy the increased requirements. In addition, the statute provided that anyone who voted in a party primary could not qualify to run as an independent candidate: "One must forgo his right to vote in his party primary if he thinks he might later wish to become an independent candidate."[21]

But the ruling in *Fairley v. Patterson* on the switch from district to at-large elections was the most far-reaching and was the one that established the principle of minority vote dilution. Under that statute, no one was prevented from voting for any office or candidate, and no one was required to forgo the right to vote. The change did not deny anyone the right to cast a ballot; it only diluted the impact of black voters' voting strength. In this instance, the Court extended the vote-dilution principle of the one-person, one-vote decisions, which on their face did not involve a racial deprivation, to cover instances of racial discrimination through vote dilution: "The right to vote can be affected by a dilution of voting power as well as by an absolute prohibition on casting a ballot. See *Reynolds v. Sims*, 377 U.S. 533, 555 (1964). Voters who are members of a racial minority might well be in the majority in one district, but in a decided minority in the county as a whole. This type of change could therefore nullify their ability to elect the candidate of their choice just as would prohibiting some of them from voting."[22]

The critical element was the denial to minority voters of "their ability to elect the candidate of their choice," and this line expresses the essence of the minority vote dilution principle. Although stated in the context of a switch from district to at-large elections, the principle is not easily confined to that context. Isn't the ability of minority voters to elect the candidate of their choice nullified by at-large election systems that had been in place before 1965, if black voters are sufficiently concentrated so that they could constitute a majority in a single-member district or city ward? Isn't it nullified if black voters are in the majority in a district that is split up and divided among several districts, so that the former black majority is so fragmented that black voters lack a majority in any of the new districts? Isn't it nullified if black voters constitute a citywide majority in a municipality, and that majority is reduced to a minority by municipal annexations?

Thus, the Supreme Court's focus in the Mississippi case of *Fairley v. Patterson* on the ability of minority voters "to elect the candidate of their choice" involved an enormous conceptual breakthrough in voting rights jurisprudence that has profoundly influenced the course of voting rights litigation down to the present time.

After the *Allen* decision, the principle of minority vote dilution went the full circle. From being first announced as the statutory Voting Rights Act standard for section 5 preclearance, it became the constitutional standard for Fourteenth Amendment voting rights violations under the *White-Zimmer* standard, then was undermined in *City of Mobile v. Bolden* when the Supreme Court held that proof of discriminatory intent was required, and finally was reinstated by Congress in 1982 as the statutory standard for determining a violation of section 2 of the Voting Rights Act.

After the *Allen* decision, the Supreme Court elevated this minority vote dilution principle, first developed in the context of the applicability of section 5 to switches to at-large elections, to a principle of constitutional law in cases challenging at-large election systems that were not covered by section 5. At-large election challenges started coming to the Supreme Court from areas not covered by section 5 of the Voting Rights Act, and this required the Supreme Court to resolve the question of whether at-large elections that diluted black voting strength violated constitutional guarantees.

In *Whitcomb v. Chavis*, decided in 1971, the Supreme Court rejected black voters' claim that at-large elections for state legislators in Indianapolis, Indiana, diluted the voting strength of black ghetto residents in violation of the Fourteenth and Fifteenth Amendments. The Court perceived the defeat of black candidates "more as a function of losing elections than of built-in bias against poor Negroes" in the absence of evidence that black voters had been discriminated against or otherwise excluded from political participation.[23] "Nor does the fact that the number of ghetto residents who were legislators was not in proportion to ghetto population satisfactorily prove invidious discrimination absent evidence and findings that ghetto residents had less opportunity than did other Marion County residents to participate in the political processes and to elect legislators of their choice."[24] Although the Supreme Court held that no constitutional violation had been proven, the Court nonetheless left the implication that constitutional vote dilution claims would be sustained where minority voters could produce sufficient evidence that they "had less opportunity than . . . other . . . residents to participate in the political processes and to elect legislators of their choice."

The case that met this test was decided two years later when, in *White v. Regester*, the Texas legislative reapportionment case, the Supreme Court struck down as unconstitutional at-large legislative elections in Dallas and Bexar (San Antonio) counties. Adopting the standard first articulated in a statutory context in *Allen* and in a constitutional context in *Whitcomb*, the Supreme Court in *White v. Regester* held that "the plaintiffs' burden is to produce evidence to support findings that the political processes leading to nomination and election were not equally open to participation by the group in question—*that its members had less opportunity than did other residents in the district to participate in the political processes and to elect legislators of their choice.*"[25] In what has become known as the "totality of the circumstances" test, the Supreme Court held that this test had been met by evidence showing a past history of racial discrimination against blacks and Mexican-Americans in voting; electoral mechanisms that handicapped minority candidates, such as a majority vote requirement and a place system requiring candidates to run for a place or post on the ballot; low levels of minority representation; racial discrimination in the slating of candidates; racial campaign tactics; and unresponsiveness of white elected officials to minority interests—all of which made it more difficult for minority voters to elect candidates of their choice and showed that at-large elections operated in a discriminatory manner.[26]

The *White v. Regester* decision constituted a critical advance in the development of the minority vote dilution principle because for the first time the Supreme Court applied it in a constitutional context to hold that at-large elections violated the Fourteenth Amendment. This advance had enormous implications since there are structural devices that dilute minority voting strength that are not covered by the section 5 preclearance requirement, either because they were adopted before the Voting Rights Act became law or because they are implemented in states not covered by section 5 (both of which applied in the Texas case). In addition, there was nothing in the Supreme Court's decision to indicate that the legal standard was restricted to at-large elections, meaning that it could be equally applied to challenge racial gerrymandering and other devices that diluted minority voting strength.

From 1973 to 1980 this *White v. Regester* standard that focused on whether the challenged election system provided minority voters "less opportunity . . . to participate in the political processes and to elect legislators of their choice" was the chief vehicle for constitutional challenges to discriminatory at-large elections and racial gerrymandering throughout the South. The principal decision implementing this standard in the Fifth Circuit, which covered most of the South, was *Zimmer v. McKeithen,*[27] and the standard became known as the *White-Zimmer* standard. Scores of successful lawsuits were filed, primarily in the South, striking down discriminatory at-large voting systems and gerrymandered election districts.[28]

The success of these efforts was soon curtailed, however, when in 1980 a divided Supreme Court in *City of Mobile v. Bolden* dealt the minority vote dilution principle a serious blow.[29] The Court held that under both the Fourteenth Amendment and the Voting Rights Act proof of discriminatory intent was required and rejected the evidentiary factors relied upon in *White v. Regester,* such as a past history of discrimination and low levels of black electoral success, as providing circumstantial evidence of discriminatory intent. Under the prior case law, minority plaintiffs could win upon proof of discriminatory intent or discriminatory effect. For example, there is nothing in the Supreme Court's decision in *White v. Regester* stating that proof of discriminatory intent is required. For voting rights advocates, the *Bolden* decision was a disaster that gutted the minority vote dilution principle. Under the *Bolden* decision, voting rights plaintiffs were required to prove not only that a challenged voting law dilutes minority voting strength but also that this was the intent of those who adopted it or kept it in place.

This reversal was symptomatic of the trend on the Burger Court during the 1970s of cutting back on legal protections against racial discrimination. During the late 1960s and early 1970s the Court had been somewhat ambivalent on whether proof of discriminatory intent was required to prove a Fourteenth Amendment violation. Although some decisions appeared to be based on an intent standard, for example, *Wright v. Rockefeller*, the New York redistricting case, the Court did not require discriminatory intent to prove a one-person, one-vote violation in the reapportionment cases, which also were based on the equal protection clause of the Fourteenth Amendment, and had even criticized the intent standard in 1971 in *Palmer v. Thompson*, the Jackson, Mississippi, swimming pool closing case.[30] Then, beginning with *Washington v. Davis*, a 1976 case alleging employment discrimination in the Washington, D.C., police department,[31] the Court began to rule that proof of discriminatory intent was a necessary element of a Fourteenth Amendment violation. Thus, the *Bolden* decision was the culmination of a fairly recent development in Supreme Court jurisprudence, beginning in 1976, of requiring strict proof of discriminatory intent in racial discrimination cases brought under the Fourteenth Amendment.

Discriminatory intent is very difficult to prove in court because ultimately it requires proof of what was in the minds of the legislators or other public officials when they adopted or decided to retain a voting law that disadvantages minority voters. Direct proof of discriminatory intent is often difficult or impossible to obtain because white public officials intent on discriminating usually do not admit to violations of the law or make public statements signaling their unconstitutional purposes. Indeed, the record of the Mississippi Legislature's massive resistance session described in chapter 2 shows that as early as 1966 there was an effort on the part of legislators to keep their discriminatory motives under wraps to prevent successful court challenges to their actions. In the absence of direct "smoking gun" evidence, victims of discriminatory voting laws must resort to circumstantial evidence that provides what courts and commentators have called "inferences," "suspicions," and "likelihoods" of discriminatory intent. When court rulings must rely on such factors, southern federal judges who are unsympathetic to civil rights claims are unlikely to find discriminatory intent.[32]

Further, the illicit purposes of laws adopted or maintained with a discriminatory intent can frequently be disguised. A plausible, nonracial justification can be offered for almost any racially discriminatory voting law. Thus, the sponsors of several of Mississippi's massive resistance laws stated publicly that the bills were being passed simply to satisfy the one-person, one-vote requirement, to elect officials who would have a countywide perspective, to promote efficiency in government, and the like. In most cases, in the absence of direct evidence of a racial purpose, courts have been willing to accept these pretexts as a complete defense to a claim of intentional discrimination. Further, the discriminatory intent standard is made more difficult by limitations on proving it, including practical difficulties in ascertaining the motives of legislators who may have adopted a discriminatory voting law 100 years ago and court rules of "legislative immunity" that prevent attorneys for minority voters from cross-examining legislators regarding their motives.[33]

The Mississippi cases discussed in the earlier chapters show that the discriminatory intent standard provided little protection for black voting rights in Mississippi. The intent issue frequently arose in the Mississippi litigation, but in all but one of the cases (*Stewart v. Waller*, in which there was direct evidence of racial motivation[34]) the courts ruled against minority voters' claims of discriminatory intent even in the face of strong evidence of racial purpose. (Prior to 1980, proof of discriminatory intent could be used to establish a constitutional violation, and attorneys raised the issue where they thought it could be proved, although it was not necessarily required under the *White-Zimmer* standard.) Thus, in the congressional redistricting case, *Connor v. Johnson*, the district court sustained the 1966 plan and the Supreme Court rejected black voters' appeal, despite strong evidence of discriminatory intent.[35] This case showed the lack of any firmly established and consistently applied legal standards governing what kinds of evidence are admissible to prove discriminatory intent and the broad discretion granted to district judges in admitting or rejecting evidence. The *Connor* court held that newspaper reports of the legislative debates—even in the absence of an official transcript—could not be used to prove discriminatory intent, and the Supreme Court summarily affirmed its decision, while the district court in *Stewart v. Waller* relied heavily on the press reports of the 1962 debate on the Mississippi law requiring at-large municipal elections to strike the law down.

In *Kirksey v. Board of Supervisors of Hinds County*, described in chapter 5, the district court and the Court of Appeals for the Fifth Circuit initially accepted the road-and-bridge equalization formula as a justification for splitting up black population concentrations and depriving black voters of a voting majority in any district in a county that was 40 percent black.[36] The Fifth Circuit sitting *en banc*—after seven years of litigation—ultimately held the gerrymandered county redistricting plan unconstitutional. But its decision was based not on a ruling that the plan was adopted for a discriminatory intent—indeed, the Fifth Circuit accepted the district court's finding that it was not intentionally discriminatory[37]—but because the plan perpetuated a past history of intentional denial to black voters of equal access to the political process.[38]

In *Kirksey v. City of Jackson*, challenging at-large city council elections, no black candidate had been elected to the Jackson city council since at-large elections were instituted in 1912, despite the fact that Jackson was 40 percent black. In the face of historical and contemporary evidence that the at-large system had been adopted and maintained for a racial purpose, the federal courts repeatedly upheld Jackson's at-large voting system.[39] Those responsible for adopting the at-large system were not the state legislators or the city council but Jackson's voters—at-large elections had been adopted by citywide referendum in 1911, and a proposal for ward voting had been rejected by citywide referendum in 1977. But after the Supreme Court's *Bolden* decision the Fifth Circuit in a bizarre ruling held that the voters' motivation in adopting and maintaining at-large elections was completely immune from judicial inquiry, thereby preventing the black voter plaintiffs from exploring the motives of those who were responsible for the discriminatory voting system.[40] Jackson's at-large city council voting system was not dismantled until after 1982, when a second lawsuit filed pursuant to the 1982 amendment to section 2 of the Voting Rights Act, described below, made citywide voting legally untenable.[41]

In 1982, two years after the *Bolden* decision, the Supreme Court in *Rogers v. Lodge*, a constitutional challenge to at-large elections in Burke County, Georgia, retreated somewhat from the extreme position it had taken in the *Mobile* case.[42] The Supreme Court did not rescind the discriminatory intent requirement. But the Court made discriminatory intent easier to prove by ruling that direct evidence was not required. The Court held that the discriminatory intent standard could be met by circumstantial evidence accepted in the *White-Zimmer* line of cases, such as a past history of discrimination, racially polarized voting, and discriminatory electoral mechanisms, that, the Court ruled, provided indirect evidence of discriminatory intent.

The Court's reconsideration of the level of proof necessary to prove discriminatory intent was probably the result of a number of factors. Criticism of the *Bolden* decision was heated and widespread among legal scholars and in the civil rights community.[43] The *Harvard Law Review* called the decision "a serious setback" for minority voting rights and accused the Court of "belittling the voting rights of minority voters."[44] Criticisms focused on the break with prior precedent, including the *White v. Regester* decision, the difficulty of proving discriminatory intent, and the lack of direction in the Court's opinion regarding how the new standard was to be applied. The *Rogers v. Lodge* ruling was also, in part, a response to what was happening in Congress. The extensive criticisms of the *Bolden* decision were aired in congressional hearings when the Voting Rights Act came up for renewal in 1982 and persuaded Congress to amend section 2 of the Voting Rights Act in 1982 to eliminate proof of discriminatory intent.[45] These congressional hearings were going on when the *Rogers* case was argued in the Supreme Court, and the decision was handed down just two days after the section 2 amendment was signed into law. Finally, there had been a shift in personnel on the Supreme Court and a change of views. Justice Potter Stewart, the author of the principal opinion in *Bolden*, retired before *Rogers v. Lodge* was decided, and Chief Justice Warren Burger changed his position—he had agreed with the Stewart opinion in *Bolden* rejecting circumstantial proof of discriminatory intent but then joined the majority opinion by Justice Byron White in *Rogers* allowing it.

By 1982, however, this change in the legal standard came too late. Congress already had amended section 2 of the Voting Rights Act to eliminate the necessity of proving discriminatory intent, which made the question of what evidence satisfied the intent standard a moot point.

Congress reacted to the *Bolden* decision by amending section 2 of the Voting Rights Act to strike down the discriminatory intent requirement and by substituting an easier-to-prove "results" test. Although discriminatory intent remains a requirement for proving a constitutional violation, the new statute prohibits any voting law "which *results* in a denial or abridgement of the right of any citizen of the United States to vote on account of race or color [or language minority status]." In section 2(b) of the statute, Congress provided that a violation is established if, "based on the totality of the circumstances," minority voters show that they "have less opportunity than other members of the electorate to participate in the political process *and to elect representatives of their choice.*"

The House and Senate committee reports indicate that the purpose in adopting this statute was to restore the *White-Zimmer* legal standard for proving minority vote dilution that prevailed before the *City of Mobile v. Bolden* decision. The Senate Judiciary Committee report lists three reasons why Congress thought that proving discriminatory intent to establish a voting rights violation was the wrong test. First, if a voting law operates today to deny minority voters an equal opportunity to participate in the political process, "what motives were in an official's mind 100 years ago is of the most limited relevance." Second, Congress considered the intent test unnecessarily divisive because it requires the federal courts to label state or local officials as racists in order to grant relief. Third, Congress thought that the intent test placed "an inordinately difficult burden" on voting rights plaintiffs because of the difficulties of gathering evidence of discriminatory intent.[46] The Judiciary Committee cited the Fifth Circuit's decision in the Jackson case barring inquiry into the motives of the voters who voted for at-large elections and defendants' ability to provide nonracial justifications for discriminatory laws as examples of the difficulties of proving discriminatory intent.[47]

Since 1982 section 2 has been phenomenally successful in eliminating racially discriminatory barriers to equal minority political participation. It has been used by blacks, Hispanics, and American Indians to challenge discriminatory voting laws. It has been applied in both the North and the South to strike down such voting procedures as discriminatory congressional redistricting and legislative reapportionment plans, at-large county elections, at-large and gerrymandered city council districting schemes in northern and southern cities, at-large state judicial elections, and discriminatory voter registration procedures that limit black citizens' opportunities to register to vote.

In amending section 2 in 1982, Congress for the first time enacted into a federal statute applicable nationwide the minority vote dilution principle first announced in 1969 in the Mississippi cases decided in the *Allen* decision. The legal standard first developed in the litigation struggles of black Mississippi voters and candidates to overcome that state's massive resistance program thus ultimately was adopted as a nationwide statutory prohibition against vote-dilution mechanisms. This debt was recognized when, in both the House and Senate committee reports supporting the 1982 section 2 amendment, Congress cited the *Allen* decision as the source of the minority vote dilution principle.[48]

The white Mississippi legislators who framed Mississippi's massive resistance response to the Voting Rights Act surely did not anticipate that their actions ultimately would result in a national legal standard prohibiting minority vote dilution. Their massive resistance strategy also produced two additional unintended consequences: it all but guaranteed that the temporary provisions of the Voting Rights Act that were originally to last only five years—including the section 5 preclearance requirement—would be extended in 1970 and subsequently, and it greatly expanded the scope of the section 5 preclearance requirement and the enforcement role of the Justice Department.

Extensions of the Voting Rights Act

When the *Allen* case was decided in 1969, the temporary enforcement provisions of the Voting Rights Act that were enacted for a five-year period—including the preclearance procedures of section 5—were due to expire the following year.[49] If the uncompromising opposition to black political participation that had characterized the policies of southern states prior to 1965 had abated, there would have been serious question whether the enforcement procedures were still needed. Indeed, the Nixon administration as part of its "Southern strategy" to appease southern states strongly opposed the extension of section 5 when it came up for renewal in 1970.[50] But the *Allen* decision and other proof that southern legislatures were acting to dilute black voting strength and frustrate the political aspirations of black voters[51] convinced Congress that continued strong actions were necessary to ensure voting rights to blacks.

The evidence of Mississippi's massive resistance played a pivotal role. In the absence of Justice Department support for continuing the protections of section 5, the United States Commission on Civil Rights provided the leading official federal government support for extending section 5. Howard Glickstein, acting staff director of the commission, in his leadoff testimony before the House Judiciary subcommittee cited as prime examples of the continuing need for federal preclearance the Mississippi massive resistance legislation switching to at-large county elections, facilitating the consolidation of predominantly black and predominantly white counties, and gerrymandering district lines.[52] Further, the *Allen* decision was frequently mentioned during the congressional hearings and was cited in the House Judiciary Committee report, the only written committee report filed in support of the extension bill, as showing that section 5 was still needed.[53] The outcome of the *Allen* case all but guaranteed that Congress would vote in 1970 to extend the enforcement provisions of the Voting Rights Act for another five years. Thus, the Mississippi Legislature's recalcitrance in refusing to accept the black vote backfired and resulted in the continuation of federal oversight of election-law changes within the state and other covered states. In addition, Congress, in extending the special enforcement provisions of the Voting Rights Act in 1970, removed any doubt about its intention regarding the scope of section 5. Members of Congress in the House committee report and legislative debates on the 1970 extension of the act extensively cited with approval the Supreme Court's interpretation of section 5 in the *Allen* case. In effect, Congress in 1970 ratified the Supreme Court's broad construction of section 5 as consistent with the congressional intent.

When the act came up for renewal in 1975, and again in 1982, Mississippi's continued resistance to the act's guarantees, including its resistance after the *Allen* decision, described in chapters 3, 4, and 5, continued to play a critical role in persuading Congress that section 5 should be further extended. Mississippi's continued use of discriminatory multimember legislative districts, efforts to switch to at-large county elections, racial gerrymandering in county redistricting, and discriminatory at-large municipal elections all were laid out in the congressional hearings in 1975 and 1981–82 and cited in the congressional committee reports and Civil Rights Commission studies as examples showing that federal preclearance was still needed.[54] The Senate Judiciary Committee report supporting the 1975 extension of the act specifically cited *Connor v. Waller*, one of the Supreme Court decisions in the long-running Mississippi legislative reapportionment case, as reiterating rulings "which make Section 5 the front line defense against voting discrimination."[55]

Section 5 and Justice Department Enforcement

Before the *Allen* decision, as voting rights attorney David Hunter has noted, section 5 had "remained practically dormant for several years."[56] The Justice Department had received only 251 submissions of voting-law changes—mostly from South Carolina (114) and Georgia (63)—had lodged only four section 5 objections, and had filed only one lawsuit to force a state to comply with section 5.[57] Mississippi, along with Louisiana and North Carolina, taking the position that section 5 covered only changes in voter registration procedures, had ignored section 5 altogether and had not submitted anything. The Supreme Court's decision in the *Allen* case, holding that the federal preclearance requirement applied to changes that altered a state's voting laws "in even a minor way" and that diluted black voting strength, as well as changes that affected registration and voting, greatly expanded the section's scope. Two years later, in another Mississippi case brought by LCDC attorney Armand Derfner, *Perkins v. Matthews*, the Supreme Court reaffirmed the *Allen* decision and held that changes in polling place locations, municipal annexations, and a change from ward to citywide elections of municipal aldermen in Canton, Mississippi, all were changes affecting voting that were subject to federal preclearance.[58]

The *Allen* decision had enormous significance for black voters' struggle against discriminatory voting laws in the South. After the *Allen* decision, section 5 became "the most frequently used portion of the Voting Rights Act" to protect against discrimination in voting.[59] Since 1968 more than 130,000 voting-law changes have been submitted to the Justice Department for section 5 review, and the department, through section 5 objections, has blocked implementation of over 600 submissions involving over 2,000 discriminatory voting-law changes (see table 6.1). Currently, the department each year reviews an average of 4,000 submissions containing an average of 13,000 voting-law changes submitted for preclearance by covered jurisdictions. Most section 5 objections have been lodged against discriminatory municipal annexations (1,088), changes in the method of electing officials (472), and redistricting plans (248).[60] But the impact of this section 5 review process goes beyond the statistics reflecting the number of section 5 objections. Section 5 also has a deterrent effect; covered states and localities are deterred from adopting discriminatory voting laws they know will not pass muster under section 5.

The *Allen* decision not only expanded the coverage of section 5 and the responsibility of covered jurisdictions to submit voting-law changes for federal preclearance, but it also forced the Department of Justice once again to make voting rights a central focus of its civil rights enforcement responsibilities. In October 1969, the Nixon administration reorganized the department's civil rights division to accommodate this new enforcement responsibility. Previously, the Civil Rights Division had been organized into geographical regions with attorneys in each region handling all types of civil rights litigation within their region. The 1969 reorganization created functional sections, and a Voting Section was established with the primary responsibility for reviewing section 5 submissions. This reorganization permitted division attorneys to become specialized and to gain functional expertise in the fast-developing field of voting rights law.[61] The *Allen* decision and the 1970 extension of section 5 by Congress forced the department to improve section 5 enforcement, so that by 1975 Assistant Attorney General J. Stanley Pottinger reported to Congress that "today enforcement of §5 is the highest priority of our Voting Section."[62]

Today, with over eighty supervisory staff, attorneys, and research analysts, the Voting Section is the largest of the five subject-matter sections in the Justice Department's civil rights division. In February

Table 6.1. Department of Justice Section 5 Objections, 1965–1988

Year	Number of Changes Submitted	Number of Objections	Number of Changes Objected to
1965	1	0	0
1966	26	0	0
1967	52	0	0
1968	110	4	6
1969	134	15	16
1970	255	3	3
1971	1,118	52	86
1972	942	32	52
1973	850	27	37
1974	988	34	73
1975	2,078	40	138
1976	7,472	64	151
1977	4,007	36	104
1978	4,675	39	49
1979	4,750	26	45
1980	7,340	32	54
1981	7,132	24	33
1982	14,287	49	109
1983	12,416	48	71
1984	16,489	42	109
1985	14,418	23	172
1986	21,898	32	639
1987	15,321	24	85
1988	18,957	23	135
Total	155,716	669	2,167

Source: U.S. Department of Justice, Voting Section statistics.

1976 the Voting Section itself was reorganized, and a Section 5 Unit was established within the Voting Section to review the growing number of section 5 submissions. To conserve attorney resources, this unit is staffed primarily by nonattorney research analysts who are supervised and trained by attorneys to conduct the processing and initial case analysis of section 5 submissions.[63]

The expansion of section 5 coverage effectuated by the *Allen* decision also resulted in the Justice Department's promulgation of its first section 5 regulations in 1971. The 1971 regulations were the result of pressure from an unusual combination of forces and involved a serious conflict over section 5 review standards between the administration and civil rights forces.

After *Allen*, the strongest demands for section 5 regulations came from conservative southern attorneys representing covered states and localities who complained to administration officials about the lack of any formalized preclearance procedures. In addition, Congressman Don Edwards of California, a strong supporter of the Voting Rights Act, scheduled hearings of his newly created House Judiciary Subcommittee on Civil Rights Oversight to hear complaints from civil rights groups concerning the Justice Department's lack of section 5 enforcement.[64]

The Nixon administration, having failed in its effort to prevent Congress from extending section 5 in 1970, then attempted to weaken section 5 through lax administrative enforcement. The issues of Justice Department enforcement and the substantive standards of the new section 5 regulations came to a head when the Justice Department failed to lodge a section 5 objection to one of the centerpieces of Mississippi's massive resistance program, the open primary law. The open primary law, which was originally passed by the Mississippi Legislature in 1966 but vetoed by Governor Paul Johnson, abolished party primaries and established a majority vote requirement to win elective office. If no candidate received a majority vote in the general election, a runoff was required. Historically, Mississippi had required a majority vote only to win party primaries, not to win in the general election. This meant that independent black candidates could possibly win office in the general election with less than a majority of the votes if the white vote was split between white party nominees. It was this potential window of opportunity for independent black candidates that the Mississippi Legislature attempted to close by enacting the open primary law.

In 1970 the Mississippi Legislature reenacted the open primary law, and this time it was signed into law by Governor John Bell Williams. The two bills were adopted after black leader Charles Evers won a plurality of the vote in a 1968 special congressional election and after debate in the 1970 legislature concerning "Negro bloc voting" and the potential for "a minority candidate with a minority vote" to win in the general election.[65] When the statutes were submitted to the Justice Department for section 5 preclearance, Assistant Attorney General Jerris Leonard wrote a letter to Mississippi attorney general A. F. Summer in which he neither objected to nor approved the change, indicating that he was unable to determine within the sixty-day period provided by section 5 for Justice Department objections whether the new laws were racially discriminatory or not. Writing that the issue was "extremely complex," Leonard noted that there were "some indications" of a discriminatory purpose but that the facts "do not conclusively establish that [the statutes] are afflicted with a racial purpose or that there is no other compelling reason for the State to have adopted them." He stated that he was "not prepared at this time . . . to make any determination of the validity or invalidity" of the statutes under the Voting Rights Act.[66]

Leonard's failure to object to the open primary laws had grave implications for section 5 enforcement. His letter indicated that he would not object even though there was evidence of a racially discriminatory purpose because the evidence was conflicting and he could not conclusively determine that the laws were racially motivated. But section 5 itself puts the burden of proof on the state or locality adopting the change to prove that the change is *not* racially discriminatory. Leonard's ruling, in effect, shifted the burden of proof to those opposing the change to prove conclusively that the laws had a racial purpose; his ruling amounted to a de facto repeal of section 5. The ruling came at a particularly critical time, since southern states were just beginning the processes of state legislative reapportionment and local redistricting following the 1970 census, and a number of Mississippi counties had instituted reregistration schemes that required all voters to reregister to vote.

Ironically, the usefulness of the section 5 enforcement process in blocking voting-law changes was saved by the hostility of three Mississippi federal judges to the preclearance requirement. After Leonard informed the Mississippi attorney general of his nondecision, Charles Evers and other black Mississippi voters, represented by the Lawyers' Committee for Civil Rights Under Law, then filed a lawsuit, *Evers v. State Board of Election Commissioners*, in district court in Mississippi seeking an injunction against the new statutes because they had not been subjected to proper section 5 review. The plaintiffs argued that, just as in section 5 judicial proceedings before the D.C. district court, the Justice Department was required to place the burden of proof on the submitting jurisdiction to show that the change was not racially discriminatory. If the evidence was conflicting, the state had not met its burden of proof, and a section 5 objection must be lodged, they contended.

The three-judge district court, with Circuit Judge Charles Clark presiding, and also including District Judges Dan M. Russell, Jr., and Walter L. Nixon, Jr., surprisingly agreed with the plaintiffs and blocked implementation of the open primary law.[67] Their unsigned opinion burned with their personal hostility to section 5, referring to the statute as embodying a "vicious 'conquered province' theory" and remarking on "the State of Mississippi's humiliation in bringing its laws to Washington for bureaucratic approval."[68] But given the Supreme Court precedents of the *Allen* and *Perkins* decisions, which as judges they were bound to enforce, they directed their hostility instead to what they called "an obtuse, patronizing failure by the federal government official to discharge the duties Congress placed upon him."[69] The court ruled that Leonard's response was inadequate:

> The problem for Mississippi in the case at bar is that having done what Congress humbled her to do, she did not receive a letter of approval, or a disapproval or a mere failure to interpose an objection within the statutory time. Rather, she received a lengthy, Pilate-like response in which the Attorney General recognized he had the very duty we declare the statute imposed upon him, bemoaned Congress's failure to accept his predecessor's suggestion to leave the matter to the courts, declared that he was not prepared to make the determinations required by the act, but made no literal objection.[70]

The judges held that section 5 required the attorney general to make a determination whether the change was discriminatory and ordered that the new statutes were in "a state of suspended animation" because they "have not been subjected to the required federal scrutiny."[71]

The *Evers* decision could not have come at a more propitious time. Prior to the *Evers* decision, the administration had been circulating draft regulations that, consistent with Leonard's letter, shifted the burden of proving discrimination to the Justice Department and those opposing the change and required an affirmative finding of racially discriminatory purpose or effect before a section 5 objection could be made.[72] In Washington, a bipartisan group of senators who had led the effort to extend the Voting Rights Act in 1970, led by Senators Philip Hart of Michigan, Hugh Scott of Pennsylvania, and Jacob

Javits of New York, began negotiations with Leonard's successor as assistant attorney general, David Norman, to reverse the department's position on section 5 enforcement. They threatened the administration with adverse publicity "to make another Carswell situation out of this" (a reference to the public outcry against President Nixon's unsuccessful nomination of southern federal judge Harold Carswell to the Supreme Court) and to accuse the administration of selling out black voters in the South by de facto repeal of section 5. Republican leaders in Congress also became concerned that the proposed regulations, if implemented, could become a political liability for northern Republicans in the upcoming 1972 elections. As historian Steven Lawson has noted, "With a presidential election approaching in 1972, the Republican regime had to decide whether to follow a course that led to new recruits among white southerners at the expense of established GOP lawmakers from civil rights constituencies in the North."[73]

In the face of the adverse legal precedent supplied by the *Evers* case, the threat of opposition and adverse publicity from leading Republicans in Congress as well as national civil rights organizations, and scheduled oversight hearings by Representative Don Edwards in the House of Representatives, the administration decided that its draft regulations were legally and politically untenable and reversed its position. A month after the *Evers* decision, and on the first day of the Civil Rights Oversight Subcommittee hearings, the Justice Department released a new draft of its proposed section 5 regulations. The new draft placed the burden of proof on the jurisdiction submitting the change for section 5 review and specifically provided that "if the evidence as to the purpose or effect of the change is conflicting, and the Attorney General is unable to resolve the conflict within the 60-day period, he shall, consistent with the above described burden of proof applicable in the District Court, enter an objection and so notify the submitting authority."[74]

The regulations were issued in final form in September 1971 and updated in January 1981 and January 1987.[75] The Justice Department section 5 regulations describe what types of voting-law changes must be precleared, establish what must be contained in a section 5 submission from a covered state or locality, and provide administrative procedures for the processing of submissions.

The *Allen* decision thus resulted in the establishment of a federal enforcement bureaucracy to implement section 5, with a separate administrative unit within the Justice Department to review submitted changes and comprehensive federal regulations establishing coverage and administrative procedures for section 5 reviews. The bureaucracy, however, is not large or oppressive. The Section 5 Unit currently consists of about fifteen persons, mostly research analysts, and the vast majority of submitted changes are promptly precleared (only an average of slightly more than 2 percent of the submitted changes per year have been objected to).[76]

Despite this enforcement structure, as the episode involving Mississippi's open primary laws shows, whether the section 5 preclearance requirement is effective in blocking discriminatory voting-law changes depends on the quality of enforcement by the assistant attorney general in charge of the Civil Rights Division. Although the Voting Rights Act gives the attorney general the power to object, this power has been delegated to the assistant attorney general in charge of the Justice Department's civil rights division. This political appointee has broad decision-making power whether or not to object to a submitted change. He or she alone makes the final decision; he or she may or may not follow a staff recommendation to object. After the *Evers* decision, the Supreme Court ruled that administrative decisions not to object cannot be challenged in federal court.[77] When the Nixon administration left office, the quality of section 5 enforcement improved under the Ford and Carter administrations, although even the Justice Department policies under those administrations have been criticized.[78] The Reagan administration, however, was notable for its retreats and defaults in voting rights enforcement, and assistant attorney general William Bradford Reynolds was denied confirmation by the Senate Judiciary Committee as associate attorney general in 1985 in part because of his poor record in voting rights enforcement. Although Reynolds did object to a number of discriminatory voting-law changes, he also to an unprecedented degree failed to object to changes that subsequently were struck down by federal courts as racially discriminatory, overruled staff recommendations to object to discriminatory changes, and sided with covered jurisdictions in litigation aimed at enforcing the Voting Rights Act.[79]

The *Allen* decision also expanded the role of the U.S. District Court for the District of Columbia in reviewing voting-law changes adopted by states and localities covered by section 5. If a state or locality desires to contest a Justice Department section 5 objection, or wants to bypass the Justice Department review process altogether, it must file a lawsuit in the D.C. district court for a judicial declaration that the voting-law change is not racially discriminatory in purpose or effect. This exclusive grant of jurisdiction to the D.C. district court removes southern federal judges who might be hostile to voting rights enforcement from the section 5 review process. These section 5 lawsuits must be defended by Justice Department attorneys, although minority voters who are affected by the voting-law changes generally are permitted to intervene in such cases to oppose judicial approval of discriminatory laws. Because the D.C. district court has been considered to be one of the more liberal courts in the country, and because historically it has had more black judges than most district courts in the South, relatively few section 5 declaratory judgment cases have been filed. However, because appeals from D.C. district court decisions go directly to the Supreme Court, and because the Supreme Court has agreed to grant full appeals and render written opinions in a high proportion of these cases, this section 5 preclearance litigation has had a substantial impact on the legal standards governing section 5 review.[80]

Criticism of Section 5 and the Principle of Minority Vote Dilution

Most of the criticism of the *Allen* decision interpretation of the scope of section 5 to include electoral law changes not directly related to the act of voting has come from three sources: southern judges, officials of jurisdictions subject to the section 5 preclearance requirement and their representatives in Congress, and a few conservative scholars.

Supreme Court Justice Hugo Black, an Alabama native, although one of the strongest defenders of civil rights on the Warren Court, was extremely vocal in his criticism of the *Allen* decision when it was handed down. His criticism was leveled not so much at the principle of minority vote dilution but at the section 5 mechanism that required federal preclearance of voting-law changes. He agreed that if section 5 were valid, each of the voting-law changes involved in *Allen* was covered by the preclearance requirement.[81] Nevertheless, in the *Allen* case he reiterated his views expressed in his original dissent in *South Carolina v. Katzenbach*,[82] the 1966 Supreme Court case that upheld the constitutionality of section 5. Section 5, he believed, was reminiscent of the military occupation of the South during the Reconstruction period, treated southern states like "conquered provinces," required them to "go to a United States Attorney General or a District of Columbia court with hat in hand begging for permission to change their laws," and constituted an unconstitutional interference with state sovereignty.[83]

Although, as the decision in the *Evers* case described above indicates, other southern federal judges agreed with Justice Black's views, no other Supreme Court Justice joined his dissent in *Allen*.[84] As the Court's majority opinion in *South Carolina v. Katzenbach* made clear, the majority considered section 5 to be "clearly a legitimate response to the problem." There was a demonstrated need for section

5. Case-by-case litigation had proven to be inadequate to overcome the systematic resistance to minority voting rights, and Congress was justified in shifting "the advantage of time and inertia from the perpetrators of the evil to its victims." Further, section 5's coverage was narrowly tailored to those states and political subdivisions which in the past had used literacy tests and other discriminatory voter registration restrictions, which had depressed rates of voter registration and voting, and where future voting discrimination was most likely to occur.[85]

The efficacy of section 5's preclearance requirement was clearly demonstrated by the *Allen* decision and subsequent Supreme Court decisions. Although Justice Black again dissented in the *Perkins* case, involving municipal annexations, polling place changes, and at-large elections in Canton, Mississippi, the Court's two most recent appointees, Justice Harry Blackmun and Chief Justice Warren Burger, accepted the *Allen* decision as binding in the *Perkins* decision and concurred with the majority opinion.[86] However, Justice Lewis Powell of Virginia, after his appointment to the Supreme Court in 1972, agreed with Justice Black's criticism that section 5 is "a serious intrusion, incompatible with the basic structure of our system, for federal authorities to compel a State to submit its legislation for *advance* review."[87] Although Justice Powell has received praise for his fairness, even-handedness, and willingness to follow Supreme Court precedents in civil rights cases while on the Court, he remained hostile to section 5. He was the author of Supreme Court decisions limiting the scope of section 5 and frequently dissented from Supreme Court decisions applying the *Allen* precedent and expanding it.[88]

Similar criticisms were voiced by conservative and southern members of Congress when section 5 came up for renewal in 1970, 1975, and 1982.[89] However, this criticism was unavailing as Congress extended section 5 all three times. But by 1982 the expansion of the black electorate and the increase in the number of black elected officials produced by the Voting Rights Act had a definite political impact. There was little opposition to the extension of section 5 based on the "conquered province" rhetoric—even the Reagan administration supported a ten-year extension. The act's extension was passed overwhelmingly by both houses of Congress, and as shown on table 6.2, a majority of most southern delegations, even senators and representatives who had opposed extension in the past, were aware of the political impact of the black vote and voted for the extension. The Voting Rights Act has thus become the political instrument of its own perpetuation.

Some conservative scholars have criticized the *Allen* decision and the minority vote dilution principle embodied in it. Their criticisms

Table 6.2. Votes of Congressional Delegations from States Covered by Section 5 of the Voting Rights Act on Passage of the Act in 1965 and Its Extension in 1970, 1975, and 1982

	1965			1970			1975			1981–82		
	For	Against	Not Voting	For	Against	Not Voting	For	Against	Not Voting	For	Against	Not Voting
Alabama	0	10	0	1	9	0	3	6	0	5	4	0
Alaska	3	0	0	0	3	1	3	0	0	3	0	0
Georgia	2	10	0	1	9	2	3	7	2	10	2	0
Louisiana	2	4	1	2	6	2	5	4	1	10	0	0
Mississippi	0	7	0	0	7	0	0	6	1	5	2	0
North Carolina[a]	0	12	1	3	9	1	12	1	0	9	3	1
South Carolina	0	8	0	0	6	2	6	2	0	8	0	0
Virginia	1	11	0	2	10	0	2	10	0	2	10	0
Additional whole states covered in 1975												
Arizona							3	1	2	3	2	1
Texas							15	7	4	23	2	1

Note: This table omits states in which only a few counties or cities are covered.

[a] Forty counties covered.

resurrect the long-discredited argument that the *Allen* decision was an unjustified expansion of the scope of section 5, and these critics contend that the minority vote dilution principle abuses the democratic process and constitutes an invidious racial preference for minority voters.

One leading conservative critic of these developments is political scientist Abigail Thernstrom in her book *Whose Votes Count?* published in 1987.[90] Thernstrom argues, first, that the only purpose of the Voting Rights Act was to secure the right to register and vote, and the Supreme Court's expansive interpretation of section 5 in the *Allen* decision violated the original intent of Congress: "The initial understanding of section 5 thus envisioned objections only to innovations involving registration and the mechanics of voting. Quite suddenly, however, a much broader view emerged—one that allowed the Department of Justice to review annexations, new district lines, and other changes affecting minority voting strength."[91] The *Allen* decision, she contends, "marked a radical change in the meaning of the act. . . . Thus the door was opened to unprecedented federal involvement in local electoral matters."[92]

Thernstrom's argument rests on a very selective reading of the legislative history of the Voting Rights Act. In arguing that Congress intended that section 5 should be "narrowly defined,"[93] she gives undue emphasis to isolated statements of civil rights leaders in the congressional hearings and ignores those authoritative portions of the legislative history that Chief Justice Earl Warren relied upon in the *Allen* decision in concluding that Congress intended section 5 to have the broadest possible scope.[94] Thus, Thernstrom omits the fact that the statutory description of covered categories was expanded to include any "standard, practice, or procedure" because Senator Fong was concerned that the reference only to "procedure" in the original draft was too narrow, and she omits Attorney General Katzenbach's response that the coverage "was intended to be all-inclusive of any kind of practice."[95] She also neglects to note that Congress failed to engraft any exceptions onto section 5, even though Katzenbach agreed that some types of changes could be excluded, another point that persuaded the Supreme Court that Congress intended to include all changes, regardless of how minor.[96] Legal scholar and voting rights attorney Pamela Karlan and historian Peyton McCrary also have pointed out that Thernstrom's argument is undermined by the fact that *Gomillion v. Lightfoot*, the Tuskegee, Alabama, gerrymandering case, and changes in the boundaries of voting districts were discussed in the House hearings and in the House Judiciary Committee report.[97]

Thus, Thernstrom clearly is wrong when she argues that the Supreme Court in the *Allen* decision exceeded the congressional mandate. The thrust of her argument is that the *Allen* case was wrongly decided, but, in contradiction to her argument, Thernstrom then concedes that the *Allen* decision "was both correct and inevitable."[98] Chief Justice Warren's central point, that the right to vote can be affected as much by dilution as by denial, "did have merit." She recognizes, as the Mississippi cases illustrate, that at-large voting does nullify black voters' ability to elect candidates of their choice when "white voters consistently voted as a bloc against candidates (white or black) preferred by blacks. Elections would then amount to a racial census, with the result that blacks in a majority-white jurisdiction would have nothing to lose by remaining home on election day. The breakdown of registrants by race would determine the outcome."[99]

Moreover, the argument over whether the *Allen* case was correctly decided is now merely academic. What Thernstrom also fails to note is that today the question of what Congress intended in 1965 is a moot point. When Congress extended section 5 in 1970, 1975, and 1982, it voted down all amendments to repeal or limit the scope of section 5 and fully endorsed the Supreme Court's interpretation of section 5 in the *Allen* decision. These actions fully confirm that the Supreme Court's decision was correct and give continuing congressional endorsement to the broad interpretation of section 5 coverage. Similarly, subsequent Supreme Court decisions have reaffirmed the *Allen* precedent.

The more serious challenge raised in Thernstrom's book goes to the question of the minority vote dilution principle itself. By accepting this dilution principle, Thernstrom contends, "*Allen v. Board of Elections* began the process by which the Voting Rights Act was reshaped into an instrument for affirmative action in the electoral sphere."[100] Thus, she attempts to make minority voting rights an "affirmative action issue": it "is perhaps the most debatable, yet the least debated, of all affirmative action issues."[101] She charges that the minority vote dilution principle grants minorities an "entitlement" to proportional representation and operates to shield minority candidates from electoral competition: "The question is: How much special protection from white competition are black candidates entitled to?"[102] In her view, the conditions that required this protection for minority voting rights have "all but disappeared,"[103] and such protection hampers efforts to achieve a color-blind society by "categorizing individuals for political purposes along racial lines and sanctioning group membership as a qualification for office."[104] In an earlier article that was expanded into her book, Thernstrom charged that Chief Justice War-

ren, in the *Allen* decision, "is envisioning color-coordinated politics—
the color of the candidate unfailingly matching the color of his con-
stituency," and that incorporating this "depressing political assumption into the Voting Rights Act is costly, for it produces a society in
which political interests are defined by racial or ethnic identity and
representation is guaranteed in proportion to groups' numerical
strength."[105] Thernstrom contends that this "may inhibit political integration" and lessens "the pressure for . . . interracial, interethnic
coalitions."[106] She does not set out a specific solution to remedy the
evils she projects, except to suggest that statutory protections for minority voting rights should be cut back and limited to rare and extreme cases in which minorities are completely "isolated" and totally
excluded from any electoral influence.[107]

Thernstrom's arguments make factual assertions and assumptions
that are inconsistent with the history and reality of southern politics,
as set out in this book, that produced this remedy. First, as the discussion in chapter 2 and the subsequent chapters indicates, it was not
the *Allen* court that first introduced the question of race into politics
or defined political interests by racial identity. The history of southern
politics is the history of racial suppression of the black vote. The *Allen*
decision was a response to the race-conscious actions of the Mississippi Legislature that attempted to nullify the Voting Rights Act by
enacting the 1966 massive resistance legislation to negate black voting strength. To deny black voters a remedy for such voting discrimination in the name of avoiding "a society in which political interests
are defined by racial or ethnic identity" would be both to ignore the
purpose and effect of that massive resistance legislation and to re-
ward the perpetrators of this discrimination by granting them victory.

Second, the minority vote dilution principle grants minority voters
a remedy from discrimination, not an entitlement to proportional
representation. Discriminatory vote-dilution mechanisms are adopted
with the purpose or effect of depriving minority voters of the opportunity to elect candidates of their choice; the vote-dilution principle
identifies the violation and redresses the deprivation. It is not a question of providing black candidates with "special protection from
white competition." As Richard Engstrom and Michael McDonald
have pointed out, the essence of a racial vote dilution claim is that
"the electoral system in a particular political jurisdiction structures
electoral competition unfairly" so as to "impair the ability of minority
group voters to convert their votes into the election of candidates of
their choice."[108] So long as governmental units continue to structure
the electoral process unfairly in a manner that denies minority voters
an equal opportunity to elect candidates of their choice, judicial intervention will continue to be required.

To label this judicial intervention as granting minority voters a racial preference or an improper "entitlement" to "special protection from white competition" grossly mischaracterizes the history of white efforts to impede minority electoral participation and the functions of remedies for voting discrimination. Thernstrom's argument rests on a preference for the status quo, which she assumes is "the work of a democratic process."[109] But is it the work of the "democratic process" for an all-white Mississippi Legislature (from which blacks have been excluded by systematic denial of the right to vote) to pass statutes that prevent black voters from electing candidates of their choice to office? Do whites have a stronger "entitlement" to a discriminatory status quo that should not be trampled by judicial efforts on the part of diluted minority voters? Moreover, creating majority-black districts as a remedy for illegal vote dilution does not structure electoral competition unfairly but simply gives both white and black candidates an opportunity to compete for black votes and gives black voters an opportunity to hold their elected officials—white or black—electorally accountable.

The 1982 amendment to section 2 of the Voting Rights Act—the statutory embodiment of the minority vote dilution principle—expressly disavows any intent on the part of Congress to create a right to proportional representation. The statute expressly states, "*Provided,* That nothing in this section establishes a right to have members of a protected class elected in numbers equal to their proportion in the population."[110] The Supreme Court has held that to obtain judicial relief under section 2, proof of minority underrepresentation alone is not sufficient. Minority voters must prove that under the "totality of circumstances" the challenged law operates in a discriminatory manner, and this requires, among other factors, evidence that white bloc voting denies minority voters an equal opportunity to elect representatives of their choice.[111] This requirement points up yet another inconsistency in Thernstrom's argument. As previously noted, Thernstrom concedes that vote-dilution claims have merit in a "setting . . . in which white voters consistently voted as a bloc against candidates (white or black) preferred by blacks." Because section 2 requires such proof, the 1982 statute in fact satisfies Thernstrom's condition under which vote-dilution claims "have merit," though she continues to criticize the statute throughout her book.

Nor has the operation of the minority vote dilution principle for the past twenty years resulted in proportional representation for blacks. According to the Joint Center for Political Studies' 1989 national roster of black elected officials, black elected officials hold only 646 of Mississippi's 4,950 elective offices, or only about 13 percent, in a state that is 35 percent black in population and 31 percent black in voting-age population.[112] Black elected officials constitute only 13 percent of the membership of the Mississippi Legislature (22 out of 174), only 17 percent of the total number of county supervisors (68 out of 410), and only 18 percent of the total number of city council members (282 out of 1,529). Thus, for Mississippi, the minority vote dilution principle has not come even close to producing a society in which "representation is guaranteed in proportion to groups' numerical strength." If anything, black citizens have a valid complaint that the legal and political system still has failed to provide them with political equality, and that they continue to be victimized by the racism of a political system that confines them to black representation only in black majority districts.

Finally, the rhetoric of arguments such as Thernstrom's that call for a rollback of legal protections for minority voting rights in the name of eliminating what she calls "entitlements" to "proportional representation" is uncomfortably reminiscent of the courtroom rhetoric of Mississippi's state attorney general in defending the state's massive resistance program. In 1966, Mississippi attorney general Joe T. Patterson, in defending the state legislature's gerrymandered congressional districts, argued to the court that granting the *Connor* plaintiffs relief would be equivalent to manipulating the electoral process to "guarantee the election of Negro candidates" and provide "a segregated congressional district in favor of the non-white population." Viewed in the Mississippi context described in the preceding chapters, the vote-dilution principle performed a useful service in opening up the political process to equal black voter participation in the face of successive actions to nullify it. But for the judicial intervention taken to protect the black vote, the Mississippi Legislature would have been successful in its efforts to maintain white supremacy in Mississippi politics. Mike Espy, Mississippi's first black member of Congress in this century, would never have been elected; the state legislature, which now has twenty-two black legislators, would have remained all white or almost all white; and Mississippi's black voters would never have been able to elect sixty-eight black county supervisors.

In sum, the struggle of black voters in Mississippi to overcome the state's massive resistance program played a decisive role in awakening the Supreme Court, the Congress, and the nation as a whole to the need to protect minority voting rights from denial through vote dilution. The Mississippi litigation brought home the realization that the struggle for the minority vote was entering a new phase, and that the literacy tests and the poll taxes had been replaced by a second generation of more sophisticated devices that permitted black voters to vote but discounted the weight of their ballots. The Mississippi struggle invigorated the section 5 preclearance requirement as a strong protection against discriminatory new voting-law changes and helped establish new national legal standards for protecting against minority vote dilution devices that were not covered by section 5.

The country soon saw that the important principles of minority vote dilution this litigation established could not be confined to Mississippi. At-large elections that perpetuate all-white government and prevent black voters from electing candidates of their choice are equally discriminatory whether they are in Forrest County, Mississippi, Dallas County, Texas, or Springfield, Illinois. The Mississippi struggle thus triggered a national movement for the elimination of racially discriminatory vote dilution mechanisms that involves both litigation and legislation and that continues at work today to make the right to vote a reality for minority voters throughout the country.

7 Race and Mississippi Politics
Changes and Continuities

Historically, race has been the central theme of Mississippi politics. Writing in 1949, political scientist V. O. Key, Jr., concluded that "the beginning and the end of Mississippi politics is the Negro."[1] This author has surveyed elements of the racial politics of Mississippi for the past thirty years, beginning with the suppression of the black vote in the early 1960s and the passage of the Voting Rights Act of 1965 that liberated black citizens from their bondage of disfranchisement. The author has demonstrated that despite the fact that large numbers of black citizens soon became registered to vote they found that they were unable to elect more than a handful of black candidates to office. The political massive resistance statutes of the 1966 session of the Mississippi Legislature, together with existing discriminatory election structures such as at-large municipal elections, erected strong barriers to the effectiveness of the new black vote. Black citizens were able to register and vote, but in many parts of the state they were unable to elect candidates of their choice to office.

Overcoming these barriers took years of litigation, and despite the hostility of some Mississippi federal judges this litigation ultimately was largely successful. Among other successes, the large multimember state legislative districts were broken up into smaller single-member districts statewide, at-large election of county supervisors and school board members was struck down, extensive racial gerrymandering of county supervisors' district lines was successfully challenged, and at-large elections for city council members were widely eliminated. Once these barriers were struck down, large numbers of black candidates were able to win election to legislative, county, and city offices. Mississippi, which previously had the lowest number of black elected officials of any state in the nation, became the state with the highest number. Beyond its impact in increasing the number of black officials in the state, this litigation also had an enormous impact on national voting rights policy and advanced the expansion of the legal protections for minority voting rights nationwide.

This concluding chapter looks at several questions raised by the changes which have occurred: What overall impact has this dramatic emergence of black political participation had on the politics of Mississippi? Has it diminished racism as a factor in state politics in any significant way? Has the legal struggle for minority voting rights run its course, or are there barriers that remain? And finally, what do the events described indicate regarding the existence of a national consensus that minority votes should not be diluted? At this point in time, it may be too early to give definitive answers to such complex, ultimate questions, but some tentative responses may be suggested.

The Impact of Black Political Emergence

First, the most immediate impact of the increase in black voter registration after 1965 and the increase in black elected officials was a decline in the systematic use of terrorism by whites as a method of political and social control of black Mississippians noted in chapter 1. As Frances Fox Piven and Richard A. Cloward point out in their book *Poor Peoples' Movements*, violence and intimidation—whether in the form of police violence, lynch mobs, individual attacks on blacks, arbitrary imprisonment, or economic intimidation—historically have been the primary methods by which whites have enforced the political and social caste system in the South to keep blacks in their place. "In the South," the authors note, "the deepest meaning of the winning of democratic political rights is that the historical primacy of terror as a means of social control has been substantially diminished."[2] Using a wide variety of sources, political scientist David C. Colby has documented that white violence in Mississippi reached its peak during 1964 and 1965 in reaction to the high level of civil rights activity in the state and dropped dramatically after 1965. Colby notes that much of the economic intimidation and attacks against blacks during this period was specifically aimed at preventing blacks from registering and voting. But once Mississippi's black people gained the vote and began to elect public officials, the violence subsided because further use of violent methods was futile, and black people now had the political and legal means to counter it.[3]

This is not to say that racial violence against blacks in Mississippi has been eliminated. Historically, Mississippi has had a violent society, and individual and group acts of racial violence continue to occur. During 1988 the first black fraternity house on Fraternity Row at the University of Mississippi was destroyed by fire, and black Representative Mike Espy's house was vandalized and defaced with racial epithets. Incidents such as these have served, as Georgia writer Anne

Siddons told V. S. Naipaul in referring to the attack on black marchers in Forsyth County, Georgia, as shocking reminders that "*it*, the
Southern violence, wasn't dead."[4] But the black political emergence
has, to a great extent, mitigated the opportunities of whites to use
violence systemically as a method of political and social control without fear of punishment or retribution.

A second impact of the black political emergence has been to curtail the use of racial demagoguery in political campaigns as a technique for winning elections. In the early part of this century Mississippi was the home of two of the most virulent racial demagogues in
American history—James K. Vardaman and Theodore G. Bilbo. After
the *Brown v. Board of Education* decision in 1954, Mississippi had a suc-
cession of gubernatorial campaigns in which the winning candidate
was the one who was the most successful in appealing to the racist
sentiments of white voters—Ross Barnett in 1959, Paul Johnson, Jr.,
in 1963, and John Bell Williams in 1967. In the 1971 governor's race,
for the first time in the modern history of the state the two leading
candidates—William Waller and Charles Sullivan—did not campaign
as segregationists. Waller's election in 1971 marked the beginning of
the transition in Mississippi politics to ending the dominance of traditional segregationist rhetoric in statewide campaigns.[5] After 1971,
none of the winning candidates for governor have employed open racial rhetoric in their campaigns, and in fact the candidates have appealed to black voters to get elected. This reflects the increased political importance of the black vote but also the fact that, to a great
extent, segregationist campaigning has become an exercise in futility.
Candidates can no longer credibly pledge to keep the public schools
segregated when the public schools have been desegregated by court
order.

Although the most vicious racial demagoguery has been eliminated as a successful tactic in statewide races, it continues to appear
in covert, disguised forms. Jerry Himelstein has shown that the rhetorical themes used by white Mississippi politicians in their die-hard
defense of white political supremacy and racial segregation in the
1950s and 1960s are still being invoked in sanitized forms that avoid
overt references to race through the use of code words and other con-
cealed messages that appeal to lingering antiblack sentiments.[6] Thus,
changes that would benefit blacks, such as eliminating at-large elections, are opposed because they would upset an alleged existing state
of racial harmony and produce discord and divisiveness, would lead
to federal court and Justice Department intervention in local affairs,
and are the products of outside agitation. In the 1950s and 1960s,
these themes would be accompanied by overt racial references and

derogatory remarks concerning blacks; now the racial references are omitted, but the rhetorical themes still are used. Himelstein argues that these themes continue as "code words" that communicate "a well-understood but implicit meaning to part of a public audience while preserving for the speaker deniability of that meaning by reference to its denotative explicit meaning." In other words, they function as "rhetorical winks."[7]

Racial campaigning also continues to occur through white in-group references and appeals to Mississippi's "traditions." Thus, Republican Webb Franklin won the 1982 race in the Second Congressional District over black legislator Robert Clark by appealing to white votes with the campaign slogan "He's One of Us" and with a television ad with this voice-over narrative:

> You know, there's something about Mississippi that outsiders will never, ever understand. The way we feel about our family and God, and the traditions that we have. There is a new Mississippi, a Mississippi of new jobs and new opportunity for all our citizens [video pan of black factory workers]. We welcome the new, but we must never, ever forget what has gone before [video pan of Confederate monuments]. We cannot forget a heritage that has been sacred through our generations.[8]

A third impact is the change in white state leadership produced by the important, sometimes decisive, influence of black voting in statewide elections, despite the fact that black voters do not have a statewide black majority. Once black voters reached 28 to 30 percent of the statewide electorate, they gained the power frequently to supply the margin of victory in statewide races between competing white candidates. After 1971, black voters had substantial influence in gubernatorial voting and were part of the winning coalition that elected Cliff Finch governor in 1975, William Winter in 1979, Bill Allain in 1983, and Ray Mabus in 1987. In the 1987 governor's race, Mabus received only about 40 percent of the white vote but was elected in what news reporters describe as "one of the narrowest gubernatorial campaign victories in Mississippi history" because he won at least 90 percent of the black vote.[9] This "swing vote" influence extends to some local offices as well in which black votes may be able to determine which of the competing white candidates gets elected, even when blacks do not have the majority voting power necessary to elect a black candidate. The statewide black vote was not sufficient, however, to prevent the election of Republican Trent Lott in 1988 to the U.S. Senate seat vacated by the retirement of Senator John Stennis. Black voters generally supported Lott's opponent, Democratic representative Wayne Dowdy. But Lott, who had instigated a number of the Reagan administration's anti–civil rights policies while in the House of Representatives, such as persuading the administration to attempt to restore tax-exempt status to segregated public schools, carried the state.

The political empowerment of black voters has also produced changes in the black leadership of the state as well. To a substantial extent the leadership roles of the civil rights leaders of the 1960s, such as Aaron Henry and Charles Evers, have been superseded by a younger generation of black elected officials, including Hinds County Supervisor Bennie Thompson, Representative Mike Espy, state Democratic party Chair Ed Cole, and others.[10] The election of these black officials to office has put them in positions of public exposure, prominence, and political influence to provide new political leadership in the state. The leadership authority of some of the civil rights veterans of the 1960s persists, however. Henry continues to wield clout by retaining his post as state president of the NAACP, and civil rights activists such as Henry J. Kirksey continue to influence black public opinion by raising important issues of concern to the black community.

A fourth impact relates to the issue of whether there has been any significant change in white attitudes on racial matters. Overall, the increase in black voting and the number of black elected officials is one significant element in the totality of changes in Mississippi in the past twenty years that have influenced white attitudes. The reaction of the all-white legislature in 1966 was evidence of the pervasive fear in the white community of blacks holding elective office, a fear stemming in part from the Reconstruction myth that black officials were illiterate, incompetent, and corrupt.[11] The election of large numbers of capable black officials has disproven this myth and mitigated this paranoid aversion to blacks holding office.

Other significant changes that have affected Mississippi society and white attitudes include the state's increased urbanization and industrialization, public school desegregation, generational turnover, in-migration of whites from outside the state, and the influence of television, among other factors. These changes, of which the black political movement is a major element, have produced significant changes in white attitudes on racial issues. A 1981 Mississippi State University survey reported that 68 percent of whites surveyed were in favor of school integration, 60 percent were for open housing, and 67 percent were in favor of the Voting Rights Act.[12] The survey apparently did not ask white Mississippians such questions as whether they would send their children to a predominantly black school or welcome a black family moving in next door, to which the positive responses would likely be much lower. But at least these survey results show that the overall attitudes of white Mississippians on racial issues are now much closer to those of whites in other southern states and to whites nationally.

Nevertheless, racism has not been eliminated as a critical element in Mississippi politics. Racial prejudice continues to be demonstrated in statewide votes on public policy issues and in racial bloc voting for candidates. In 1987 there was a statewide referendum on whether to repeal the section of Mississippi's state constitution banning interracial marriages. In a sense, the issue was moot; the section had long since been rendered unenforceable by Supreme Court decisions. Nonetheless, 48 percent of Mississippi's voters voted in favor of retaining the ban on interracial marriages. Two years later, Mississippi had a statewide referendum on whether to repeal the state's poll tax that had been voided twenty-four years earlier by the Voting Rights Act. Although a majority of the voters supported repealing the unenforceable poll tax, 42 percent voted to retain it.

In state and local elections, which can be considered as ultimate polls of racial attitudes, strict patterns of racially polarized voting continue to prevail, and the vast majority of white voters still consistently refuse to vote for black candidates. As the discussion in chapter 5 shows, the black state legislators, county supervisors, city council members, and other black elected officials generally have been elected from majority-black districts. The evidence produced in a recent lawsuit challenging at-large election of state court judges showed that in the area in which the vast majority of black officials have been elected (generally the western portion of the state), there were only nineteen black elected officials from districts that were less than 65 percent black, and statewide, there were only four black elected officials who have been elected in majority-white districts.[13] The persistence of white bloc voting and the continued need for 65 percent black districts was again demonstrated in the state judicial elections held in the spring of 1989. As described later in this chapter, a federal district court in Mississippi struck down at-large elections for state court judges in eight judicial districts for dilution of black voting strength. The district court then adopted a redistricting plan devised by a court-appointed expert that divided these multimember judicial districts into single-member districts, fourteen of which were majority-black in population. However, citing Espy's 1986 success and the election of a handful of black officials from districts that were less than 65 percent black, the district judge ruled that districts higher than 65 percent black should be "avoided." He reasoned that "packing of all minority voters into one sub-district would leave them without influence in other sub-districts and would further racially politicize these judicial elections."[14] As a result, only three of the fourteen majority-black districts were over 65 percent black. The consequences of placing a 65-percent cap on these judicial districts, when previously that percentage had been considered the minimum necessary for black voters to elect candidates of their choice, were disastrous for all but a few black judicial candidates in the spring 1989 elections. Although seventeen black candidates ran for state court judgeships, only five were elected. Three of the five who won were elected in districts that were over 65 percent black. The defeat of most of the black candidates prompted one of the attorneys for the plaintiffs, Carroll Rhodes, to remark, "In spite of some black leaders' allegations that there is no more discrimination in Mississippi, these election results are a clear indication that discrimination is alive and well in Mississippi and will probably be around for some time to come."[15]

This means that although Mississippi leads the nation in the number of black elected officials, this fact alone does not indicate that state politics are biracial. Unlike some other southern states in which black mayors and other officials have been elected as the result of biracial voting coalitions, Mississippi politics at the voting level continues to remain strictly divided along racial lines. Mississippi, the testing ground for minority voting rights and the barometer of civil rights progress, remains in a transitional period without true biracial politics.

Elements of the recent past continue to reappear. In 1986 the Mississippi Legislature passed a law—touted as an education reform measure—requiring countywide referendums in each county on whether to switch from election to appointment of the county school superintendent, a statute almost identical (but without requiring the change in particular counties) to the massive resistance statute enacted in 1966 that was involved in the *Allen* case.[16] (All the counties voted the change down.) Similarly, in 1986, as part of a revamping of the state election code, the state legislature passed a statute requiring independent candidates for office to qualify to run at the same time as party candidates,[17] a provision that had been contained both in the independent candidate law that was before the Supreme Court in the *Allen* case and in the open primary laws. Although similar provisions had received section 5 objections by prior administrations, both of them were precleared by the Reagan administration's Justice Department. Whether these statutes represent the beginning of a new effort to dilute black voting power in Mississippi remains to be seen. But certainly the Reagan administration's approval of these two measures in the face of an extensive record of prior section 5 objections to almost identical measures has the potential for encouraging renewed attempts to discriminate by covered jurisdictions.

The Continuing Struggle for Equal Voting Rights

The continued polarization of Mississippi politics also indicates that blacks remain dependent upon voting rights litigation to remove the remaining barriers to equal black political participation. Two recent court cases in Mississippi show that this legal struggle is a continuing one, and that litigation continues to be required. The two most recent statewide cases in Mississippi have involved challenges to the state's continued restrictions on voter registration and to the at-large election of state court judges.

The voter registration case brought voting rights litigation in Mississippi full circle, from the Justice Department's voter registration cases of the 1960s, through litigation against the full spectrum of structural barriers, and back to voter registration. In 1987 the district court in *Mississippi State Chapter, Operation PUSH v. Allain*, a lawsuit promoted by the Reverend Jesse Jackson and filed by black voters represented by the NAACP Legal Defense Fund and the Lawyers' Committee for Civil Rights Under Law, held that there were still racially discriminatory barriers to voter registration in Mississippi that violated section 2 of the Voting Rights Act. The court ruled that in spite of the gains in black voter registration under the 1965 act, only 54 percent of Mississippi's eligible black population was registered to vote, as compared with 79 percent of the eligible white population, because of continued discriminatory restrictions on the right to register to vote.[18] Despite the Voting Rights Act's prohibitions against discriminatory tests and the poll tax, Mississippi was able to retain its "dual registration" requirement, one of the elements of the Mississippi Plan of 1890, that required voters who live in cities and towns to register first with the county circuit clerk to vote in federal, state, and county elections and again with the municipal clerk to vote in municipal elections. Further, Mississippi was able to retain a state statute, enacted in 1955 with a series of discriminatory statutes after the Supreme Court's *Brown v. Board of Education* decision, that prevented the circuit clerks from registering voters outside their offices in the absence of the express permission of the county board of supervisors. Prior law had made satellite registration mandatory in each statewide election year.[19]

The court ruled that both statutes were enacted for a discriminatory purpose and had a discriminatory impact. Substantial numbers of black voters apparently were not informed of the dual registration requirement when they registered to vote with the circuit clerks or were otherwise unaware of the requirement, and disproportionate numbers of black voters have been denied the ballot in municipal elections in Mississippi because they had failed to register again with their municipal clerks.[20] (Although the Mississippi Legislature amended the dual registration requirement in 1984 after this lawsuit was filed to make it less restrictive by appointing some municipal clerks deputy county registrars, some vestiges of the requirement remained.) Further, the prohibition on satellite registration restricted voter registration to the circuit clerk's offices during regular business hours during the week. Because disproportionate numbers of black people in Mississippi work in blue-collar and service jobs for an hourly wage, they are less likely to be able to leave their jobs during the workweek to register to vote. In addition, large numbers of black families lack their own transportation necessary to get to the county courthouse to register to vote. Black poverty in Mississippi continues to be so pervasive that 27.8 percent of all black households have no motor vehicle available at home for household use, as compared with only 6.76 percent of all white families.[21] The court victory in *Mississippi State Chapter, Operation PUSH v. Allain* was the first successful challenge to statewide voter registration procedures for restrictions on time and place of registration and established an important precedent that can be used nationwide to challenge similar restrictions.[22]

In the second case, *Martin v. Allain/Mabus*, black voters represented by the same two legal organizations filed two lawsuits challenging at-large election of state court judges. Voting rights attorney Robert B. McDuff has said that at-large judicial elections "have created one of the last enclaves of segregation among elected officials in state and local government."[23] As late as 1988, of Mississippi's 102 state court trial judges (circuit, chancery, and county court judges), only one was black, and this judge—Circuit Judge Fred L. Banks, Jr., of Hinds County—was appointed to the position by Governor Bill Allain to fill a vacancy. In 1987 the district court in Mississippi ruled that judicial elections were covered by section 2 of the Voting Rights Act and held that at-large judicial elections in districts in which majority-black single-member districts could be created had to be dismantled.[24] The *Martin* decision was the first case in the country to strike down at-large judicial elections for violation of section 2 of the Voting Rights Act, and it has spawned similar lawsuits in Louisiana, Alabama, Texas, Ohio, Illinois, and North Carolina.[25]

Both of these Mississippi cases, *PUSH v. Allain* and *Martin v. Allain/Mabus*, show that more than twenty years after the Voting Rights Act was passed discriminatory barriers continue to deny black voters the opportunity to register to vote and to elect candidates of their choice and that new law is still being made in Mississippi in the voting rights area.

The National Consensus on Voting Rights

During the period described in this book, a broad-based national consensus, crossing party and ideological lines, appeared to develop that supported strong statutory and judicial protection for minority voting rights that played a critical role in the results achieved, symbolized by the passage of the Voting Rights Act in 1965, its extension in 1970 and 1975, and the extension and strengthening of the act in 1982. When the Voting Rights Act came up for renewal in 1981–82, the nation had the most conservative president in decades, the administration strongly opposed the civil rights coalition's bill, and Senator Strom Thurmond of South Carolina, long an opponent of civil rights legislation, was chair of the Senate Judiciary Committee. Despite all this, the Senate Judiciary Committee reported out, Congress passed, and President Reagan signed into law the strongest Voting Rights Act ever that extended the protections of section 5 for twenty-five years (the longest previous extension had been for seven years), and that amended section 2 to overrule the *Mobile* decision and eliminate the necessity of proving discriminatory intent.

Similarly, the Supreme Court, once it realized the enormity of the problem of negation of black votes in the South, developed new legal principles that extended the vote-dilution principle of the one-person, one-vote decisions, first to section 5 of the Voting Rights Act, and then to the Fourteenth Amendment itself. In the Mississippi Legislature reapportionment case, during a period in which the Court was becoming more conservative on civil rights matters generally, the Court repeatedly reversed adverse decisions of the district court and employed extraordinary procedures, such as shortening schedules for briefs and oral argument, and even more extraordinary, entertaining petitions for mandamus, to force the district court into ordering nondiscriminatory single-member districts for the state legislature. The almost total exclusion of black representation, in a state that was 35 percent black, was apparently too much even for some of the Court's most conservative members (although none of these actions were taken totally without dissents). To be sure, the Court took a decidedly backward step in *City of Mobile v. Bolden* when it ruled that Mobile's at-large election system was not unconstitutional without direct evidence of discriminatory intent. But the widespread outcry against the *Mobile* decision in the legal literature and in Congress forced the Court to reverse itself in *Rogers v. Lodge* to make discriminatory intent easier to prove. Then, after the section 2 amendment, the Court accepted the new "results" test and made proof of voting discrimination even easier in *Thornburg v. Gingles.*[26]

The dramatic increase in the number of black elected officials—which is still continuing—today is one of the strongest and most enduring legacies of the civil rights movement of the 1960s. In an era in which other civil rights gains, including busing for school desegregation and hiring quotas, are increasingly criticized and jeopardized, strong protections for minority voting rights appear to be thriving. Why? Certainly the civil rights movement of the 1960s brought into clearer focus the contradiction between the nation's democratic ideals and the denial of the vote to blacks, and the nation's governmental institutions acted to make democratic principles a reality. Today it is difficult to argue that blacks and other minorities should not be allowed to vote or, once minorities have the right to vote, barriers to allowing minority voters to elect candidates of their choice should not be removed. Further, the dramatic increases in black registration in the South and in the number of black elected officials throughout the country have multiplied the number of constituencies of state legislators and members of Congress in which the black vote is a critical political factor. Certainly the growth in black voting and black elected officials in South Carolina has greatly mitigated Thurmond's opposition to civil rights. The Reagan administration depended on southern Democrats in the U.S. Senate to support the nomination of Robert Bork to the Supreme Court. Yet all the southern Democrats, with the exception of Ernest Hollings of South Carolina, who previously had committed himself for Bork, voted against the nomination despite the fact that they were under intense pressure from white constituents to confirm Bork.

Moreover, white opposition to remedies protecting minority voting rights is not as pronounced as it is to the remedies developed in other civil rights areas. Contrary to the argument of Thernstrom and others, the question of strong protections for minority voting cannot properly be characterized—and is not widely perceived—as an affirmative action issue because the impact on the personal lives of most whites is substantially less than, say, busing or hiring quotas. The creation of majority-black single-member districts may dislodge incumbent white officials who are replaced by black officials (although this does not always happen). But, as Karlan and McCrary have pointed out, white politicians are not widely perceived as "victims" of "reverse discrimination." No individual officeholder has an entitlement to elective office.[27]

Further, strong protection for minority voting rights rarely threatens white political dominance. In no state legislature and in only a few of the most heavily black counties and cities have blacks gained a majority of the legislative seats. Thus, in most instances the creation of single-member districts or the elimination of gerrymandered districts has produced, not black control, but power-sharing among white and black legislators. Initially, particularly in the Deep South, any power-sharing at all was strenuously resisted, but as more black officials have been elected to office, southern whites generally appear to have come to terms with the necessity of black representation and sharing power with black officials. For example, in Jackson, Mississippi, when the section 2 lawsuit appeared to make the change to single-member districts inevitable, influential elements of the white political leadership and downtown business establishment supported the referendum to change Jackson's form of government. In part, they wanted to retain the ability to draw the district lines, but they also apparently believed that black representation in city government would end the controversy over exclusion of black representation and create a more stable environment for business growth and development.[28]

Whether this national consensus will continue depends upon several elements: continued growth in minority registration, political organizing, and the number of minority elected officials; a responsive president and Congress; and the continued responsiveness of the federal judiciary to minority voting rights. Certainly, the development of favorable judicial principles by the Supreme Court has been a vital element in the changes which have taken place, and continued progress is dependent upon the appointment of Supreme Court justices who have convincing records of civil rights commitment. This book has shown that full judicial protection against minority vote dilution has been critical to ensuring representative government and the proper functioning of the democratic process. Any effort to limit this judicial protection or to roll back the limited advances that have been made would have the most profound implications for the future of democratic government and race relations in this country.

Notes

Introduction

1. Cavanagh and Stockton, *Black Elected Officials*, p. 1; Joint Center for Political Studies, *Black Elected Officials* (1989), table 4.

2. Joint Center for Political Studies, *Black Elected Officials* (1989), table 3.

3. Quoted in Gamarekian, "One Woman's Chronicle," *New York Times*, Aug. 31, 1987.

4. See, e.g., Engstrom and McDonald, "The Election of Blacks to Southern City Councils"; Davidson and Korbel, "At-Large Elections and Minority Group Representation," and studies cited.

5. See, e.g., Engstrom and McDonald, "Quantitative Evidence in Vote Dilution Litigation."

6. See, e.g., Morris, *The Politics of Black America*, pp. 14–16 and sources cited.

7. Jones, "A Frame of Reference for Black Politics," p. 9.

8. Quotation from filmed speech reproduced in the television series *Eyes on the Prize: America's Civil Rights Years*, program 5, "Mississippi: Is This America? (1962–1964)," produced by Henry Hampton.

9. United States Commission on Civil Rights, *Voting in Mississippi*, pp. 13–19; *Voting Rights: Hearings before the Senate Comm. on the Judiciary*, 89th Cong., 1st Sess., pt. 2, pp. 1175–445 (1965).

10. Lawson, *Black Ballots*, p. 330.

11. Ibid., p. 338.

12. Lawson, *In Pursuit of Power*, p. xii.

13. See, e.g., Davidson and Korbel, "At-Large Elections and Minority Group Representation," pp. 71–79 and studies cited.

14. Engstrom and McDonald, "The Election of Blacks to Southern City Councils," p. 245.

15. See, e.g., Ely, *Democracy and Distrust*, pp. 117, 135.

16. See Lawson, *Black Ballots*.

17. Tushnet, "Commentary," p. 120.

18. *Voting Rights Act: Hearings Before the Subcomm. on the Constitution of the Senate Comm. on the Judiciary*, 97th Cong., 2d Sess., pp. 228–43 (testimony of Walter Berns); pp. 423–46 (testimony of Barry R. Gross); pp. 647–64 (testimony of John Bunzel); pp. 1332–65 (testimony of James F. Blumstein) (1982)

19. Thernstrom, *Whose Votes Count?*, pp. 20–27.

20. Ibid., pp. 5, 27.

21. Ibid., pp. 238–39.

Chapter 1

1. Quoted in Raines, *My Soul Is Rested*, p. 241.

2. McMillan, "Black Enfranchisement in Mississippi," pp. 362–63. In addition to the McMillan article, the descriptions of voter registration efforts in Mississippi contained in this chapter are taken from Branch, *Parting the Waters*, pp. 712–25; Carson, *In Struggle*, pp. 77–81, 86–87; and other sources cited.

3. Quoted in Tomkins, "Profiles (Marian Wright Edelman)," p. 61.

4. Department of Justice, 1964 Status Report, reprinted in *Voting Rights: Hearings before the Senate Comm. on the Judiciary*, 89th Cong., 1st Sess., pt. 2, p. 1302.

5. United States Commission on Civil Rights, *Voting in Mississippi*, pp. 70–71.

6. McMillan, "Black Enfranchisement in Mississippi," p. 362.

7. Lewis and *New York Times*, *Portrait of a Decade*, p. 204.

8. Quoted in ibid., p. 221.

9. *Brown v. Board of Education*, 347 U.S. 483 (1954), 349 U.S. 294 (1955).

10. Southern Education Reporting Service, *Statistical Summary*, pp. 40–43.

11. Sarratt, *The Ordeal of Desegregation*, p. 299.

12. McMillan, *The Citizens' Council*, p. 11.

13. Senate Concurrent Resolution 126, Miss. Legislature, 1956, reprinted in 1 *Race Relations Law Reporter* 440 (1956).

14. House Bill 31, Miss. Laws, 1956.

15. Miss. Code Ann. sec. 4065.3 (1942) (1956 Recomp.).

16. Miss. Code Ann. secs. 9028-31 through 9028-48 (1942) (1956 Recomp.).

17. Declaration of Constitutional Principles, 102 Cong. Rec. 3948, 4004 (March 12, 1956), reprinted in 1 *Race Relations Law Reporter* 435 (1956).

18. Black, *Southern Governors and Civil Rights*, p. 349.

19. Quoted in Loewen and Sallis, *Mississippi: Conflict and Change*, p. 264.

20. Southern Education Reporting Service, *Statistical Summary*, p. 43.

21. United States Commission on Civil Rights, *Political Participation*, pp. 12–13.

22. Ibid.

23. See McMillan, "Black Enfranchisement in Mississippi."

24. "Interview with SNCC Leader: Voter Registration Drive Moves Forward Painfully," *New America*, Feb. 6, 1963, p. 5, quoted in Carson, *In Struggle*, p. 78.

25. Colby, "Protest and Party," pp. 8–9; Carson, *In Struggle*, pp. 97–98.

26. McMillan, "Black Enfranchisement in Mississippi," p. 367. The 1964 Mississippi "Freedom Summer" activities are described in McAdam, *Freedom Summer*; King, *Freedom Song*, chap. 10; and Carson, *In Struggle*, chaps. 8 and 9.

27. King, *Freedom Song*, p. 419.

28. Ibid., pp. 367–436; Carson, *In Struggle*, pp. 111–24; Colby, "Protest and Party," pp. 12–14.

29. Carson, *In Struggle*, pp. 123–29.

30. Stavis, "A Century of Struggle," pp. 640–64; McMillan, "Black Enfranchisement in Mississippi," p. 368.

31. Delegate McLaurin of Sharkey County, Jackson *Clarion Ledger*, Sept. 25, 1890, quoted in United States Commission on Civil Rights, *Voting in Mississippi*, p. 3.

32. Kousser, *The Shaping of Southern Politics*, pp. 139–45; Key, *Southern Politics*, pp. 537–38; Wharton, *The Negro in Mississippi*, pp. 213–14; Kirwan, *Revolt of the Rednecks*, pp. 68–72; United States Commission on Civil Rights, *Voting in Mississippi*, pp. 3–6.

These discriminatory franchise restrictions were supplemented with a state legislative reapportionment plan that increased the number of white constituencies, an electoral college scheme for gubernatorial elections, and a "dual registration" requirement that allowed municipalities to establish their own registration procedures. Kousser, *The Shaping of Southern Politics*, p. 143; Kirwan, *Revolt of the Rednecks*, pp. 78–84.

33. United States Commission on Civil Rights, *Voting in Mississippi*, pp. 8–9.

34. Quoted in ibid., p. 5.

35. Ibid., pp. 9–10, 13–19, 67–68.

36. Ibid; see also, Colby, "The Voting Rights Act," pp. 124–28.

37. See United States Commission on Civil Rights, *Hearings Held in Jackson, Mississippi*, vol. 1, *Voting*; United States Commission on Civil Rights, *Voting in Mississippi*, pp. 21–39.

38. *Voting in Mississippi*, pp. 9–10.

39. Ibid., pp. 18–19.

40. Black, *Southern Governors and Civil Rights*, pp. 58–66, 180–84, 208–12, 260–66.

41. United States Commission on Civil Rights, *Political Participation*, app. VI, p. 218.

42. See Garrow, *Protest at Selma*, pp. 15–30.

43. *Voting Rights: Hearings Before the Senate Comm. on the Judiciary*, 89th Cong., 1st Sess., pt. 1, pp. 9, 12–14 (1965).

44. H.R. Rep. No. 439, 89th Cong., 1st Sess. (1965), reprinted in 1965 U.S. Code Cong. & Ad. News 2437, 2440–44.

45. Other elements of the "Mississippi Plan," including the durational residency requirement and the four-month voter registration deadline subsequently were struck down by the courts in constitutional litigation. However, although the Voting Rights Act eliminated the discriminatory voter registration tests and the poll taxes, it left standing voter registration procedures such as the "dual registration" requirement and restrictions on time and place of registration that had been enacted to restrict black registration and that had a racially discriminatory effect. These were later challenged and invalidated by the federal district court in Mississippi, *Mississippi State Chapter, Operation PUSH v. Allain*, 674 F. Supp. 1245 (N.D. Miss. 1987).

46. United States Commission on Civil Rights, *Political Participation*, pp. 12–13.

47. Mississippi does not keep any official statewide voter registration sta-

tistics by race, and therefore any such statistics are estimates. These statistics are estimates reported by the Voter Education Project that generally have been used in studies of black political participation in the South. Any estimates of black voter registration rates should be viewed with caution. For example, a number of studies have shown that survey data reported by the Bureau of the Census in its Current Population Reports are subject to serious question because persons surveyed tend to overreport voting and registration, and blacks tend to overreport in a far greater proportion than whites, even controlling for socioeconomic status and other factors. See, e.g., Abramson and Claggett, "Race-Related Differences in Self-Reported and Validated Turnout," *Journal of Politics* 46 (1984): 719; Shingles, "Black Consciousness and Political Participation: The Missing Link," *American Political Science Review* 75 (1981): 76; Katosh and Traugott, "The Consequences of Validated and Self-Reported Voting Measures," *Public Opinion Quarterly* 45 (1981): 519.

A 1986 analysis using the results from the federal jury selection process in Mississippi found that only 54 percent of eligible blacks in the Northern District of Mississippi were registered to vote. Lichtman, "Analysis of Racial Distinctions in Voter Registration Rates, State of Mississippi," Ex. P-130 in *Mississippi State Chapter, Operation PUSH v. Allain*, 674 F. Supp. 1245, 1252–55 (N.D. Miss. 1987).

48. Hamer, *To Praise Our Bridges: An Autobiography of Mrs. Fanny Lou Hamer* quoted in Carson et al., *Eyes on the Prize*, p. 135.

49. Salamon and Van Evera, "Fear, Apathy, and Discrimination," p. 1290.

50. Matthews and Prothro, *Negroes and the New Southern Politics*, pp. 308–24.

51. Salamon and Van Evera, "Fear, Apathy, and Discrimination," p. 1293.

52. Ibid., pp. 1293–1301. But see Kernell, "Comment"; and Salamon and Van Evera, "Fear Revisited."

Chapter 2

1. Gene Wirth, "Study Negro in Politics," Jackson *Clarion-Ledger*, Jan. 12, 1958.

2. "Negroes' Bloc Proves Small," *Clarion-Ledger/Jackson Daily News*, June 17, 1962. [The Jackson *Clarion-Ledger* and the *Jackson Daily News* published a joint Sunday edition, the *Clarion-Ledger/Jackson Daily News*.]

3. For accounts of massive resistance in education, see Bartley, *The Rise of Massive Resistance*, and Muse, *Virginia's Massive Resistance*.

4. In 1965 in an effort to avoid Voting Rights Act coverage, Governor Paul B. Johnson, Jr., persuaded the state legislature to simplify the literacy test by repealing the "read and understand" requirement and to repeal other elements of the 1962 legislation. See Bass and DeVries, *The Transformation of Southern Politics*, p. 206.

5. Secretary of State, *Mississippi: Official and Statistical Register, 1964–1968*, pp. 63–74, 80–105.

6. United States Commission on Civil Rights, *Political Participation*, p. 22.

7. See Loewen and Sallis, *Mississippi: Conflict and Change*, pp. 6–7, 15–18;

Key, *Southern Politics,* chap. 11, "Mississippi: The Delta and the Hills."

8. Roy Reed, "Delta Negroes Threaten Whitten's Seat in House," *New York Times,* Apr. 3, 1966; Frank E. Smith, *Congressman from Mississippi.*

9. In 1964, in *Reynolds v. Sims,* 377 U.S. 533, 577, the Supreme Court held that the equal protection clause of the Fourteenth Amendment required state legislatures to make a good faith effort to construct legislative districts in both houses of the state legislature "as nearly of equal population as is practicable."

10. Engstrom, "The Supreme Court and Equi-Populous Gerrymandering."

11. Charles M. Hills, "House Seeks Methods of Redistricting State," Jackson *Clarion-Ledger,* Jan. 7, 1966.

12. Hills, Jackson *Clarion-Ledger,* Jan. 14, 1966.

13. James Saggus, AP wire story, "No Senate Hearing Seen on 'Redistricting Bill,'" Jackson *Clarion-Ledger,* Jan. 19, 1966.

14. Memphis *Commercial Appeal,* Jan. 16, 1966.

15. Saggus, "No Senate Hearing," Jackson *Clarion-Ledger,* Jan. 19, 1966.

16. William L. Chaze, "Senate Approves Redistricting Bill," Jackson *Clarion-Ledger,* Feb. 16, 1966.

17. Jackson *Clarion-Ledger,* Feb. 15, 1966. Also, Kenneth Toler, "Negro Strength Remains Intact In Reseat OK," Memphis *Commercial Appeal,* Feb. 16, 1966; Jackson *Clarion-Ledger,* Feb. 16, 1966.

18. "Redistrict Bill Goes to House," Memphis *Commercial Appeal,* Feb. 17, 1966.

19. Hills, Jackson *Clarion-Ledger,* Mar. 8, 1966; Chaze, Jackson *Clarion-Ledger,* Apr. 5, 1966; James Saggus, "Redistricting Deadline Near," *Jackson Daily News,* Apr. 5, 1966; *Jackson Daily News,* Apr. 7, 1966.

20. *Jackson Daily News,* Apr. 7, 1966.

21. See Parker, "Racial Gerrymandering and Legislative Reapportionment," pp. 86–99. The terms were first coined in the context of nonracial gerrymandering in Tyler, "Court versus Legislature," pp. 390, 400.

22. See, e.g., *Zimmer v. McKeithen,* 485 F.2d 1297, 1303 (5th Cir. 1973) (*en banc*), *aff'd on other grounds sub nom. East Carroll Parish School Board v. Marshall,* 424 U.S. 636 (1976); *Moore v. Leflore County Board of Election Commissioners,* 502 F.2d 621 (5th Cir. 1974).

23. See Parker, "The Mississippi Congressional Redistricting Case."

24. Parker, "County Redistricting in Mississippi." See, e.g., *Kirksey v. Board of Supervisors of Hinds County,* 554 F.2d 139 (5th Cir. 1977) (*en banc*), *cert. denied,* 434 U.S. 968 (1977).

25. *Stewart v. Waller,* 404 F. Supp. 206 (N.D. Miss. 1975) (three-judge court).

26. Miss. Laws, 1966, ch. 290, amending Miss. Code Ann. sec. 2870 (1956 Recomp.). Boards of supervisors could switch to at-large elections by order of the board. The move could be blocked only if 20 percent of the county's voters filed a petition objecting to the switch within sixty days after it was adopted and the switch was voted down in a countywide referendum.

27. Dana B. Brammer, *A Manual for Mississippi County Supervisors.* 2d ed. University, Miss.: University of Mississippi Bureau of Governmental Research, 1973.

28. W. F. Minor, New Orleans *Times-Picayune,* Jan. 1966.

29. Kenneth Toler, "Legislature Gives Final OK on Bill Ending Primaries," Memphis *Commercial Appeal*, May 18, 1966.

30. Jackson *Clarion-Ledger*, May 16, 1966.

31. *Mississippi House Journal*, 1966 Regular Session, p. 678; *Mississippi Senate Journal*, 1966 Regular Session, p. 1049.

32. *Extension of the Voting Rights Act of 1965: Hearings before the Subcommittee on Constitutional Rights of the Senate Comm. on the Judiciary*, 94th Cong., 1st Sess., p. 149 (1975).

33. Miss. Laws, 1966, ch. 404, codified as Miss. Code Ann. sec. 6271-03.5 (1956 Recomp.) (Supp. 1966). Countywide school board elections were mandated in Hancock, Lowndes, Lincoln, Lafayette, Warren, and Wayne counties and permitted at the local option of the school boards in Benton and Marshall counties.

34. Miss. Laws, 1966, ch. 428, approved June 15, 1966 (Leflore County); Miss. Laws, 1966, ch. 431, approved May 10, 1966 (Coahoma and Washington counties).

35. House Bill 183, Miss. Laws, 1966, ch. 406, approved June 17, 1966, codified as Miss. Code Ann. sec. 6271-08 (1956 Recomp.) (Supp. 1966).

36. Lawyers' Committee for Civil Rights Under Law, Memorandum for the Attorney General of the United States, pp. 17–18 (n.d.), attached to Section 5 comment letter from Louis F. Oberdorfer to Attorney General John N. Mitchell, May 15, 1969.

37. Mississippi Constitution, art. 14, sec. 271 (1942).

38. Henry Harris, West Point *Times-Leader*, reprinted as "A Guest Editorial: Consolidation of Counties," Jackson *Clarion-Ledger*, Apr. 15, 1966.

39. New Orleans *Times-Picayune*, May 24, 1966.

40. "Mississippi Revives County Merger Plan," Memphis *Commercial Appeal*, June 9, 1966; *Jackson Daily News*, June 8, 1966; Jackson *Clarion-Ledger*, June 9, 1966; New Orleans *Times-Picayune*, June 9, 1966.

41. See n. 40 above.

42. "Mississippi Election Panel Rejects Negro Candidates," *New York Times*, Oct. 7, 1964; Colby, "Protest and Party," pp. 24–25.

43. House Bill 68, Miss. Laws, 1966, ch. 613, approved June 15, 1966, amending Miss. Code Ann. sec. 3260 (1956 Recomp.).

44. UPI, "Election Bill Passes House," Memphis *Commercial Appeal*, Feb. 16, 1966.

45. United States Commission on Civil Rights, *Political Participation*, pp. 145–46.

46. House Bills 435 and 793, Miss. Legislature, 1966 Regular Session. Although labeled "open primary" bills by the press, the bills were not true open primary measures in the sense of opening up primary elections to participation by all voters regardless of party affiliation. The bills actually abolished party primaries.

47. Andrew Reese, Jr., UPI wire story, Feb. 22, 1966.

48. Veto message, May 26, 1966, *Mississippi House Journal*, 1966 Regular Session, pp. 1111–12.

49. James Saggus, AP wire story, May 27, 1966.

50. Ibid.

51. See Parker and Phillips, *Voting in Mississippi*, pp. 72–79.

52. Between 1890 and 1962, at least ten counties had been subdivided to provide separate legislative representation for parts of counties, a form of gerrymandering designed to offset the disproportionate representation from the majority-black delta counties and to create majority-white districts in predominantly black areas by carving out predominantly white enclaves. See Miss. Code Ann. sec. 3326 (1942) (1956 Recomp.); Kirwan, *Revolt of the Rednecks*, pp. 83–84; Kirwan, "Apportionment in the Mississippi Constitution of 1980."

53. *Connor v. Johnson*, 256 F. Supp. 962 (S.D. Miss. 1966) (three-judge court).

54. James Saggus, AP, "Committee Approves Formula for House," Jackson *Clarion-Ledger*, Nov. 16, 1966.

55. Senate Bill 1504, Miss. Laws, 1966–67 Sp. Sess., ch. 41, approved Dec. 1, 1966, codified at Miss. Code Ann. secs. 3326, 3327 (1956 Recomp.) (Supp. 1966); *Connor v. Johnson*, 265 F. Supp. 492 (S.D. Miss. 1967) (three-judge court); Parker and Phillips, *Voting in Mississippi*, pp. 20–21.

56. A. B. Albritton, "Senate Okays Reapportion," Jackson *Clarion-Ledger*, Nov. 19, 1966.

57. Ibid.; John Hall, AP wire story, "Seat Plans May Face Revisions," Jackson *Clarion-Ledger*, Nov. 21, 1966.

58. Garland, "Taste of Triumph," p. 25.

59. In 1875 the white Democratic forces seized power across the state, drove black public officials from office, and maintained control of the electoral process through force and violence until 1890, when the new state constitution disfranchised Mississippi's black citizens. In a few heavily black counties, however, some black officeholders continued to be elected after 1875 under the "fusion" principle under which the whites continued to allow some blacks to be elected, usually to relatively minor posts. See Wharton, *The Negro in Mississippi*, chaps. 13 and 14; Kirwan, *Revolt of the Rednecks*, chap. 1.

60. Walton, *Invisible Politics*, pp. 18–19.

61. See United States Commission on Civil Rights, *Political Participation*; Parker and Phillips, *Voting in Mississippi*.

62. Carmichael and Hamilton, *Black Power*, p. 87.

63. Quoted in Thomas R. Brooks, *Walls Come Tumbling Down*, p. 273.

64. Lawson, *In Pursuit of Power*, pp. 50–63; Carson, *In Struggle*, pp. 207–11.

65. Carson, *In Struggle*, p. 215.

66. Ladner, "What Black Power Means to Negroes in Mississippi," p. 148.

67. Ibid., pp. 143–46, 151–52.

68. Ibid., p. 146. A number of studies have demonstrated that the effects of low socioeconomic status can be overcome by a sense of group or racial self-consciousness. Group or racial self-consciousness can overcome the expectation of decreased political participation normally associated with low socioeconomic status. See studies cited in Pinderhughes, "Legal Strategies for Voting Rights," pp. 530–33; Shingles, "Black Consciousness and Political Participation," pp. 76–91.

69. "Mississippi Is Pondering Potential of High Increase in Negro Voters," Memphis *Commercial Appeal*, July 11, 1967.

70. United States Commission on Civil Rights, *Political Participation*, p. 13.

71. Black, *Southern Governors and Civil Rights*, pp. 181–84; John Pearce, AP wire story, Oct. 1967.

72. Freedom Information Service (FIS), *Mississippi Newsletter*, Aug. 4, Aug. 1, Nov. 10, 1967, FIS Library, Jackson, Miss.

73. See Dittmer, "The Politics of the Mississippi Movement"; Bass and DeVries, *The Transformation of Southern Politics*, pp. 205–6.

Dittmer describes the split as reflecting age, class, gender, and lifestyle differences between supporters of the two groups. The NAACP represented the traditional, older, predominantly male, established black leadership in the state, with roots in the black middle class and in the urban areas. The MFDP and SNCC were new groups, whose members were younger, which encouraged the development of new, indigenous black leaders, many of whom were women, who were poorer and less well educated, with roots in the rural, plantation areas of the state.

In addition, some white northern liberal supporters of the civil rights movement in Mississippi in the early 1960s attempted to drive a wedge between the NAACP and SNCC and to isolate the MFDP with "red-baiting" based on SNCC's growing militancy, its policy of not excluding leftists from its ranks, and its association with left-wing groups such as the National Lawyers' Guild, which had provided legal support for Mississippi organizing efforts. See Dittmer, "The Politics of the Mississippi Movement," pp. 82, 88; Carson, *In Struggle*, pp. 136–40, 180–83.

However, as Dittmer notes, "What liberal and conservative critics failed to realize (or pretended not to see) was that down in Mississippi the fledgling Freedom Democratic party was struggling to steer a middle course between the SNCC radicals and NAACP conservatives." Dittmer, "The Politics of the Mississippi Movement," p. 89. Despite the alienation of SNCC activists from electoral politics, the MFDP under chair Lawrence Guyot remained active in electoral politics, supported the Johnson-Humphrey ticket in Mississippi in 1964, and sponsored the challenge to Mississippi's all-white congressional delegation in 1965.

74. Guyot and Thelwell, "Toward Independent Political Power," pp. 246–48, 252–54.

75. Ibid., p. 252. For an analysis of the significance of the MFDP efforts to build an independent black political movement, see Carmichael and Hamilton, *Black Power*, chap. 4.

76. Ted Poston, "Black Power Loser in Miss. Vote—Evers," *New York Times*, May 3, 1967.

77. FIS, *Mississippi Newsletter*, Aug. 4, Aug. 11, and Nov. 10, 1967; "Mississippi Is Pondering Potential of High Increase," Memphis *Commercial Appeal*, July 11, 1967.

78. Memphis *Commercial Appeal*, July 11, 1967.

79. Garland, "Taste of Triumph," p. 26.

80. William Peart, "Jackson Report: Negro Vote Is Now Potent in the State,"

Greenville *Delta Democrat-Times*, Nov. 13, 1967.

81. National Committee for Free Elections in Mississippi, "Negro Election Victories in Mississippi—1967," n.d. (mimeo), FIS Library.

82. "Independent Candidates File Suit," Jackson *Clarion-Ledger*, Oct. 10, 1967; "19 Denied Slots on Miss. Ballot," New Orleans *Times-Picayune*, Oct. 28, 1967.

83. FIS, *Mississippi Newsletter*, Aug. 4, Aug. 11, and Nov. 10, 1967.

84. United States Commission on Civil Rights, *Political Participation*, p. 218.

85. FIS compilation, "Votes Received by Black Candidates and Their Opponents in the Democratic Primary Elections, August 8 and August 29, 1967, in Mississippi," Sept. 1967, FIS Library.

86. See n. 83 above.

87. Robert G. Clark Interview.

88. Howard D. Hamilton, "Legislative Constituencies," pp. 331–32.

89. United States Commission on Civil Rights, *Political Participation*, pp. 104–11.

90. Kousser, "The Undermining of the First Reconstruction," pp. 31–37.

Chapter 3

1. See chap. 5.

2. For about two years, beginning in 1963, the National Lawyers' Guild, a national organization of progressive lawyers, also had an office in Jackson. The National Lawyers' Guild was active in defending criminal prosecutions involving civil rights workers and litigated the civil rights lawsuit that unsuccessfully challenged the closing of Jackson's swimming pools and other public recreation facilities to avoid desegregation, *Palmer v. Thompson*, 402 U.S. 217 (1971). Interview with Carolyn Parker, former guild office secretary, May 29, 1986.

3. For example, in the most recent account, Doug McAdam's *Freedom Summer*, only LCDC is mentioned, and this is because the organization was named in a telegram from Edward Koch of New York, who was an LCDC volunteer, to Pennsylvania governor David Lawrence, chair of the credentials committee of the 1964 Democratic National Convention (*Freedom Summer*, p. 156). Mary King in *Freedom Song* mentions the Lawyers' Committee twice and LCDC only once (*Freedom Song*, pp. 355, 418). Clayborne Carson, who devotes two chapters to the Freedom Summer Project in *In Struggle*, fails to mention either of these lawyers' groups.

4. For example, Steven Lawson in *In Pursuit of Power* mentions the Lawyers' Committee only three times, twice in footnotes (*In Pursuit of Power*, pp. 177, 348 n. 52, 359 n. 41), and fails to mention LCDC at all.

5. Watters and Cleghorn, *Climbing Jacob's Ladder*, p. 146 n. 18.

6. For a fuller discussion of the work of the Lawyers' Committee, see Lawyers' Committee for Civil Rights Under Law, *10 Year Report*, and Vose, *Guide to the Microfilm Edition*.

A fuller analysis of the case loads of these civil rights legal organizations can be found in Stewart and Heck, "The Day-To-Day Activities of Interest Group Lawyers," pp. 173–81; Heck and Stewart, "Ensuring Access to Justice."

7. Interview with Alvin J. Bronstein, former director of the Jackson LCDC office, May 23, 1986; see Vose, *Guide to the Microfilm Edition*, pp. 46–47; Meier and Rudwick, *CORE*, p. 271.

8. Two full-time attorneys originally staffed the Inc. Fund's Jackson office. One of them was Marian Wright Edelman, the first black woman to pass the Mississippi bar and later to become the nationally known head of the Children's Defense Fund. In 1968 the Inc. Fund office became the biracial Jackson law firm of Anderson, Banks, Nichols & Leventhal, although the national organization continued to pay the office a monthly retainer to defray salary and civil rights litigation expenses.

The Inc. Fund litigated almost all of the private school desegregation cases (those not filed by the Justice Department) in the state. School desegregation cases made up about 80 percent of its docket. The Inc. Fund also handled landmark cases challenging racial discrimination in the provision of municipal services and state-supplied textbooks for racially segregated private schools.

Interviews with Melvyn R. Leventhal, former NAACP Legal Defense Fund staff attorney and former partner, Anderson, Banks, Nichols & Leventhal, Nov. 2, 1985 and June 23, 1986.

9. In contrast, the federal judges of the District Court for the Northern District of Mississippi at the time, William C. Keady and Orma R. Smith, generally were considered to be fair-minded judges who gave civil rights plaintiffs a fair hearing on their claims, although even they did not always rule in favor of black plaintiffs in civil rights cases.

10. Bass and DeVries, *The Transformation of Southern Politics*, p. 199.

11. In contrast, there were a number of southern federal judges on both the Court of Appeals for the Fifth Circuit and the district courts who were dedicated to upholding the law and who repeatedly ruled for civil rights plaintiffs in sustaining racial discrimination claims. Bass, *Unlikely Heroes*; Peltason, *Fifty-Eight Lonely Men*.

12. 1963 television address, transcript, p. 5 (May 16, 1963). For an extensive analysis of Coleman's campaign rhetoric, see Black, *Southern Governors and Civil Rights*, pp. 58–66, 208–12. The "strong segregationist" label is Black's.

13. Bill Simpson, "Gloves Removed in Talks," *Clarion-Ledger/Jackson Daily News*, June 23, 1963, p. 1.

14. Jack Shearer, Jr., "Campaign Pace Hits New, Higher Tempo," Jackson *Clarion-Ledger*, July 24, 1963, p. 16.

15. Mary Ann Pardue, "CR Advocates Oppose Coleman As U.S. Judge," Jackson *Clarion-Ledger*, July 24, 1963.

16. McMillan, "Black Enfranchisement in Mississippi," pp. 357–58; Stern, "Judge William Harold Cox and the Right to Vote in Clarke County, Mississippi"; Charles V. Hamilton, "Southern Judges and Negro Voting Rights," pp. 84–86; Note, "Judicial Performance in the Fifth Circuit," pp. 101–2, 107.

17. McMillan, "Black Enfranchisement in Mississippi," p. 357.

18. Navasky, *Kennedy Justice*, pp. 250–51.

19. "Judge Harold Cox: Dispositions by the Fifth Circuit Court of Appeals and the Supreme Court," Attachment H to Motion to Recuse and Affidavit of Personal Bias filed in *Phillips v. Joint Legislative Committee on Performance and Expenditure Review*, Civil No. J76-114C (S.D. Miss.).

20. Quoted in Charles V. Hamilton, "Southern Judges and Negro Voting Rights," pp. 86–87.

21. Quoted in "Judge in Rights Case: William Harold Cox," *New York Times*, Feb. 26, 1965.

22. Memorandum opinion, p. 3, *Bolton v. Murray Envelope Corp.*, Civil No. 72H-7 (S.D. Miss. Feb. 5, 1973).

23. See *Sanders v. Russell*, 401 F.2d 241 (5th Cir. 1968).

24. See *Singleton v. Jackson Municipal Separate School District*, 332 F. Supp. 984, 985–87 (S.D. Miss. 1971).

25. See *Alexander v. Holmes County Board of Education*, 396 U.S. 19 (1969).

26. "Ole Miss Professor Urges More Action Behind Talk," Memphis *Commercial Appeal*, Feb. 2, 1966.

27. Kirksey interview.

28. Baer, "The New Black Politics in Mississippi," p. 43.

29. Guyot and Thelwell, "The Politics of Necessity and Survival in Mississippi," p. 131.

30. Ibid., p. 130.

31. Ibid.

32. The one-person, one-vote principle was first enunciated by the Supreme Court one year earlier in *Reynolds v. Sims*, 377 U.S. 533 (1964).

33. Complaint, *Connor v. Johnson*, Civil No. 3830 (S.D. Miss. filed Oct. 19, 1965).

34. Ibid.

35. *Connor v. Johnson*, 279 F. Supp. 619, 622 n. 1 (S.D. Miss. 1966) (three-judge court).

36. 279 F. Supp. at 623–24.

37. 364 U.S. 339 (1960).

38. 279 F. Supp. at 624.

39. Jurisdictional Statement, p. 4, *Connor v. Johnson*, 386 U.S. 483 (1967).

40. State defendants' Motion to Dismiss or Affirm, pp. 14, 16, *Connor v. Johnson, supra*.

41. *Connor v. Johnson*, 386 U.S. 483 (1967).

42. Dixon, *Democratic Representation*, pp. 474–75.

43. See, e.g., *Hall v. St. Helena Parish School Board*, 197 F. Supp. 649, 652–53 and n. 8 (E.D. La. 1961) (three-judge court), *aff'd mem.*, 368 U.S. 515 (1962) (holding unconstitutional a state statute authorizing the closing of the public schools and payment of tuition grants to segregated private schools); *Loewen v. Turnipseed*, 488 F. Supp. 1138, 1148–49 (N.D. Miss. 1980) (holding unconstitutional Mississippi state agency's refusal to adopt multiracial Mississippi history textbook).

The rationale is that most southern legislatures do not keep official records of their deliberations, and therefore the press accounts of legislative debates constitute the best evidence of the legislative intent.

44. Dixon, *Democratic Representation*, pp. 456–57.

45. Ibid., p. 457.

46. *Jordan v. Winter*, 541 F. Supp. 1135 (N.D. Miss. 1982), *vac'd and remanded sub nom. Brooks v. Winter*, 461 U.S. 921 (1983), 604 F. Supp. 807 (N.D. Miss. 1984), *aff'd sub nom. Mississippi Republican Executive Committee v. Brooks*, 469 U.S. 1002 (1984).

47. Parker, "The Mississippi Congressional Redistricting Case."

48. *South Carolina v. Katzenbach*, 383 U.S. 301, 334 (1966).

49. 42 U.S.C. sec. 1973c.

50. Ibid.

51. H.R. Rep. No. 439, 89th Cong., 1st Sess., pp. 10–11 (1965), reprinted in 1965 U.S. Code Cong. & Ad. News, pp. 2440–41; *Voting Rights: Hearings Before the Senate Comm. on the Judiciary*, 89th Cong., 1st Sess., pt. 1, pp. 10–14 (testimony of Attorney General Nicholas Katzenbach).

52. *South Carolina v. Katzenbach*, 383 U.S. 301, 335 (1966).

53. *Whitley v. Johnson*, 260 F. Supp. 630 (S.D. Miss. 1966) (three-judge court).

54. *Whitley v. Johnson*, 296 F. Supp. 630 (S.D. Miss. 1967) (three-judge court).

55. *Fairley v. Patterson*, 282 F. Supp. 164 (S.D. Miss. 1967) (three-judge court); *Bunton v. Patterson*, 281 F. Supp. 918 (S.D. Miss. 1967 (three-judge court).

56. *Hearings on the Voting Rights Act (H.R. 6400) before Subcommittee No. 5 of the House Comm. on the Judiciary*, 89th Cong., 1st Sess., ser. 2, p. 74 (1965), quoted in Brief for Appellees, p. 27, *Fairley v. Patterson* decided sub nom. *Allen v. State Board of Elections*, 393 U.S. 544 (1969).

57. Brief for Appellees, p. 44, *Fairley v. Patterson, supra.*

58. *Voting Rights: Hearings on S. 1564 before the Senate Comm. on the Judiciary*, 89th Cong., 1st Sess., pt. 1, pp. 191–92 (1965), quoted in Brief for Appellants, p. 18, *Fairley v. Patterson, supra.*

59. *Hearings on the Voting Rights Act (H.R. 6400) before Subcommittee No. 5 of the House Comm. on the Judiciary*, 89th Cong., 1st Sess., ser. 2, p. 60 (1965).

60. Ibid., p. 95.

61. 42 U.S.C. sec. 1973*l*(c)(1).

62. Memorandum for the United States as Amicus Curiae, p. 12, *Fairley v. Patterson, supra.*

63. *Allen v. State Board of Elections*, 393 U.S. 544 (1969).

64. 393 U.S. at 567.

65. 393 U.S. at 566.

66. 393 U.S. at 566–67.

67. 393 U.S. at 568.

68. 393 U.S. at 554–63.

69. 393 U.S. at 571–72.

70. Section 5 objection letter from Assistant Attorney General for civil rights Jerris Leonard to Mississippi attorney general A. F. Summer, May 21, 1969.

71. Engstrom, "Racial Vote Dilution," p. 145.

72. 393 U.S. at 592–93.

73. *Reynolds v. Sims*, 377 U.S. 533, 555 (1964).

74. 393 U.S. at 569.

75. Engstrom, "Racial Vote Dilution," p. 146; Note, "The Voting Rights Act of 1965 and Minority Access to the Political Process," pp. 129, 142.

76. Statement of the Mississippi Freedom Democratic Party, Mar. 5, 1969, p. 1 (mimeo) (emphasis added).

Chapter 4

1. George Bundy Smith, "The Failure of Reapportionment."

2. Ibid., p. 640.

3. Ibid.

4. Ibid.

5. *Whitcomb v. Chavis*, 403 U.S. 124, 142 (1971).

6. See Dixon, *Democratic Representation*, pp. 461–63, 470–84, 503–12; Howard D. Hamilton, "Legislative Constituencies," pp. 323–26; *Whitcomb v. Chavis*, 403 U.S. at 157–60 and sources cited in n. 38.

7. Dixon, *Democratic Representation*, p. 504.

8. Discriminatory multimember districts were eliminated in 1970s litigation in all southern states except Arkansas, Florida, North Carolina, South Carolina (state senate), and Virginia. Multimember districts were struck down in these states in the next round of reapportionment litigation in the 1980s.

9. Parker, "Racial Gerrymandering and Legislative Reapportionment," pp. 88–89.

10. *United States v. Mississippi*, 444 U.S. 1050, 1053 (1980) (dissenting opinion).

11. Ibid. (footnote omitted).

12. *Fortson v. Dorsey*, 379 U.S. 433, 439 (1965); *Burns v. Richardson*, 384 U.S. 73, 88 (1966).

13. *Connor v. Waller*, 396 F. Supp. 1308, 1321 (S.D. Miss. 1975) (three-judge court).

14. *Connor v. Johnson*, 256 F. Supp. 962 (S.D. Miss. 1966) (three-judge court).

15. W. F. Minor, "Miss. Reseating Plan Attacked," New Orleans *Times-Picayune*, Jan. 10, 1967.

16. Ibid.

17. *Connor v. Johnson*, 265 F. Supp. 492 (S.D. Miss. 1967) (three-judge court).

18. W. F. Minor, "Federal Reseat Plan Is Analyzed; No 'Racial Consideration'—Judge," New Orleans *Times-Picayune*, Mar. 4, 1967.

19. 265 F. Supp. at 499.

20. 265 F. Supp. at 494.

21. Jackson *Clarion-Ledger*, Mar. 29, 1967.

22. *Connor v. Johnson*, 330 F. Supp. 506 (S.D. Miss. 1971) (three-judge court).

23. Plaintiffs' Motion for Affirmative Relief, filed May 17, 1971, *Connor v. Johnson, supra.*
24. 330 F. Supp. 506.
25. 330 F. Supp. at 518–19.
26. *Connor v. Johnson,* 402 U.S. 690, 691 (1971).
27. 402 U.S. at 692.
28. *Whitcomb v. Chavis,* 403 U.S. 124 (1971); *Kilgarlin v. Hill,* 386 U.S. 120 (1967); *Harrison v. Schaefer,* 383 U.S. 269 (1966); *Burns v. Richardson,* 384 U.S. 73 (1966); *Burnette v. Davis,* 382 U.S. 42 (1965); *Fortson v. Dorsey,* 379 U.S. 433 (1965); *Lucas v. Colorado General Assembly,* 377 U.S. 713 (1964). See *Whitcomb v. Chavis,* 403 U.S. at 142–44.
29. 403 U.S. at 144.
30. *Chapman v. Meier,* 420 U.S. 1, 19 (1975).
31. See, e.g., *East Carroll Parish School Board v. Marshall,* 424 U.S. 636, 639 (1976) (Louisiana parish redistricting); *Chapman v. Meier,* 420 U.S. 1, 17–19 (1975) (North Dakota legislative reapportionment); *Mahan v. Howell,* 410 U.S. 315, 333 (1973) (Virginia legislative reapportionment).
32. *Connor v. Johnson,* 330 F. Supp. 521 (S.D. Miss. 1971) (three-judge court).
33. *Connor v. Johnson,* 403 U.S. 928 (1971).
34. *Connor v. Williams,* 404 U.S. 549 (1972).
35. United States Commission on Civil Rights, *The Voting Rights Act: Ten Years After,* pp. 208–41.
36. *Dorsey v. Fortson,* 228 F. Supp. 259 (N.D. Ga. 1964) (three-judge court), *rev'd,* 379 U.S. 433 (1965).
37. *Fortson v. Dorsey,* 379 U.S. 433, 439 (1965).
38. Howard D. Hamilton, "Legislative Constituencies," p. 332.
39. Joint Center for Political Studies, *Black Elected Officials* (1971).
40. 411 U.S. 526 (1973).
41. Joint Center for Political Studies, *Black Elected Officials* (1976), xi.
42. *Sims v. Baggett,* 247 F. Supp. 96, 109 (M.D. Ala. 1965) (three-judge court). See United States Commission on Civil Rights, *Political Participation,* pp. 27–30.
43. *Sims v. Amos,* 336 F. Supp. 924 (M.D. Ala. 1972), *aff'd mem.,* 409 U.S. 942 (1972).
44. 336 F. Supp. at 934–35.
45. United States Commission on Civil Rights, *The Voting Rights Act: Ten Years After,* pp. 239–41.
46. *Graves v. Barnes,* 343 F. Supp. 704, 724–44 (W.D. Tex. 1972) (three-judge court), *aff'd in relevant part sub nom. White v. Regester,* 412 U.S. 755 (1973). *Connor v. Johnson* was cited at 343 F. Supp. at 736.
47. *White v. Regester,* 412 U.S. 755 (1973).
48. *Graves v. Barnes,* 378 F. Supp. 640 (W.D. Tex. 1974), *vac'd sub nom. White v. Regester,* 422 U.S. 935 (1975).
49. Quoted in Bass and DeVries, *The Transformation of Southern Politics,* p. 199.
50. After Lawrence Guyot left Mississippi in the late 1960s, Kirksey became

the driving force in the Mississippi redistricting litigation. He testified as an expert witness in a number of county redistricting cases and was the leading plaintiff, not only in the legislative reapportionment case, but also in the successful Hinds County redistricting case and the challenge to at-large city council elections in Jackson.

51. *Connor v. Waller*, 396 F. Supp. 1308 (S.D. Miss. 1975) (three-judge court).

52. 396 F. Supp. at 1321–32.

53. *Connor v. Waller*, 421 U.S. 656 (1975).

54. Ibid.

55. The issue of when a plan drawn up by a state or locality covered by section 5 and submitted to a district court for implementation in litigation is a court-ordered plan or a legislative plan has been a continuing issue in voting rights cases. See, e.g., *East Carroll Parish School Board v. Marshall*, 424 U.S. 636 (1976); *Wise v. Lipscomb*, 437 U.S. 535 (1978); and *McDaniel v. Sanchez*, 452 U.S. 130 (1981). The Court's opinion in *Connor v. Waller* foreshadowed its later conclusion in *McDaniel v. Sanchez* that the fact that a reapportionment plan is devised in response to a federal court order does not change its character as a legislative plan, subject to section 5. See 452 U.S. at 145–46.

56. Memorandum for the United States as Amicus Curiae, *Connor v. Waller*, 421 U.S. 656 (1975), pp. 17–23, Appendix B, p. B-6.

57. Section 5 objection telegram from J. Stanley Pottinger, assistant attorney general, to A. F. Summer, June 10, 1975.

58. Order Establishing Certain Temporary Districts for the Election of Senators and Representatives in the Mississippi Legislature for the Year 1975 Only, *Connor v. Waller*, Civil No. 3830(A) (S.D. Miss. July 11, 1975) (unreported).

59. Ibid., pp. 35, 40–41.

60. Order of Aug. 1, 1975, *Connor v. Waller*, *supra* (unreported).

61. The racial percentages of the Hinds County single-member districts are set out in the Appendix to the District Court's Order of July 11, 1975.

62. See *Kirksey v. Board of Supervisors of Hinds County*, 554 F.2d 139 (5th Cir. 1977) (en banc), *cert. denied*, 434 U.S. 968 (1977).

63. *Connor v. Coleman*, 425 U.S. 675 (1976).

64. *Connor v. Finch*, 419 F. Supp. 1072, 419 F. Supp. 1089, 422 F. Supp. 1014 (S.D. Miss. 1976) (three-judge court).

65. 419 F. Supp. at 1074.

66. *Connor v. Finch*, 431 U.S. 407 (1977). Justice Harry Blackmun, joined by Chief Justice Warren Burger, filed a concurring opinion expressing separate views but concurring in the judgment of the Court.

67. 431 U.S. at 413–21.

68. 431 U.S. at 422–25.

69. Parker, "Racial Gerrymandering and Legislative Reapportionment," p. 89.

70. 431 U.S. at 423.

71. Parker, "Racial Gerrymandering and Legislative Reapportionment," p. 92.

72. 431 U.S. at 424–25.
73. 431 U.S. at 422 n. 21.
74. *Mississippi v. United States*, 490 F. Supp. 569 (D.D.C. 1979) (three-judge court), *aff'd mem.*, 444 U.S. 1050 (1980).
75. E. C. Foster, "A Time of Challenge," p. 192.
76. Hester, "Mississippi and the Voting Rights Act," p. 841; *Connor v. Winter*, 519 F. Supp. 1337, 1352 (S.D. Miss. 1981) (three-judge court).
77. Parker and Phillips, *Voting in Mississippi*, p. 29.
78. Ibid., pp. 29–30.

Chapter 5

1. Dan Davis, "Newman Won't Seek Speaker's Post," Jackson *Clarion-Ledger*, Mar. 27, 1987, p. 1A.
2. The bill, the Education Reform Act, was enacted later in 1982 at a special session of the state legislature called by Governor Winter.
3. Bill Minor, "Speaker's Campaign Shaping Up," *Clarion-Ledger/Jackson Daily News*, Feb. 8, 1967, p. 3J.
4. Black and Black, *Politics and Society in the South*, pp. 126–51, 292–96.
5. Bartley and Graham, *Southern Politics and the Second Reconstruction*, pp. 191–92 and articles cited in n. 10.
6. Black and Black, *Politics and Society in the South*, p. 148.
7. Ibid., pp. 146–51.
8. Dan Davis, "Black Caucus Is Force To Be Reckoned With," Jackson *Clarion-Ledger*, Mar. 3, 1986, p. 1B.
9. Interview with state NAACP president and state representative Aaron Henry, Oct. 6, 1985; interview with Rims Barber, state legislative representative for the Children's Defense Fund, Oct. 10, 1985; Davis, "Black Caucus Is Force To Be Reckoned With," Jackson *Clarion-Ledger*, Mar. 3, 1986.
10. See n. 9 above.
11. William Rabb, "Opponents of Constitutional Convention Fear the Unknown," *Jackson Daily News*, Jan. 31, 1988; Dan Davis, "Constitution Reform Bill Stalled," Jackson *Clarion-Ledger*, May 5, 1988; Dan Davis and Joe O'Keefe, "Constitution Bill Dealt Fatal Blow," Jackson *Clarion-Ledger*, May 6, 1988.
12. See n. 11 above; Dan Davis, "Racial Confrontation Erupts in House," Jackson *Clarion-Ledger*, Feb. 15, 1986.
13. Numerous empirical studies have found continued strong patterns of racially polarized voting in Mississippi elections. See, e.g., Lichtman, "Racial Bloc Voting in Mississippi Elections"; Stekler, "Electing Blacks to Office in the South"; and Loewen, "Continued Obstacles to Black Electoral Success in Mississippi." Racially polarized voting has also been found in numerous court decisions in Mississippi voting rights cases. See, e.g., *Martin v. Allain*, 658 F. Supp. 1183, 1193–94 (S.D. Miss. 1987); *Jordan v. Winter*, 604 F. Supp. 807 (N.D. Miss. 1984) (three-judge court), *aff'd sub nom. Mississippi Republican Executive Committee v. Brooks*, 469 U.S. 1002 (1984).
14. See, e.g., *United Jewish Organizations v. Carey*, 430 U.S. 144, 164 (1977); *Ketchum v. Byrne*, 740 F.2d 1398, 1413–17 (7th Cir. 1984), *cert. denied*, 471 U.S.

1135 (1985); *Mississippi v. United States*, 490 F. Supp. 569, 575 (D.D.C. 1979) (three-judge court), *aff'd mem.*, 444 U.S. 1050 (1980).

15. See Parker, "Racial Gerrymandering and Legislative Reapportionment," pp. 108–11; *Ketchum v. Byrne*, 740 F.2d at 1413–17.

During the Reagan administration, however, Assistant Attorney General William Bradford Reynolds, the head of the Justice Department's Civil Rights Division, repudiated the use of any 65 percent standard. See *James v. City of Sarasota*, 611 F. Supp. 25, 32–33 (M.D. Fla. 1985).

16. See *Martin v. Allain*, 658 F. Supp. at 1195 (four blacks have been elected from majority-white districts, including Anderson); *Martin v. Mabus*, 700 F. Supp. 327, 333–34 (S.D. Miss. 1988) (seventeen black officials elected from majority-black districts that are less than 65 percent black).

17. Lichtman, "Racial Bloc Voting in Mississippi Elections," table 1.

18. Ibid., table 3.

19. Cavanagh and Stockton, *Black Elected Officials*, pp. 8–9.

20. Joint Center for Political Studies, *Black Elected Officials* (1989), table 7.

21. Thernstrom, *Whose Votes Count?* p. 234.

22. Black, *Southern Governors and Civil Rights*, p. 337.

23. Interview with Representative Eric Clark.

24. Cliff Treyens, "Legislature Opens Today; Sparks May Fly," Jackson *Clarion-Ledger*, Jan. 3, 1984, p. 1A; Treyens, "House Rejects Rules Change on First Day," Jackson *Clarion-Ledger*, Jan. 4, 1984, p. 1A.

25. Davis, "Black Caucus Is Force To Be Reckoned With."

26. Dan Davis, "House Strips Newman's Powers, 75–45," *Clarion-Ledger/Jackson Daily News*, Jan. 10, 1987, p. 1A.

27. Shawn McIntosh, "Unlikely Twosome," Jackson *Clarion-Ledger*, Mar. 9, 1987, p. 1A.

28. Joe O'Keefe, "Mabus Hits, Misses with Agenda Plans," *Clarion-Ledger/Jackson Daily News*, May 8, 1988; "How the House voted on selected legislation," ibid.

29. Peter Applebome, "G.O.P. Tide Rises in the South, but Democrats Say It Will Ebb," *New York Times*, Apr. 15, 1989.

30. United States Commission on Civil Rights, *Political Participation*, pp. 139–42.

31. Colby, "Protest and Party," pp. 37–40.

32. *Riddell v. National Democratic Party*, 344 F. Supp. 908 (S.D. Miss. 1972), *rev'd*, 508 F.2d 770 (5th Cir. 1975).

33. Interview with Ed Cole, Mississippi state Democratic party chair, June 6, 1989.

34. Interview with Bennie G. Thompson, Democratic National Committeeman for Mississippi, Dec. 29, 1986.

35. Loewen and Sallis, *Mississippi: Conflict and Change*, p. 323.

36. On the conflicts between the Loyalists and the Regulars before and after merger, see Lamis, *The Two-Party South*, chap. 4, "Mississippi: It's All Black and White"; Stekler, "Black Politics in the New South," chap. 4, "Black Political Power and Party Politics—The Unification of the Mississippi Democratic Party."

37. Data from section 5 comment letter from Frank R. Parker to William

Bradford Reynolds, assistant attorney general, Civil Rights Division, U.S. Department of Justice, Dec. 24, 1986.

38. Memorandum, Lawyers' Committee for Civil Rights Under Law, "Violations of Voting Rights, 1971 Mississippi General Election," Nov. 11, 1971.

39. See United States Commission on Civil Rights, *The Voting Rights Act: Unfulfilled Goals*, chap. 5; United States Commission on Civil Rights, *The Voting Rights Act: Ten Years After*, chap. 9; for racial gerrymandering in Louisiana parishes, see Halpin, "The Anti-Gerrymander."

40. U.S. Department of Justice, Civil Rights Division, "Complete Listing of Objections Pursuant to Section 5 of the Voting Rights Act of 1965," Apr. 30, 1987, Mississippi, pp. M1–M8.

41. Court record, *Kirksey v. Board of Supervisors of Hinds County*, 554 F.2d 536 (5th Cir. 1977) (*en banc*), *cert. denied*, 434 U.S. 968 (1977); section 5 objection letter to Thomas Watkins, attorney for the Hinds County Board of Supervisors, from David L. Norman, acting assistant attorney general, U.S. Department of Justice, July 14, 1971; Parker, "County Redistricting in Mississippi," pp. 406–8.

42. Henry J. Kirksey, "County Redistricting in Mississippi," (Jackson, Miss.: Lawyers' Committee for Civil Rights Under Law, n.d.), p. 2.

43. Section 5 objection letter to Watkins from Norman.

44. The board of supervisors contended that because the 1969 plan was adopted as the result of a prior lawsuit (filed by white voters) seeking equally apportioned districts, it was not covered by section 5. A Justice Department lawsuit seeking to enforce the section 5 objection was dismissed as moot when the federal district court struck down the plan for unconstitutional malapportionment in 1972.

45. *Kirksey v. Board of Supervisors of Hinds County*, 402 F. Supp. 658, 666 (S.D. Miss. 1975).

46. *Kirksey v. Board of Supervisors of Hinds County*, 402 F. Supp. 658 (S.D. Miss. 1975), *aff'd*, 528 F.2d 536 (5th Cir. 1976).

47. 554 F.2d 139 (5th Cir. 1977), *cert. denied*, 434 U.S. 968 (1977).

48. Because of numerous lawsuits to county redistricting plans drawn after the 1980 census, county supervisor elections regularly scheduled to be held in 1983 in a number of counties were postponed by court order and not held until plans were finally adopted which met federal constitutional and Voting Rights Act requirements.

49. Data supplied by Bennie G. Thompson, member of the Hinds County Board of Supervisors, Oct. 5, 1988.

50. Rice, *Progressive Cities*. The thesis that at-large voting constituted a municipal takeover by professional and business groups to advance their own interests was first advanced in the early 1960s by James Weinstein and Samuel P. Hays. See, e.g., Samuel P. Hays, "The Politics of Reform in Municipal Government in the Progressive Era," *Pacific Northwest Quarterly* 55 (October 1964): 157–69; James Weinstein, *The Corporate Ideal in the Liberal State, 1900–1918* (Boston: Beacon Press, 1968), chap. 4.

51. Rice, *Progressive Cities*, p. 118.

52. Greenville *Times*, Nov. 24, 1906, p. 1.

53. James Saggus, "Senate Approves Measure To Change City Vote Rules," Jackson *Clarion-Ledger*, Mar. 2, 1962.

54. 404 F. Supp. 206 (N.D. Miss. 1975) (three-judge court).

55. See, e.g., *Wade v. Mississippi Cooperative Extension Service*, 378 F. Supp. 1215 (N.D. Miss. 1975), *aff'd in part, vac'd in part*, 538 F.3d 508 (5th Cir. 1976) (Keady, J., ordering elimination of job discrimination against blacks in the Mississippi Cooperative Extension Service); *Loewen v. Turnipseed*, 488 F. Supp. 1138 (N.D. Miss. 1980) (Smith, J., ordering state to adopt ninth-grade Mississippi history textbook, *Mississippi: Conflict and Change*, rejected by state textbook board for racially discriminatory reasons).

56. 404 F. Supp. at 214–15.

57. 404 F. Supp. at 214, 215.

58. 461 F. Supp. 1282 (S.D. Miss. 1978), *vac'd and remanded*, 625 F.2d 21 (5th Cir. 1980), 506 F. Supp. 491 (S.D. Miss. 1981), *aff'd*, 663 F.2d 659 (5th Cir. 1981).

59. 608 F. Supp. 1448, 1454–55 (S.D. Miss. 1985).

60. Joint Center for Political Studies, *Black Elected Officials* (1989), table 4.

61. See, e.g., Karnig and Welch, *Black Representation and Urban Policy*, pp. 108–11.

62. Abney, "Factors Related to Negro Voter Turnout in Mississippi."

63. E.g., Karnig and Welch, *Black Representation and Urban Policy*, pp. 111–15.

64. Ibid., pp. 113–15.

65. See Morrison, *Black Political Empowerment*.

66. Data from testimony of Bennie G. Thompson, *Extension of the Voting Rights Act: Hearings Before the Subcommittee on Civil and Constitutional Rights of the House Comm. on the Judiciary*, 97th Cong., 1st Sess., pt. 1, pp. 552–55.

Chapter 6

1. In 1975 the Voting Rights Act was extended to protect the rights of non-English-speaking Americans, and the requirement of bilingual voter registration and elections also promoted their electoral participation.

2. United States Department of Justice, Voting Section, "Number of Changes."

3. Voting Rights Act Amendments of 1982, 96 Stat. 131, *codified at* 42 U.S.C. sec. 1973 et seq.

4. 42 U.S.C. sec. 1973(b) (1988).

5. United States Department of Justice, *Civil Rights Division*, Voting Rights section, p. 2.

6. See, e.g., *Sims v. Baggett*, 247 F. Supp. 96 (M.D. Ala. 1965) (three-judge court); *Smith v. Paris*, 257 F. Supp. 901 (M.D. Ala. 1966), *aff'd*, 386 F.2d 979 (5th Cir. 1967).

7. Kousser, "The Undermining of the First Reconstruction," pp. 31–32.

8. See *United States v. Classic*, 313 U.S. 299 (1941) (ballot-box stuffing); *Guinn v. United States*, 238 U.S. 347 (1915) (grandfather clause); *Nixon v. Hern-*

don, 273 U.S. 536 (1926) (white primary).

9. 377 U.S. 533, 579 (1964).

10. *Fortson v. Dorsey*, 379 U.S. 433, 439 (1965); *Burns v. Richardson*, 384 U.S. 73, 88 (1966).

11. Dixon, *Democratic Representation*, pp. 476–80.

12. 364 U.S. 339 (1960).

13. See *Colgrove v. Green*, 328 U.S. 549, 556 (1946).

14. Dixon, *Democratic Representation*, p. 465.

15. 376 U.S. 52 (1964).

16. 393 U.S. 544, 569 (1969).

17. United States Commission on Civil Rights, *Political Participation*, chaps. 1 and 2.

18. Ibid., pp. 19–20.

19. Historically, the Supreme Court has been reluctant to adopt new constitutional rulings because of the difficulty in overturning them. Constitutional decisions can be reversed only by the Supreme Court itself or by the difficult and cumbersome procedure of constitutional amendment. Constitutional amendments must be proposed by a two-thirds vote of both houses of Congress or by a constitutional convention convened by vote of two-thirds of the state legislatures and ratified by the legislatures or conventions of three-fourths of the states. Statutory rulings, on the other hand, can be reversed simply by an act of Congress adopting a new statute or amending an existing one.

20. 393 U.S. at 569–70.

21. 393 U.S. at 570.

22. 393 U.S. at 569.

23. 403 U.S. 124, 153.

24. 403 U.S. at 149.

25. 412 U.S. 755, 766 (1973) (emphasis added).

26. 412 U.S. at 766–67.

27. 485 F.2d 1297 (5th Cir. 1973) (*en banc*), *aff'd sub nom. East Carroll Parish School Board v. Marshall*, 424 U.S. 636 (1976).

28. See Parker, "The 'Results' Test," pp. 722–26; Bickerstaff, "Reapportionment by State Legislatures," pp. 643–51; Bonapfel, "Minority Challenges to At-Large Elections."

29. 446 U.S. 55 (1980).

30. 403 U.S. 217, 224–25 (1971). See also, *Wright v. City of Emporia*, 407 U.S. 451, 461–62 (1972).

31. 426 U.S. 229 (1976).

32. See Parker, "The 'Results' Test," pp. 740–46.

33. See S. Rep. No. 97-417, 97th Cong., 2d Sess., pp. 36–37 (1982).

34. 404 F. Supp. 206 (N.D. Miss. 1975) (three-judge court). In *Connor v. Finch*, 431 U.S. 407, 425 (1977), the Supreme Court disapproved a court-ordered Mississippi legislative reapportionment plan for the reason that "unexplained departures" from the district court's neutral guidelines for reapportionment "can lead, as they did here, to a charge that the departures are explicable only in terms of a purpose to minimize the voting strength of a

minority group." The Supreme Court did not expressly hold, however, that the plan was adopted by the district court for a racially discriminatory purpose.

35. *Connor v. Johnson*, 279 F. Supp. 619 (S.D. Miss. 1966) (three-judge court), *aff'd mem.*, 386 U.S. 483 (1967).

36. 402 F. Supp. 658 (S.D. Miss. 1975), *aff'd*, 528 F.2d 536 (5th Cir. 1976), *rev'd*, 554 F.2d 139 (5th Cir. 1977) (*en banc*), *cert. denied*, 434 U.S. 968 (1977).

37. 554 F.2d 139, 146, 151 (5th Cir. 1977) (*en banc*).

38. 554 F.2d at 148–51.

39. *Kirksey v. City of Jackson*, 461 F. Supp. 1282 (S.D. Miss. 1978), *vac'd and remanded*, 625 F.2d 21 (5th Cir. 1980), *on remand*, 506 F. Supp. 491 (S.D. Miss. 1981), *aff'd*, 663 F.2d 659 (5th Cir. 1982).

40. *Kirksey v. City of Jackson*, 663 F.2d 659 (5th Cir. 1981).

41. *Kirksey v. Danks*, 608 F. Supp. 1448 (S.D. Miss. 1985).

42. 458 U.S. 613 (1982).

43. See articles cited in Parker, "The 'Results' Test," p. 737 n. 110.

44. Comment, "The Supreme Court, 1979 Term," *Harvard Law Review* 94 (Nov. 1980): 143, 149.

45. *Voting Rights Act: Hearings Before the Subcomm. on the Constitution of the Senate Comm. on the Judiciary*, 97th Cong., 2d Sess. (1982).

46. S. Rep. No. 97-417, 97th Cong., 2d Sess., pp. 36–37 (1982).

47. Ibid., p. 37.

48. H.R. Rep. No. 97-227, 97th Cong., 1st Sess., pp. 17–18, 30 (1981); S. Rep. No. 97-417, 97th Cong., 2d Sess., p. 6 (1982).

49. These "temporary" provisions, which originally were to last only five years, were (1) the suspension of literacy tests and other voter registration tests as prerequisites to registration and voting (section 4); (2) the federal preclearance requirement (section 5); (3) the attorney general's authority to assign federal examiners (registrars) to covered jurisdictions (sections 6 and 7); and (4) the attorney general's authority to assign federal observers (poll watchers) (section 8).

50. On the opposition of the Nixon administration to the extension of section 5 in its original form in 1970, see Lawson, *In Pursuit of Power*, pp. 130ff.; Ball, Krane, and Lauth, *Compromised Compliance*, pp. 67ff.

51. See United States Commission on Civil Rights, *Political Participation*.

52. Testimony of Howard A. Glickstein, *Voting Rights Act Extension: Hearings before Subcommittee No. 5 of the House Comm. on the Judiciary*, 91st Cong., 1st Sess., p. 17 (1969).

53. H.R. Rep. No. 91-397, 91st Cong., 2d Sess. (1980), reprinted in 1970 U.S. Code Cong. & Ad. News 3280, 3284.

54. *Extension of the Voting Rights Act of 1965: Hearings before the Subcommittee on Constitutional Rights of the Senate Comm. on the Judiciary*, 94th Cong., 1st Sess., pp. 95–96 (testimony of Arthur S. Flemming, chairman of the U.S. Commission on Civil Rights), 139–86 (testimony of Frank R. Parker, Lawyers' Committee for Civil Rights Under Law), 581–83 (testimony of J. Stanley Pottinger, assistant attorney general in charge of the civil rights division, U.S. Department of Justice); S. Rep. No. 94-295, 94th Cong., 1st Sess., pp. 16–19

(1975); *Extension of the Voting Rights Act: Hearings before the Subcommittee on Civil and Constitutional Rights of the House Comm. on the Judiciary*, 97th Cong, 1st Sess. (1981); *Voting Rights Act: Hearings before the Subcomm. on the Constitution of the Senate Comm. on the Judiciary*, 97th Cong., 2d Sess. (1982); H.R. Rep. No. 97-227, 97th Cong., 1st Sess., pp. 17–20 (1981); S. Rep. No. 97-417, 97th Cong., 2d Sess., pp. 9–15 (1982); United States Commission on Civil Rights, *The Voting Rights Act: Ten Years After*, pp. 211–14, 268–87, United States Commission on Civil Rights, *The Voting Rights Act: Unfulfilled Goals*, pp. 41, 45–47, 57–58.

55. S. Rep. No. 94-295, 94th Cong., 1st Sess., p. 18 (1975).

56. Hunter, *Federal Review of Voting Changes*, p. 10.

57. *Allen v. State Board of Elections*, 393 U.S. 544, 549 n. 5, 556 n. 22 (1969); testimony of J. Stanley Pottinger, assistant attorney general, U.S. Department of Justice, *Extension of the Voting Rights Act: Hearings before the Subcommittee on Civil and Constitutional Rights of the House Committee on the Judiciary*, 94th Cong., 1st Sess., p. 182 (1975). See Engstrom, "Racial Vote Dilution," p. 144.

58. 400 U.S. 379 (1971).

59. Hunter, *Federal Review of Voting Changes*, p. 9.

60. United States Department of Justice, Voting Section, "Number of Changes."

61. See Lawson, *In Pursuit of Power*, pp. 162–63; Ball, Krane, and Lauth, *Compromised Compliance*, pp. 68–69.

62. Statement of J. Stanley Pottinger, assistant attorney general, Civil Rights Division, U.S. Department of Justice, *Extension of the Voting Rights Act of 1965: Hearings before the Subcommittee on Constitutional Rights of the Senate Comm. on the Judiciary*, 94th Cong., 1st Sess. (1975), p. 581.

63. Ball, Krane, and Lauth, *Compromised Compliance*, pp. 78–81.

64. Ibid., pp. 72–73; Lawson, *In Pursuit of Power*, ch. 6.

65. Parker and Phillips, *Voting in Mississippi*, pp. 72–77.

66. Section 5 letter from Jerris Leonard, assistant attorney general, Civil Rights Division, U.S. Department of Justice, to A. F. Summer, Mississippi attorney general, Sept. 21, 1970.

67. *Evers v. State Board of Election Commissioners*, 327 F. Supp. 640 (S.D. Miss. 1971) (three-judge court), *appeal dism'd*, 450 U.S. 1001 (1972).

68. 327 F. Supp. at 641.

69. Ibid.

70. 327 F. Supp. at 642.

71. 327 F. Supp. at 644.

72. Washington Research Project, *The Shameful Blight*, p. 144.

73. Lawson, *In Pursuit of Power*, pp. 168–70.

74. Department of Justice, Administration of Voting Rights Act of 1965, Notice of Proposed Rule Making, *The Enforcement of the Voting Rights Act: Hearings before the Civil Rights Oversight Subcommittee of the House Comm. on the Judiciary*, 92d Cong., 1st Sess., pp. 28–29 (1971). See Lawson, *In Pursuit of Power*, pp. 158–74.

75. Department of Justice, Procedures for the Administration of Section 5 of the Voting Rights Act of 1965, 36 Fed. Reg. 18186 (Sept. 10, 1971); 46 Fed.

Reg. 870 (Jan. 5, 1981); 52 Fed. Reg. 486 (Jan. 6, 1987). The section 5 regulations are codified at 28 C.F.R. Part 51.

76. Ball, Krane, and Lauth, *Compromised Compliance*, p. 137.

77. *Morris v. Gressette*, 432 U.S. 491 (1977).

78. Ball, Krane, and Lauth, *Compromised Compliance*, pp. 152–211.

79. See *Nomination of William Bradford Reynolds to Be Associate Attorney General of the United States: Hearings before the Senate Comm. on the Judiciary*, 99th Cong., 1st Sess., pp. 268–76 (statement on behalf of the Lawyers' Committee for Civil Rights Under Law), 374–445 (statement of Lani Guinier, assistant counsel, NAACP Legal Defense and Educational Fund), 449–69 (statement of Frank R. Parker, director, Voting Rights Project, Lawyers' Committee for Civil Rights Under Law) (1985).

80. See McDonald, "The 1982 Extension of Section 5," pp. 30–61; Engstrom, "Racial Vote Dilution," pp. 147–63.

81. *Allen v. State Board of Elections*, 393 U.S. 544, 595 (Black, J., dissenting).

82. 383 U.S. 301, 355–62 (1966).

83. 393 U.S. at 595–97.

84. Justice John Harlan also dissented in part in the *Allen* case. His dissent was based not on Justice Black's rhetoric, but on his reading of the legislative history of the 1965 act. See 393 U.S. at 582–94.

85. 383 U.S. at 327–29.

86. *Perkins v. Matthews*, 400 U.S. 379, 397 (1971).

87. *Georgia v. United States*, 411 U.S. 526, 545 (1973) (Powell, J., dissenting).

88. See, e.g., *City of Pleasant Grove v. United States*, 479 U.S. 462, 472–80 (1987) (Powell, J., dissenting); *City of Lockhart v. United States*, 460 U.S. 125 (1983) (Powell, J., for the Court); *City of Port Arthur v. United States*, 459 U.S. 159, 169–75 (1982) (Powell, J., dissenting).

89. See Lawson, *In Pursuit of Power*, pp. 134–58, 237–52, 283–92.

90. Thernstrom's analysis has been criticized in several book reviews, including Karlan and McCrary, "Book Review"; James Turner, "Illusory Cabal at the Polls?" *Washington Times*, Mar. 8, 1988, p. F4; Adam Clymer, "Black Ballots," *New York Times Book Review*, Oct. 18, 1987, p. 40; and Margaret Edds, "Debating the Effects of the Voting Rights Act," *Washington Post Book World*, Sept. 27, 1987, p. 7.

A number of conservative scholars also criticized section 5 and the minority vote dilution principle in testimony in opposition to the amendment and extension of the Voting Rights Act in 1982. See *Voting Rights Act: Hearings before the Subcommittee on the Constitution of the Senate Comm. on the Judiciary*, 97th Cong., 1st Sess., pp. 228–42 (testimony of Professor Walter Berns, American Enterprise Institute), 423–46 (testimony of Professor Barry Gross, City University of New York), 542–60 (testimony of Professor Susan McManus, University of Houston), 1332–64 (testimony of Professor James F. Blumstein, Vanderbilt University Law School) (1982).

91. Thernstrom, *Whose Votes Count?* p. 22.

92. Ibid., p. 25.

93. Ibid., p. 21.

94. *Allen v. State Board of Elections*, 393 U.S. at 566–69.

95. 393 U.S. at 566.
96. 393 U.S. at 568.
97. Karlan and McCrary, "Book Review," pp. 756–57.
98. Thernstrom, *Whose Votes Count?* p. 30.
99. Ibid., p. 23.
100. Ibid., p. 27.
101. Ibid., p. 9.
102. Ibid., p. 5.
103. Ibid., pp. 1–3, 23.
104. Ibid., p. 242.
105. Thernstrom, "The Odd Evolution of the Voting Rights Act," pp. 58, 60.
106. Thernstrom, *Whose Votes Count?* pp. 242–43.
107. Ibid., pp. 23, 238–40.
108. Engstrom and McDonald, "Quantitative Evidence in Vote Dilution Litigation," p. 369.
109. Thernstrom, *Whose Votes Count?* p. 78.
110. 42 U.S.C. sec. 1973(b).
111. *Thornburg v. Gingles*, 478 U.S. 30 (1986).
112. Joint Center for Political Studies, *Black Elected Officials* (1989), table 2. The total number of elective offices in Mississippi is taken from U.S. Bureau of the Census, *1987 Census of Governments, Popularly Elected Officials in 1987*, Preliminary Report (Dec. 1988), p. 6.

Chapter 7

1. Key, *Southern Politics*, p. 229.
2. Piven and Cloward, *Poor Peoples' Movements*, p. 182.
3. Colby, "White Violence and the Civil Rights Movement," pp. 31–48.
4. Quoted in *New York Times Book Review*, Feb. 19, 1989, p. 35, from V. S. Naipaul, *A Turn in the South*.
5. Black, *Southern Governors and Civil Rights*, pp. 65–66.
6. Himelstein, "Rhetorical Continuities in the Politics of Race."
7. Ibid., p. 156.
8. *Mississippi Republican Executive Committee v. Brooks*, 469 U.S. 1002, 1005 n. 3 (1984) (Stevens, J., concurring).
9. Dan Davis, "Black Vote Key in Many Races—Including Mabus'," *Clarion-Ledger/Jackson Daily News*, Oct. 23, 1988.
10. Dan Davis, "Younger, Better Educated People Next in Line," Jackson *Clarion-Ledger*, Oct. 25, 1988.
11. See Current, Introduction to Garner, *Reconstruction in Mississippi*.
12. Shaffer, "A Traditionalist Political Culture in Transition," table 1.
13. *Martin v. Allain*, 658 F. Supp. 1183, 1195 (S.D. Miss. 1987); *Martin v. Mabus*, 700 F. Supp. 327, 333–34 (S.D. Miss. 1988).
14. *Martin v. Mabus*, 700 F. Supp. at 333–34.
15. Beverly Canerdy, "Black Candidates Appear to Do Poorly in Judicial Races," Jackson *Clarion-Ledger*, June 21, 1989.

16. Miss. Laws, 1986, ch. 492, sec. 203, codified at Miss. Code Ann. sec. 37-9-12 (1987 Supp.).

17. Miss. Laws, 1986, ch. 495, secs. 109, 110, and 336, codified at Miss. Code Ann. secs. 23-15-359, 23-15-361 (1972) (Special Pamphlet, Mississippi Election Code).

18. 674 F. Supp. 1245, 1255 (N.D. Miss. 1987).

19. 674 F. Supp. at 1248–52.

20. 674 F. Supp. at 1255.

21. 674 F. Supp. at 1255–56.

22. See Piven and Cloward, *Why Americans Don't Vote*, detailing the history and continued impact of voter registration restrictions in the United States, contributing to the low turnout in elections.

23. Interview with Robert B. McDuff, Feb. 28, 1989.

24. *Martin v. Allain*, 658 F. Supp. 1183 (N.D. Miss. 1987); also, *Martin v. Mabus*, 700 F. Supp. 327 (N.D. Miss. 1988).

25. Sherman, "Is Mississippi Turning?"

26. 478 U.S. 30 (1976).

27. Karlan and McCrary, "Book Review," p. 776.

28. For the same reasons a decade earlier, after years of opposing busing for public school desegregation and after the Supreme Court's *Swann v. Charlotte-Mecklenburg County Board of Education* decision endorsing busing, Jackson business interests supported a busing plan to integrate the city schools to bring about a peaceful end to the desegregation controversy and to improve the economic climate. See Charles Sallis and John Quincy Adams, "Desegregation in Jackson, Mississippi," in *Southern Businessmen and Desegregation*, ed. Jacoway and Colburn (Baton Rouge: Louisiana State University Press, 1982), pp. 253–54.

Bibliography

Congressional Materials

U.S. House of Representatives

H.R. Rep. No. 439, 89th Cong., 1st Sess. (1965). Reprinted in 1965 U.S. Code Cong. & Ad. News 2437.

H.R. Rep. No. 91–397, 91st Cong., 2d Sess. (1980). Reprinted in 1970 U.S. Code Cong. & Ad. News 3280.

H.R. Rep. No. 97–227, 97th Cong., 1st Sess. (1981).

Hearings on the Voting Rights Act (H.R. 6400) before Subcommittee No. 5 of the House Comm. on the Judiciary, 89th Cong., 1st Sess., ser. 2 (1965).

Voting Rights Act Extension: Hearings before Subcommittee No. 5 of the House Comm. on the Judiciary, 91st Cong., 1st Sess., ser. 3 (1969).

The Enforcement of the Voting Rights Act: Hearings before the Civil Rights Oversight Subcommittee of the House Comm. on the Judiciary, 92d Cong., 1st Sess., ser. 8 (1971).

Extension of the Voting Rights Act of 1965: Hearings before the Subcommittee on Constitutional Rights of the Senate Comm. on the Judiciary, 94th Cong., 1st Sess. (1975).

U.S. Senate

S. Rep. No. 94–295, 94th Cong., 1st Sess. (1975). Reprinted in 1975 U.S. Code Cong. & Ad. News 774.

S. Rep. No. 97–417, 97th Cong., 2d Sess. (1982). Reprinted in 1982 U.S. Code Cong. & Ad. News 177.

Voting Rights: Hearings on S. 1564 before the Senate Comm. on the Judiciary, 89th Cong., 1st Sess. 2 parts. (1965).

Extension of the Voting Rights Act of 1965: Hearings before the Subcommittee on Constitutional Rights of the Senate Comm. on the Judiciary, 94th Cong., 1st Sess. (1975).

Voting Rights Act: Hearings before the Subcommittee on the Constitution of the Senate Comm. on the Judiciary, 97th Cong., 2d Sess., ser. J-97-92 (1982).

Nomination of William Bradford Reynolds To Be Associate Attorney General of the United States: Hearings before the Senate Comm. on the Judiciary, 99th Cong., 1st Sess., ser. J-99-29 (1985).

Court Cases

Alexander v. Holmes County Board of Education, 396 U.S. 19 (1969).

Allen v. State Board of Elections, 393 U.S. 544 (1969).

Brown v. Board of Education, 347 U.S. 483 (1954), 349 U.S. 294 (1955).
Bunton v. Patterson, 281 F. Supp. 918 (S.D. Miss. 1967) (three-judge court), rev'd sub nom. *Allen v. State Board of Elections,* 393 U.S. 544 (1969).
Burns v. Richardson, 384 U.S. 73 (1966).
City of Lockhart v. United States, 460 U.S. 125 (1983).
City of Mobile v. Bolden, 446 U.S. 55 (1980).
City of Pleasant Grove v. United States, 479 U.S. 462 (1987).
City of Port Arthur v. United States, 459 U.S. 159 (1982).
Colgrove v. Green, 328 U.S. 549 (1946).
Connor v. Coleman, 425 U.S. 675 (1976).
Connor v. Coleman, 440 U.S. 612 (1979), 441 U.S. 792 (1979).
Connor v. Finch, 431 U.S. 407 (1977).
Connor v. Johnson, 256 F. Supp. 962 (S.D. Miss. 1966) (three-judge court), 265 F. Supp. 492 (S.D. Miss. 1967) (three-judge court), 330 F. Supp. 521 (S.D. Miss. 1971) (three-judge court), stay granted, 402 U.S. 690 (1971), further stay denied, 403 U.S. 928 (1971), vac'd sub nom. *Connor v. Williams,* 404 U.S. 549 (1972), *Connor v. Waller,* 396 F. Supp. 1308 (S.D. Miss. 1975) (three-judge court), rev'd, 421 U.S. 656 (1975), Civil No. 3830(A) (S.D. Miss. Orders of July 11, 1975, August 1, 1975) (three-judge court) (unreported), *Connor v. Finch,* 419 F. Supp. 1072, 419 F. Supp. 1089, 422 F. Supp. 1014 (S.D. Miss. 1976) (three-judge court), rev'd, 431 U.S. 407 (1977), 469 F. Supp. 693 (S.D. Miss. 1979) (three-judge court) (state legislative reapportionment).
Connor v. Johnson, 279 F. Supp. 619 (S.D. Miss. 1966) (three-judge court), aff'd mem., 386 U.S. 483 (1967) (congressional redistricting).
Connor v. Johnson, 402 U.S. 690 (1971).
Connor v. Waller, 421 U.S. 656 (1975).
Dorsey v. Fortson, 228 F. Supp. 259 (N.D. Ga. 1964) (three-judge court), rev'd sub nom. *Fortson v. Dorsey,* 379 U.S. 433 (1965).
Evers v. State Board of Election Commissioners, 327 F. Supp. 640 (S.D. Miss. 1971) (three-judge court), appeal dism'd, 450 U.S. 1001 (1972).
Fairley v. Patterson, 282 F. Supp. 164 (S.D. Miss. 1967) (three-judge court), rev'd sub nom. *Allen v. State Board of Elections,* 393 U.S. 544 (1969).
Fortson v. Dorsey, 379 U.S. 433 (1965).
Georgia v. United States, 411 U.S. 526 (1973).
Gomillion v. Lightfoot, 364 U.S. 399 (1960).
Graves v. Barnes, 343 F. Supp. 704 (W.D. Tex. 1972) (three-judge court), aff'd in part, rev'd in part sub nom. *White v. Regester,* 412 U.S. 755 (1973).
Graves v. Barnes, 378 F. Supp. 640 (W.D. Tex. 1974), vac'd sub nom. *White v. Regester,* 422 U.S. 935 (1975).
Guinn v. United States, 238 U.S. 347 (1915).
Jordan v. Winter, 541 F. Supp. 1135 (N.D. 1982) (three-judge court), vac'd and remanded sub nom. *Brooks v. Winter,* 461 U.S. 921 (1983), on remand, 604 F. Supp. 807 (N.D. Miss. 1984) (three-judge court), aff'd sub nom. *Mississippi Republican Executive Committee v. Brooks,* 469 U.S. 1002 (1984).
Ketchum v. Byrne, 740 F.2d 1398 (7th Cir. 1984), cert. denied, 471 U.S. 1135 (1985).

Kirksey v. Board of Supervisors of Hinds County, 402 F. Supp. 658 (S.D. Miss. 1975), aff'd, 528 F.2d 536 (5th Cir. 1976), rev'd, 554 F.2d 139 (5th Cir. 1977) (en banc), cert. denied, 434 U.S. 968 (1977).

Kirksey v. Board of Supervisors of Hinds County, 544 F.2d 139 (5th Cir. 1977) (en banc), cert. denied, 434 U.S. 968 (1977).

Kirksey v. City of Jackson, 461 F. Supp. 1282 (S.D. Miss. 1978), vac'd and remanded, 625 F.2d 21 (5th Cir. 1980), 506 F. Supp. 491 (S.D. Miss. 1981), aff'd, 663 F.2d 659 (5th Cir. 1981).

Kirksey v. Danks, 608 F. Supp. 1448 (S.D. Miss. 1985).

McDaniel v. Sanchez, 452 U.S. 130 (1981).

Martin v. Allain, 658 F. Supp. 1183 (S.D. Miss. 1987).

Martin v. Mabus, 700 F. Supp. 327 (S.D. Miss. 1988).

Mississippi v. United States, 490 F. Supp. 569 (D.D.C. 1979) (three-judge court), aff'd mem., 444 U.S. 1050 (1980).

Mississippi State Chapter, Operation PUSH v. Allain, 674 F. Supp. 1245 (N.D. Miss. 1987).

Moore v. Leflore County Board of Election Commissioners, 502 F.2d 621 (5th Cir. 1974).

Morris v. Gressette, 432 U.S. 491 (1977).

Palmer v. Thompson, 403 U.S. 217 (1971).

Perkins v. Matthews, 400 U.S. 379, 397 (1971).

Reynolds v. Sims, 377 U.S. 533 (1964).

Riddell v. National Democratic Party, 334 F. Supp. 908 (S.D. 1972), rev'd, 508 F.2d 770 (5th Cir. 1975).

Rogers v. Lodge, 458 U.S. 613 (1982).

Sanders v. Russell, 401 F.2d 241 (5th Cir. 1968).

Sims v. Amos, 336 F. Supp. 924 (M.D. Ala. 1972) (three-judge court), aff'd mem., 409 U.S. 942 (1972).

Sims v. Baggett, 274 F. Supp. 96 (M.D. Ala. 1965) (three-judge court).

Smith v. Allwright, 321 U.S. 649 (1944).

Smith v. Paris, 257 F. Supp. 901 (M.D. Ala. 1966), aff'd, 386 F.2d 979 (5th Cir. 1967).

South Carolina v. Katzenbach, 383 U.S. 301 (1966).

Stewart v. Waller, 404 F. Supp. 206 (N.D. Miss. 1975) (three-judge court).

Thornburg v. Gingles, 478 U.S. 30 (1986).

United Jewish Organizations v. Carey, 430 U.S. 144 (1977).

United States v. Classic, 313 U.S. 299 (1941).

Washington v. Davis, 426 U.S. 229 (1976).

Whitcomb v. Chavis, 403 U.S. 124 (1971).

White v. Regester, 412 U.S. 755 (1973).

Whitley v. Johnson, 260 F. Supp. 630 (S.D. Miss. 1966) (three-judge court), 296 F. Supp. 630 (S.D. Miss. 1967) (three-judge court), rev'd sub nom. *Allen v. State Board of Elections*, 393 U.S. 544 (1969).

Wise v. Lipscomb, 437 U.S. 535 (1978).

Wright v. Rockefeller, 376 U.S. 52 (1964).

Zimmer v. McKeithen, 485 F.2d 1297 (5th Cir. 1973) (en banc), aff'd sub nom. *East Carroll Parish School Board v. Marshall*, 424 U.S. 636 (1976).

Interviews

Allain, Bill A. Interview with author. October 10, 1985. Jackson, Mississippi.
Barber, Rims. Interview with author. October 10, 1985. Jackson, Mississippi.
Bronstein, Alvin J. Interview with author. May 23, 1986. Washington, D.C.
Clark, Eric C. Interview with author. October 11, 1985. Jackson, Mississippi.
Clark, Robert G. Interview with author. October 12, 1985. Jackson, Missis-
   sippi.
Cole, Ed. Telephone interview with author. June 6, 1989.
Henry, Aaron E. Interview with author. October 6, 1985. Clarksdale, Missis-
   sippi.
Keady, William C. Interview with author. October 5, 1985. Greenville, Mis-
   sissippi.
Kirksey, Henry J. Interview with author. October 9, 1985. Jackson, Missis-
   sippi.
Leventhal, Melvyn R. Interview with author. November 2, 1985; June 23,
   1986. New York, New York.
Parker, Carolyn T. Telephone interview with author. May 29, 1986.
Thompson, Bennie G. Interview with author. October 12, 1985. Jackson,
   Mississippi. Telephone interview with author. December 29, 1986.

Newspapers

Greenville *Delta Democrat-Times*
Greenville *Times* (1906)
Jackson *Clarion-Ledger*
Jackson Daily News
Memphis *Commercial Appeal*
New Orleans *Times-Picayune*
New York Times

Books, Articles, and Unpublished
Dissertations and Papers

Abney, Glenn F. "Factors Related to Negro Voter Turnout in Mississippi."
   Journal of Politics 37 (November 1974): 1057–63.
Baer, Charles H. "The New Black Politics in Mississippi: A Quantitative
   Analysis." Ph.D. dissertation, Northwestern University, 1970.
Ball, Howard, Dale Krane, and Thomas P. Lauth. *Compromised Compliance:
   Implementation of the 1965 Voting Rights Act.* Westport, Conn.: Greenwood
   Press, 1982.
Bartley, Numan V. *The Rise of Massive Resistance.* Baton Rouge: Louisiana
   State University Press, 1969.
Bartley, Numan V., and Hugh D. Graham. *Southern Politics and the Second Re-
   construction.* Baltimore: Johns Hopkins University Press, 1975.

Bass, Jack. *Unlikely Heroes*. New York: Simon & Schuster, 1981.

Bass, Jack, and Walter DeVries. *The Transformation of Southern Politics: Social Change and Political Consequence since 1945*. New York: Basic Books, 1976.

Bickerstaff, Steve. "Reapportionment by State Legislatures: A Guide for the 1980's." *Southwestern Law Journal* 34 (June 1980): 608–86.

Black, Earl. *Southern Governors and Civil Rights: Racial Segregation as a Campaign Issue in the Second Reconstruction*. Cambridge, Mass.: Harvard University Press, 1976.

Black, Earl, and Merle Black. *Politics and Society in the South*. Cambridge, Mass.: Harvard University Press, 1987.

Blacksher, James U., and Larry T. Menefee. "From *Reynolds v. Sims* to *City of Mobile v. Bolden*: Have the White Suburbs Commandeered the Fifteenth Amendment?" *Hastings Law Journal* 34 (September 1982): 1–64.

Bonapfel, Paul W. "Minority Challenges to At-Large Elections: The Dilution Problem." *Georgia Law Review* 10 (1976): 353–90.

Branch, Taylor. *Parting the Waters: America in the King Years, 1954–64*. New York: Simon & Schuster, 1988.

Brooks, Gary, and William Claggett. "Black Electoral Power, White Resistance, and Legislative Behavior." *Political Behavior* 3 (1981): 49–68.

Brooks, Thomas R. *Walls Come Tumbling Down: A History of the Civil Rights Movement, 1940–1970*. Englewood Cliffs, N.J.: Prentice Hall, 1974.

Carmichael, Stokely, and Charles V. Hamilton. *Black Power: The Politics of Liberation in America*. New York: Vintage Books, 1967.

Carson, Clayborne. *In Struggle: SNCC and the Black Awakening of the 1960's*. Cambridge, Mass.: Harvard University Press, 1981.

Carson, Clayborne, David J. Garrow, Vincent Harding, Darlene Clark Hine, and Toby Kleban Levine, eds. *A Reader and Guide: Eyes on the Prize, America's Civil Rights Years*. New York: Penguin Books, 1987.

Cavanagh, Thomas E., and Denise Stockton. *Black Elected Officials and Their Constituencies*. Washington, D.C.: Joint Center for Political Studies, 1983.

Colby, David C. "Protest and Party: A Revisionist Study of the Mississippi Freedom Democratic Party." Paper prepared for presentation at the Southern Political Science Association Convention, Nashville, Tenn., November 1985.

———. "The Voting Rights Act and Black Registration in Mississippi." *Publius* 16 (Fall 1986): 123–37.

———. "White Violence and the Civil Rights Movement." In *Blacks in Southern Politics*, edited by Laurence W. Moreland, Robert P. Steed, and Tod A. Baker, pp. 31–48. New York: Praeger, 1987.

Current, Richard N. Introduction to reprint edition of James W. Garner, *Reconstruction in Mississippi*. Baton Rouge: Louisiana State University Press, 1968.

Davidson, Chandler, and George Korbel. "At-Large Elections and Minority Group Representation." In *Minority Vote Dilution*, edited by Chandler Davidson, pp. 65–84. Washington, D.C.: Howard University Press, 1984.

Derfner, Armand. "Racial Discrimination and the Right to Vote." *Vanderbilt Law Review* 26 (April 1973): 523–84.

Dittmer, John. "The Politics of the Mississippi Movement, 1954–1964." In

The Civil Rights Movement in America, edited by Charles W. Eagles, pp. 65–93. Jackson: University Press of Mississippi, 1986.

Dixon, Robert G., Jr. *Democratic Representation: Reapportionment in Law and Politics*. New York: Oxford University Press, 1968.

Edds, Margaret. *Free at Last: What Really Happened When Civil Rights Came to Southern Politics*. Bethesda, Md.: Adler & Adler, 1987.

Ely, John Hart. *Democracy and Distrust: A Theory of Judicial Review*. Cambridge, Mass.: Harvard University Press, 1980.

Engstrom, Richard L. "The Supreme Court and Equi-Populous Gerrymandering: A Remaining Obstacle in the Quest for Fair and Effective Representation." *Arizona State Law Journal* 1976, no. 2 (1977): 277–319.

————. "Racial Vote Dilution: Supreme Court Interpretations of Section 5 of the Voting Rights Act." *Southern University Law Review* 4 (Spring 1978): 139–64.

Engstrom, Richard L., and Michael D. McDonald. "Quantitative Evidence in Vote Dilution Litigation: Political Participation and Polarized Voting." *Urban Lawyer* 17 (Summer 1985): 369–77.

————. "The Election of Blacks to the Southern City Councils: The Dominant Impact of Electoral Arrangements." In *Blacks in Southern Politics*, edited by Laurence W. Moreland, Robert B. Steed, and Tod A. Baker, pp. 245–58. New York: Praeger, 1987.

Evers, Charles. *Evers*. New York: World Publishing Co., 1971.

Foster, E. C. "A Time of Challenge: Afro-Mississippi Political Developments since 1965." *Journal of Negro History* 68 (Spring 1983): 185–200.

Foster, Lorn S. "The Voting Rights Act: Black Voting and the New Southern Politics." *Western Journal of Black Studies* 7, no. 3 (1983): 120–29.

Garland, Phyl A. "A Taste of Triumph for Black Mississippi." *Ebony* 23 (February 1968): 25–32.

Garrow, David J. *Protest at Selma: Martin Luther King, Jr., and the Voting Rights Act of 1965*. New Haven: Yale University Press, 1978.

Guyot, Lawrence, and Mike Thelwell. "The Politics of Necessity and Survival in Mississippi." *Freedomways* 6 (Second Quarter, 1966): 120–32.

————. "Toward Independent Political Power," *Freedomways* 6 (Third Quarter, 1966): 246–54.

Halpin, Stanislaus A. "The Anti-Gerrymander: The Impact of Section 5 of the Voting Rights Act upon Louisiana Parish Redistricting." Ph.D. dissertation, George Washington University, 1978.

Hamilton, Charles V. "Southern Judges and Negro Voting Rights: The Judicial Approach to the Solution of Controversial Social Problems." *Wisconsin Law Review* 65 (Winter 1965): 72–102.

Hamilton, Howard D. "Legislative Constituencies: Single Member Districts, Multi-Member Districts, and Floterial Districts." *Western Political Quarterly* 20 (1967): 321–40.

Heck, Edward V., and Joseph Stewart, Jr. "Ensuring Access to Justice: The Role of Interest Group Lawyers in the Campaign for Civil Rights." *Judicature* 66 (August 1982): 84–94.

Hester, Kathryn Healy. "Mississippi and the Voting Rights Act: 1965–1982." *Mississippi Law Journal* 52 (December 1982): 803–76.

Himelstein, Jerry. "Rhetorical Continuities in the Politics of Race: The Closed Society Revisited." *Southern Speech Communication Journal* 48 (Winter 1983): 153–66.

Hunter, David H. *Federal Review of Voting Changes: How to Use Section 5 of the Voting Rights Act.* 2d ed. Washington, D.C.: Joint Center for Political Studies, 1975.

Joint Center for Political Studies. *Black Elected Officials: A National Roster.* 18 vols. Washington, D.C.: Joint Center for Political Studies, 1970–89.

Jones, Mack H. "A Frame of Reference for Black Politics." In *Black Political Life in the United States,* edited by Lenneal J. Henderson, Jr., pp. 7–20. San Francisco: Chandler, 1972.

Karlan, Pamela S., and Peyton McCrary. "Book Review, Without Fear and Without Research: Abigail Thernstrom on the Voting Rights Act." *Journal of Law and Politics* 4 (Spring 1988): 751–77.

Karnig, Albert K., and Susan Welch. *Black Representation and Urban Policy.* Chicago: University of Chicago Press, 1980.

Kernell, Sam. "Comment: A Re-Evaluation of Black Voting in Mississippi." *American Political Science Review* 67 (December 1973): 1307–18.

Key, V. O., Jr. *Southern Politics in State and Nation.* New York: Knopf, 1949.

King, Mary. *Freedom Song: A Personal Story of the 1960s Civil Rights Movement.* New York: William Morrow & Co., 1987.

Kirwan, Albert D. "Apportionment in the Mississippi Constitution of 1890." *Journal of Southern History* 14 (1948): 234–46.

———. *Revolt of the Rednecks: Mississippi Politics: 1876–1925.* 1951. Reprint. Gloucester, Mass.: Peter Smith, 1964.

Kousser, Morgan J. *The Shaping of Southern Politics: Suffrage Restriction and the Establishment of the One-Party South, 1880–1910.* New Haven: Yale University Press, 1974.

———. "The Undermining of the First Reconstruction: Lessons for the Second." In *Minority Vote Dilution,* edited by Chandler Davidson, pp. 27–46. Washington, D.C.: Howard University Press, 1984.

Ladner, Joyce. "What Black Power Means to Negroes in Mississippi." In *The Transformation of Activism,* edited by August Meier, pp. 131–54. Chicago: Aldine Publishing Co., 1970.

Lamis, Alexander. *The Two-Party South.* New York: Oxford University Press, 1984.

Lawson, Steven R. *Black Ballots: Voting Rights in the South, 1944–1969.* New York: Columbia University Press, 1976.

———. *In Pursuit of Power: Southern Blacks and Electoral Politics 1965–1982.* New York: Columbia University Press, 1985.

Lawyers' Committee for Civil Rights Under Law. *10 Year Report.* Washington, D.C.: Lawyers' Committee for Civil Rights Under Law, 1973.

Lewis, Anthony, and the *New York Times. Portrait of a Decade: The Second American Revolution.* New York: Random House, 1964.

Lichtman, Allan J. "Racial Bloc Voting in Mississippi Elections: Methodology and Results." Trial exhibit presented in *Martin v. Allain,* 658 F. Supp. 1183 (S.D. Miss. 1987).

Loewen, James W. "Continued Obstacles to Black Electoral Success in Mississippi." *Civil Rights Research Review* 9 (Fall–Winter 1981): 24–39.

Loewen, James W., and Charles Sallis, eds. *Mississippi: Conflict and Change.* Rev. ed. New York: Pantheon Books, 1980.

McAdam, Doug. *Freedom Summer.* New York: Oxford University Press, 1988.

———. *Political Process and the Development of Black Insurgency, 1930–1970.* Chicago: University of Chicago Press, 1982.

McDonald, Laughlin. "The 1982 Extension of Section 5 of the Voting Rights Act of 1965: The Continued Need for Preclearance." *Tennessee Law Review* 51 (Fall 1983): 1–82.

———. "The Quiet Revolution in Minority Voting Rights." *Vanderbilt Law Review* 42 (May 1989): 1249–97.

McMillan, Neil R. *The Citizens' Council: Organized Resistance to the Second Reconstruction, 1954–1964.* Urbana: University of Illinois Press, 1971.

———. "Black Enfranchisement in Mississippi: Federal Enforcement and Black Protest in the 1960's." *Journal of Southern History* 43 (August 1977): 351–72.

Matthews, Donald R., and James W. Prothro. *Negroes and the New Southern Politics.* New York: Harcourt, Brace & World, 1966.

Meier, August, and Elliot Rudwick. *CORE: A Study in the Civil Rights Movement, 1942–1968.* New York: Oxford University Press, 1973.

Mississippi Secretary of State, *Official and Statistical Register,* 1964–1968, 1968–1972, 1972–1976, 1976–1980, 1980–1984, 1984–1988, 1988–1992 (Jackson, Miss.: Secretary of State, 1964, 1968, 1972, 1976, 1980, 1985, 1989).

Morris, Milton D. *The Politics of Black America.* New York: Harper & Row, 1975.

Morrison, Minion K. C. *Black Political Empowerment.* Albany: State University of New York Press, 1987.

Muse, Benjamin. *Virginia's Massive Resistance.* Bloomington: Indiana University Press, 1961.

Naipaul, V. S. *A Turn in the South.* New York: Alfred A. Knopf, 1988.

Navasky, Victor S. *Kennedy Justice.* New York: Atheneum Publishing Co., 1971.

Note. "Judicial Performance in the Fifth Circuit." *Yale Law Journal* 73 (1963): 90–133.

Note. "The Voting Rights Act of 1965 and Minority Access to the Political Process." *Columbia Human Rights Law Review* 6 (Spring 1974): 129–53.

Parker, Frank R. "County Redistricting in Mississippi: Case Studies in Racial Gerrymandering." *Mississippi Law Journal* 44, no. 3 (1973): 391–424.

———. "The Mississippi Congressional Redistricting Case: A Case Study in Minority Vote Dilution." *Howard Law Journal* 28, no. 2 (1985): 397–415.

———. "Racial Gerrymandering and Legislative Reapportionment." In *Minority Vote Dilution,* edited by Chandler Davidson, pp. 85-113. Washington, D.C.: Howard University Press, 1984.

———. "The 'Results' Test of Section 2 of the Voting Rights Act: Abandoning the Intent Standard." *Virginia Law Review* 69 (May 1983): 715–64.

Parker, Frank R., and Barbara Y. Phillips. *Voting in Mississippi: A Right Still Denied.* Washington, D.C.: Lawyers' Committee for Civil Rights Under Law, 1981.

Peltason, Jack W. *Fifty-Eight Lonely Men: Southern Federal Judges and School Desegregation.* New York: Harcourt, Brace, 1962.

Pinderhughes, Dianne M. "Legal Strategies for Voting Rights: Political Science and the Law." *Howard Law Journal* 28, no. 2 (1985): 515–40.

Piven, Frances Fox, and Richard A. Cloward. *Poor Peoples' Movements: Why They Succeed, How They Fail.* New York: Vintage Books, 1977.

————. *Why Americans Don't Vote.* New York: Pantheon, 1988.

Race Relations Law Reporter, 12 vols. Nashville, Tenn.: Vanderbilt University School of Law, 1956–67.

Raines, Howell. *My Soul Is Rested: The Story of the Civil Rights Movement in the Deep South.* New York: Penguin Books, 1977.

Rice, Bradley Robert. *Progressive Cities: The Commission Government Movement in America, 1901–1920.* Austin: University of Texas Press, 1971.

Salamon, Lester M., and Stephen Van Evera. "Fear, Apathy, and Discrimination: A Test of Three Explanations of Political Participation." *American Political Science Review* 67 (December 1973): 1288–1306.

————. "Fear Revisited: Rejoinder to 'Comment' by Sam Kernell." *American Political Science Review* 67 (December 1973): 1319–26.

Sarratt, Reed. *The Ordeal of Desegregation: The First Decade.* New York: Harper & Row, 1966.

Shaffer, Stephan D. "A Traditionalist Political Culture in Transition: The Case of Mississippi." Paper presented at the annual meeting of the American Political Science Association, Washington, D.C., September 3–6, 1987.

Sherman, Rorie. "Is Mississippi Turning?" *National Law Journal* (February 20, 1989): 1, 24–27.

Shingles, Richard D. "Black Consciousness and Political Participation: The Missing Link." *American Political Science Review* 75 (1981): 76–91.

Smith, Frank E. *Congressman from Mississippi.* New York: Pantheon, 1964.

Smith, George Bundy. "The Failure of Reapportionment: The Effect of Reapportionment on the Election of Blacks to Legislative Bodies." *Howard Law Journal* 18 (1975): 639–84.

Southern Education Reporting Service. *Statistical Summary, State by State, of School Segregation-Desegregation in the Southern and Border Area from 1954 to the Present.* Nashville, Tenn.: Southern Education Reporting Service, 1967.

Stavis, Morton. "A Century of Struggle for Black Enfranchisement in Mississippi: From the Civil War to the Congressional Challenge of 1965—and Beyond." *Mississippi Law Journal* 57, no. 3 (December 1987): 591–676.

Stekler, Paul J. "Black Politics in the New South: An Investigation of Change at Various Levels." Ph.D. dissertation, Harvard University, 1983.

————. "Electing Blacks to Office in the South: Black Candidates, Bloc Voting, and Racial Unity Twenty Years after the Voting Rights Act." Paper prepared for the Center for Legal Studies on Intergovernmental Relations, Tulane Law School, 1985.

Stern, Gerald M. "Judge William Harold Cox and the Right to Vote in Clarke County, Mississippi." In *Southern Justice*, edited by Leon Friedman, pp. 165–86. New York: Random House, 1965.

Stewart, Joseph, Jr., and Edward V. Heck. "The Day-to-Day Activities of Interest Group Lawyers." *Social Science Quarterly* 64 (March 1983): 173–82.

Stewart, Joseph, Jr., and James F. Sheffield, Jr. "Does Interest Group Litigation Matter? The Case of Black Political Mobilization in Mississippi." *Jour-*

nal of Politics 49 (August 1987): 780–98.

Thernstrom, Abigail M. "The Odd Evolution of The Voting Rights Act." *The Public Interest* 55 (Spring 1979): 49–76.

————. *Whose Votes Count? Affirmative Action and Minority Voting Rights.* Cambridge, Mass.: Harvard University Press, 1987.

Thompson, Kenneth H. *The Voting Rights Act and Black Electoral Participation.* Washington, D.C.: Joint Center for Political Studies, 1982.

Tompkins, Calvin. "Profiles (Marian Wright Edelman): A Sense of Urgency." *The New Yorker*, March 27, 1989, pp. 48–74.

Tushnet, Mark V. "Commentary" on "Federal Law and the Courts in the Civil Rights Movement," by Charles V. Hamilton. In *The Civil Rights Movement in America*, edited by Charles W. Eagles, pp. 117–25. Jackson: University Press of Mississippi, 1986.

Tyler, Gus. "Court versus Legislature: The Sociopolitics of Malapportionment." *Law and Contemporary Problems* 27 (1962): 390–410.

United States Commission on Civil Rights. *Hearings Held in Jackson, Mississippi, February 16–20, 1965.* 2 vols. Vol. 1, *Voting*. Vol. 2, *Administration of Justice*. Washington, D.C.: Government Printing Office, 1965.

————. *Political Participation.* Washington, D.C.: Government Printing Office, 1968.

————. *Voting in Mississippi.* Washington, D.C.: Government Printing Office, 1965.

————. *The Voting Rights Act: Ten Years After.* Washington, D.C., Government Printing Office, 1975.

————. *The Voting Rights Act: Unfulfilled Goals.* Washington, D.C.: Government Printing Office, 1981.

United States Department of Justice. *Civil Rights Division: Enforcing the Law.* Washington, D.C.: U.S. Department of Justice, 1987.

————. "Number of Changes to Which Objections Have Been Interposed by Type and Year from 1965–December 31, 1988." Washington, D.C.: U.S. Department of Justice, 1988 (photocopy).

Vose, Clement E., ed. *Guide to the Microfilm Edition of Southern Civil Rights Litigation Records for the 1960s.* Middletown, Conn.: Wesleyan University, 1980.

Walton, Hanes. *Invisible Politics: Black Political Behavior.* Albany: State University of New York, 1985.

Wasby, Stephen L. *Vote Dilution, Minority Voting Rights, and the Courts.* Washington, D.C.: Joint Center for Political Studies, 1982.

Washington Research Project. *The Shameful Blight: The Survival of Racial Discrimination in the South.* Washington, D.C.: Washington Research Project, 1972.

Watters, Pat. *The South and the Nation.* New York: Vintage Books, 1969.

Watters, Pat, and Reese Cleghorn. *Climbing Jacob's Ladder: The Arrival of Negroes in Southern Politics.* New York: Harcourt, Brace, 1967.

Wharton, Vernon Lane. *The Negro in Mississippi, 1865–1890.* New York: Harper & Row, 1947.

Wirt, Frederick M. *Politics of Southern Equality: Law and Social Change in a Mississippi County.* Chicago: Aldine Publishing Co., 1970.

Index